W9-CYV-677

THE PARENT'S GUIDE TO
SOLVING SCHOOL PROBLEMS

kindergarten through middle school

ELAINE K. McEWAN

Harold Shaw Publishers
Wheaton, Illinois

All Scripture quotations, unless otherwise indicated, are from *The Living Bible,* © 1971 by Tyndale House Publishers, Wheaton, Illinois. Used by permission.

Copyright © 1992 by Elaine K. McEwan

All rights reserved. No part of this book may be reproduced or transmitted in any form or by any means, electronic or mechanical, including photocopying, recording, or any information storage and retrieval system without written permission from Harold Shaw Publishers, Box 567, Wheaton, Illinois 60189. Printed in the United States of America.

ISBN 0-87788-640-7

Cover illustrations, © 1992 by Guy Wolek

Library of Congress Cataloging-in-Publication Data

McEwan, Elaine K., 1941-
    The parent's guide to solving school problems : kindergarten through middle school / Elaine K. McEwan.
      p.   cm.
    Includes bibliographical references and index.
    ISBN 0-87788-640-7
    1. Education—United States—Parent participation.
    2. Problem solving. I. Title.
    LC225.3.M4 1992
    370.19'3—dc20   92-5143
                                                CIP

99 98 97 96 95 94 93 92

10 9 8 7 6 5 4 3 2 1

*To the parents and teachers
of Lincoln School*

Contents

INTRODUCTION
Getting Started:
A Problem-Solving Preview

I receive the telephone calls at all hours of the day and night. Some come from good friends, some from residents in the school district where I work, others from people who have heard me speak at their church or school. Sometimes the calls come in the form of questions to the regular column called *School Talk* that I write for the local paper. Sometimes the calls come in to a radio talk show where I occasionally serve as a guest expert on schooling issues. It doesn't make any difference where the parents live, how much money they have, or how educated they are. Behind each call or question is a parent who is at the end of his or her proverbial rope. They have a son or daughter who is having a problem in school and the result is turmoil at home. Sometimes when Mom and Dad don't agree on the nature of the problem, marital discord can even result.

I received one such call just last week. The mother was frantic. Her son, a bright second-grader who had been placed above grade level in math, was frustrated and unhappy about the pressure his teacher was placing on him to do more and go faster in his work. His mother had made an attempt to talk with the teacher and principal but was left with the feeling that the problem was hers, not theirs. Her son had staged a mini-rebellion and was refusing to do his homework. She was desperate for advice and turned to me. We talked for nearly half an hour. By the end of the call, we had mapped out a plan to assist her in solving the problem. It wasn't a magical solution and will probably require some fine-tuning along the way, but she was feeling empowered and in control once again.

To the casual observer, the problems that parents face on a daily basis as their children move through school can seem unimportant and petty: the playground bully, a teacher who isn't sympathetic, a homework assignment that wasn't completed on time. Parents are often accused of overreacting and overprotecting (sometimes even by their spouses). But to the individuals who are involved, school problems are often devastating and traumatic. As parents, we love our children deeply and want them to be happy and successful in school. When they aren't, we suffer along with them. The road to school success is often a rocky one, even for those "good" students, and parents need all the help they can get along the way.

Providing that help has been my goal in writing this book. As the mother of two grown children I've solved my own share of school problems. As an elementary school principal and assistant superintendent for instruction, my job has been to make sure that the children in my school and district are succeeding in school. When they're not, it's my problem to figure out why and become part of the solution. I hope to share that expertise with you in the following chapters.

In *Chapter One* we'll look at what constitutes a real school problem and figure out just who the problem belongs to. Determining ownership of the problem is the first step toward solving it. Children can have academic, social, emotional, and behavioral problems. Parents can have those same problems as well, and the personal problems of parents can sometimes have a severe impact on what happens to their children in school. Even schools can have problems. Sometimes it's a teacher, sometimes a principal, sometimes the curriculum or poor discipline. In a worst-case scenario, everyone can be involved. Those kinds of problems are the most difficult to solve because usually everyone is blaming everyone else, and no one wants to take ownership and help solve the problem. Problems can never be solved until everyone stops blaming and starts working toward positive solutions.

In *Chapter Two* we'll talk about what to do when schools aren't doing their fair share. The problems your child is having may be complicated or even caused by an ineffective school. We'll suggest some possible solutions to this major stumbling block.

Chapter Three will address the critical problems many students have with reading and writing. These basic skills are the foundation for school success, and the inability to read or write well can make school a torturous experience.

Our technological society calls for an ever-increasing understanding of math, yet many of our children can't even remember their math facts. Ways to help our children become more mathematically literate and avoid the math anxiety that plagued many of us are suggested in *Chapter Four.*

The bright child who refuses to work or the average student who just isn't motivated to learn are among the most challenging problems that parents and educators face. In *Chapter Five* we'll examine some of the reasons and suggest ways you can help your child overcome the underachievement syndrome.

Our educational world today is often defined solely by test scores and numbers. High schools are judged by their average SAT and ACT scores. College admissions and scholarship awards are given on the basis of grade-point averages and test scores. Testing begins as early as first or second grade in some school districts and your child's inability to do well on this single measure will frustrate both of you. Homework and study skills are important keys to school success also. *Chapter Six* will look at studying and test-taking and offer some keys to success in this area. It will also include some important information about children's learning styles and how they impact test-taking and studying.

One of the major schooling problems that parents and students face has nothing at all to do with learning or academics. It has to do with friends. A child's social relationships can often make or break his or her success in school. *Chapter Seven* will examine some tried and true methods for helping your child solve social problems and make friends.

Chances are if you're having discipline problems at home with your child, this problem has reared its ugly head at school as well. It is the rare child who acts out in school and is a perfect angel at home. If parents and teachers can't agree on a discipline plan together, a child has little chance of success in school. *Chapter Eight* will help you if your child is always in trouble at school. You'll learn how to develop a behavior management plan and how to turn your child's behavior around.

Children with school problems are often diagnosed with learning disabilities or attention deficit disorder. How can you tell whether your child really has one of these problems? What can you do if the diagnosis is confirmed? Clear definitions of these problems and helps for parents whose children fall into these categories will be given in *Chapter Nine.*

Chapter Ten will discuss how stress and anxiety are impacting today's student. You will find ways to help your child manage the fears that can make school a nightmare for some children.

1

WHAT'S THE PROBLEM?

And How Can We Solve It?

I'd like to consider myself somewhat of an expert on problem solving in the school setting. As a school principal I've helped many dozens of families solve all kinds of academic, social, and behavioral problems. Many of them came to my office angry and dissatisfied with the school and left with smiles on their faces, feeling that someone had been willing to listen and help them with their problem. I've learned some specific problem-solving techniques that almost always work. But I've learned some of my most valuable lessons about schooling problems from the two major mistakes I made when my own children, Emily and Patrick, faced schooling problems. I learned how emotionally involved and subjective we as parents become when our children are in pain. And I learned how important it is for school administrators to take a leadership role when parents come to school with problems. Let me explain.

When my own children (now both in college) were elementary school students, I was no different than any other parent. I wanted school to run smoothly for my children, and I wanted them to be supremely happy with every aspect of their experience. My little darlings should never have to endure hardship, discomfort, or a teacher they didn't like. I'm being a little facetious, but my statement is not without an element of truth. I remember the fall when Emily was about to enter sixth grade. The day the class assignments were posted she ran to school at breakneck speed to find out who her teacher would be for the coming year. She came home in tears. "I'm in the wrong room," she sobbed. "I know Mrs. Silver hates me," she continued. "And not a single one of my friends is in my room." The picture she painted was grim. She was certain that her final year in elementary school was ruined. I sprang into action, positive I could alleviate this terrible injustice and wave the magic wand of happiness. I'd never pulled any strings at school before, but I knew the principal would see things my way. After all, I was a fellow educator. Surely she would give me what I wanted. She owed it to me. I didn't waste a minute; I had an appointment before the tears on Emily's cheeks were dry.

I was not prepared for what I would hear, however. "I'm sorry," the principal said, "I can't accomodate your request. It just doesn't make any sense."

"But," I pleaded, "Emily is desperately unhappy."

In her infinite wisdom, this experienced educator merely smiled and nodded. "She'll get over it before the end of the week. Mrs. Silver is one of the best teachers in sixth grade.

She'll love her. I know Emily and I know the teacher. My assignment stands."

I was furious. I told the principal so in some well-chosen words that I ever after deeply regretted. She was the consumate professional and never lost her cool. Emily was in love with her new teacher in less than a week. She had totally forgotten her despair. The chagrin and embarassment I felt at seeing the principal's words come true almost overnight are still vivid in my memory even though the incident happened over ten years ago, and I now enjoy a warm, professional relationship with that individual. My experience taught me that even the most reasoned and intelligent of individuals can lose all sense of judgment and objectivity when the happiness of his child is at stake. While I always take seriously whatever parents say to me in the context of a problem-solving session, I never hold a grudge for words spoken in haste or anger. I've been there and know how it feels.

My second great *faux pas* occurred when Patrick was also in sixth grade. His grade level was the first in our community to transfer to the junior high for a new middle school program. He was nervous about leaving the friendly environment of the local elementary school, and when he started complaining about his new teacher I thought it was just a minor adjustment problem. After all, I remembered my experience with Emily and was determined not to make the same mistake twice. However, Patrick did not fall in love with his teacher. In fact with each passing day, his complaints grew more wearisome. They seemed to revolve around the teacher's treatment of other students. She reduced at least one or two to tears each day. Patrick assured me that he had never been subjected to her wrath, but I could tell that his sensitive nature caused him to live in dread that he would be the next target. I kept telling him not to worry, but he kept complaining. Our dinner hour each evening had turned into a litany of complaints against Mrs. Redstone (not her real name).

My husband said the words that he knew would prod me into action. "You're a principal," he said. "Can't you do something about this?"

I broke all the rules of effective problem solving as I barnstormed Patrick's school and once again lived to regret it. Did I go to the teacher to discuss the problem first? Of course not. Did I ask the principal to talk with the teacher to determine what could be done to solve the problem? It didn't even occur to me. I picked up the phone and, without letting the guidance counselor even identify herself, I demanded that Patrick be removed from this environment that was damaging to his psyche. The task was accomplished before the end of the day. I had, however, neglected one important step in the entire process. I'd forgotten to make Patrick part of the final decision. He was placed in a classroom without any of his friends from elementary school and with a teacher who was brand new. His only response to what I thought was a wonderful accomplishment was, "Mom, I just wanted you to listen. You didn't have to go and get me moved." My biggest mistake was defining the problem and solution without even meeting with the teacher, the principal, and the guidance counselor. Unfortunately, the officials at the middle school hadn't been as firm and thoughtful in their treatment of parents as the elementary school principal. I learned from my experience that whatever the nature of the problem, there is always time to discuss it thoughtfully with all of the parties involved and to attempt to reach an amicable solution before moving to action.

While the school problems my children encountered were not serious ones, I can call up the feelings I experienced at a moment's notice. I know the frustration and agony of having a child not want to go to school because of a real or imagined problem. I always bring forth those feelings when I'm tempted to dismiss a parent's worries as overreaction or a child's concerns as unimportant. I constantly remind myself, especially when faced with a hysterical, out-of-control parent, that this individual loves his or her child deeply and is only there because he or she cares.

Three Types of Schooling Problems

Schooling problems come in all shapes and sizes. Sometimes they can be solved with a simple telephone call or a parent-teacher conference, but all too frequently a schooling problem can grow like an out-of-control weed, choking communication between home and school, throwing up prickly thistles between parent and child, and stifling the academic growth of the student. For purposes of our discussion, a schooling problem is defined as anything that keeps a child from achieving his or her learning potential in the formal school setting. The school can be either public or private. There have been numerous books written to help parents get the most out of their child's public school experience,[1] but my research has shown that attendance at a Christian or private school doesn't necessarily guarantee smooth sailing through school waters for your child.[2] The challenge to parents faced with a possible schooling problem is threefold: 1) determining whether the problem is a real one, 2) deciding on the possible cause of the problem, and 3) finally, figuring out the steps involved in coming up with a solution. Problems are usually discovered or described by three groups: 1) children, 2) parents, and 3) teachers (or other school personnel).

Kids' problems. If parents are talking regularly with their children and listening to what they say, there are often clues regarding potential problems in their comments. I've heard many of these statements from my own children and had telephone calls from countless parents sharing similar ones.

"The teacher doesn't like me." "I don't understand a thing that's going on in that class." "I got a D on my last test in math." "Nobody in my class likes me." "I got put back in a lower reading group today." "We don't ever have any homework." "I'm in the dumb class." "I don't understand my homework assignment." All children complain about school occasionally. The skilled parent must learn to distinguish between a real problem and the everyday ups and downs of life in a school. Everything will not run smoothly for your child, and part of growing up is learning to deal with our imperfect world. But when the complaints are constant and revolve around a central theme or when they begin to affect appetite, sleep habits, or personality, that's a warning that a *schooling problem* is in the making. You need to contact your child's teacher and principal to find out what is really going on. The teacher or principal may be totally unaware of your child's feelings and may try to pass them off as unimportant or a figment of your child's imagination. But my experiences as a parent, teacher, and administator have shown that children are sensitive human beings with important perceptions about their schooling experiences. If for any reason they aren't happy in school, we need to do all we can to get to the bottom of the problem. **Any problem faced by a child at school is a real problem that must be addressed.** Sometimes all we need to do is listen and empathize.

One of the regular ways I attempted to "take the pulse of my school" as an elementary principal was to eat lunch with small groups of students. In these informal settings I would often uncover potential problems as students honestly shared their feelings about what was happening in their lives. I attempted to do the same with my own children as we talked about their daily lives at school around the dinner table. The challenge lies in sorting out what is a *real* problem that needs action and what is a *minor* problem that will solve itself given the passage of time. In many cases, children know before the rest of us that they have a problem. They just can't always explain it in ways that parents and teachers can understand. An example of just such a problem involves the little boy you met in the introduction. His mother and teacher were both unaware that his school day had become unbearable until he began to complain. He didn't just complain; he refused to go to school. The student involved had pinpointed the cause of the problem in his mind. The subject was too hard and the teacher had unreasonably high expectations. He had the solution: just stop working. The teacher, when confronted with her student's frustration, had pinpointed the cause of the problem in her mind. The parent was overprotective and the student worried too much. He just needed to relax and everything would be fine. The parent wasn't quite sure where the truth lay. She couldn't observe what was happening in the classroom. She only knew she wanted her son to stop complaining and start liking school again. Finding the "real truth" in the midst of all of these perceptions is often a task for Solomon. But parents armed with the proper information along with good questioning and problem-solving techniques can often be just the advocate their child needs to solve the problem.

Parents' problems. Sometimes parents uncover schooling problems on their own. Your children may be unaware of the problem since it does not affect them directly, but while volunteering at school or talking with other parents, you discover an issue of grave concern that involves the entire school or system. The problem may revolve around a poorly constructed curriculum, books and materials you find unacceptable, poor classroom management on the part of your child's teacher, or lack of achievement expectations in your child's classroom or school as compared to other classes in the school, or schools in the district. These *schooling problems,* while more general in nature, can often be detrimental when allowed to go unchanged. **Schooling problems that affect the overall positive attitudes of parents about the school (or school system) can often have a very detrimental effect on their children's ability to be successful and well adjusted in the school setting.** These problems are often systemic in nature and frequently take major change to remedy. In some cases, when change will take too long to benefit your child or requires an involvement of time and energy that you are unable to make, you may have to consider the selection of another schooling option. A vivid example of just such a schooling problem has been played out in the newspapers, school board meetings, and local elections of my community during the past months. A group of parents have vigorously objected to the use of a textbook series in the district's classrooms. This schooling problem did not come from the students, the majority of whom seemed largely unaffected by the curriculum until their parents raised concerns. And the teachers and administrators obviously didn't think the materials were a problem; they had chosen them in the first place. But judging from the emotional fervor of the controversy, parents were most concerned about the detrimental effects of the books on their children. After a task force reviewed the materials and recommended they be retained and the candidates who wanted to remove the materials from the classrooms were defeated in the election, a group of parents filed a lawsuit, asking that their children be allowed to select an alternate curriculum of study. Leaving aside the questions of censorship and parental choice, this group of parents must deal with the most important question of all: How will their involvement in this issue affect their child's chances for being successful and well adjusted in this school setting?

Problems identified by school personnel. The schooling problems that are most likely to strike fear in the hearts of parents, however, are those that are raised by their child's own teacher. The concern may come in the form of a telephone call, a handwritten note, or a formal report card. The phrases are usually polite and couched in educational jargon, but the meaning is quite clear: Your child isn't measuring up to some standard of behavior or achievement, and you as a parent need to do something about it.

"Mary seems a bit immature with regard to her social relationships."

"I'm concerned about John's behavior. He isn't following our classroom rules and has received more detentions than any other student in the class thus far this year."

"Sarah is falling behind in her work. She has failed the last two math tests, and if she doesn't spend more time studying for the next quiz, she might receive a failing grade."

"Your daughter can't seem to get along with anyone. She wants her own way no matter what the situation."

"We're concerned about a possible learning problem with your son, Jeremy. Please call and make an appointment for a conference at your earliest convenience."

"Jessica doesn't seem quite ready for first grade. She hasn't learned her letter sounds and often has a difficult time paying attention when we read stories in the circle."

"Ken hasn't turned in his science homework for over a week. Please give me a call right away."

As parents you've done the very best you know how. It's not as though you purposefully raised a child who can't or won't learn. It's not that you tried to bring up your child to break all the rules in the book. So, when faced with the prospect of your child's problems in school, your stomach tightens into knots, you relive your own failures as a student, and immediately begin to launch into a cycle of self-blame and recrimination or adopt a defensive position that lays the blame squarely on someone else. You've been told you're expected to do something but often just *what* is unclear. This third category of schooling problems is the most difficult and frustrating of the three. **Solutions to serious academic, social, or behavioral problems usually involve facing some difficult choices about ourselves and our children, often require large investments of time on the part of everyone involved, and may mean substantial changes in attitudes and behaviors from parents, children, and teachers.**

A problem of this nature has faced Joan and her middle-school daughter, Tammy, for most of the past school year. They've discovered that the problems Tammy has always faced in school were not really the result of her lack of paying attention or her intense interest in the social scene, but rather the result of a serious learning problem that was beginning to manifest itself in depression and self-esteem problems. Joan always knew down deep that Tammy was bright, but was puzzled by the fact that while her grades were all right, they were never outstanding. Tammy's teachers attributed it to lack of motivation and her "social butterfly" image. They weren't ready to buy a "learning problem" as the issue. After all, Tammy never really did that poorly. Extensive neurological tests and subsequent counseling revealed the depth of Tammy's problem and forced her teachers to stop blaming Tammy for her lack of motivation and start looking at ways to make learning more meaningful for her particular learning style. Joan was forced to look at an identical problem in the life of her father that had made her own growing-up years very difficult. Solving educational and learning problems is often a family affair.

Academic, social, or behavioral problems at school can frequently be manifestations of a variety of family problems as well. I recently received a Christmas greeting from a family who had moved away from my elementary school. It was a complimentary note full of praise for all I had done for the family. I remembered eight years earlier when I was attempting to help their daughter Sandra cope with fourth grade. Everyone owned a share of this particular schooling problem. Sandra was uncooperative and sullen. Her teacher was punitive and rigid. Sandra's mother was hysterical. Sandra's father had deserted the family before she was born. I attempted to move this trio through some problem-solving exercises but felt like a miserable failure. Sandra barely scraped through fourth grade, but I hung in with her and her mother. As the years unfolded and I heard news of Sandra's teenage pregnancy and her running away from home, her problems with homework and assignment completion in fourth grade seemed minor. But I also learned of the sexual abuse, alcoholism, and other dysfunctional behaviors that were a part of the home setting. They had all taken their toll on Sandra's ability to succeed in school. News of a solid remarriage for Sandra's mom, the strengthening of her religious faith, and Sandra's return to the family gave the Christmas greeting a happy note. But these changes had taken eight years of heartache and suffering to achieve. The message in Sandra's story is that schooling problems can often be symptomatic of a variety of family problems and cannot be truly solved until the family problems are faced and tackled.

In summary. Thus far we've identified three types of schooling problems: 1) those that originate with your child because of some personal difficulty or anxiety he or she is encountering at school, 2) those problems that have been identified by you, the parent, because of something you've noticed through observation or heard about in the community, and 3) the schooling problems that have been brought to your attention by school personnel because your child's academic, social, or behavioral performance is not measuring up to what his or her teacher or the school in general has defined as the norm. A simple seven-step, problem-solving process can be used in any of the three cases.

Seven-Step Problem-Solving Process

In his book, *The Interactive Parent: How to Help Your Child Survive and Succeed in the Public Schools,* Linwood Laughy sets forth this seven-step problem-solving process:[3]

☐ *STEP ONE: BEGIN TO DEFINE THE PROBLEM.* Talk it over with someone or even write it down.

☐ *STEP TWO: GATHER INFORMATION.* You may discover you don't even have a problem once you've done some research.

☐ *STEP THREE: REDEFINE THE PROBLEM.* The problem may be even worse than you thought and have several aspects.

☐ *STEP FOUR: ESTABLISH AN ACCEPTABLE OUTCOME.* Decide what you want to have happen as a result of solving the problem and make sure the outcome is measurable.

☐ *STEP FIVE: GENERATE ALTERNATIVE MEANS.* Don't just settle for one solution to the problem; your first solution may not work.

☐ *STEP SIX: ESTABLISH THE PLAN.* Make sure you detail why the plan is being prepared, who is going to participate, what specific actions each individual will take, when these activities will be performed, and where they will occur.

☐ *STEP SEVEN: IMPLEMENT THE PLAN AND EVALUATE.* Remember that all the participants have a responsibility for involvment and action in the plan.

I've used variations of this process for years with great success. The critical elements, however, are the skills of the participants in the process (administrators, teachers, and parents), not the process itself. If any subset of participants does not possess the necessary skills and desires to effectively use the process and implement the design, the results can be disastrous. Be forewarned that as you move through the problem-solving process, there are three possible scenarios that can occur.

Three Problem-Solving Scenarios

Consensus/collaboration. If *consensus/collaboration* is reached, everyone agrees on the nature of the problem and the solution. Parents are supportive of school personnel's plans and they are going to do everything they can at home to help. There is usually some type of written plan that documents what everyone will be doing. (The suggestions that are given in Chapters Three through Nine will help you as a parent do all you can to support the school in the solution of your child's school problem.) Sharon's case is a perfect example of consensus/collaboration. Every staff member of my school agreed that Sharon had a serious problem. She was in third grade and didn't know how to read. She had transferred in from a private school where her learning problems had been overlooked due to a constant shift in teaching personnel. We tested Sharon and everyone agreed that she had a learning disability. We immediately gave her special services and prescribed activities for her parents to help with at home. We shared with Sharon what her part would be in solving this problem. Everyone followed through, and by sixth grade Sharon was reading above grade level and winning awards in reading. Not every problem has such a successful resolution, but it is an example of what can happen when everyone, including the child, does his or her part.

Compromise. Sometimes there is disagreement as to the nature of the problem or the type of solution that is needed. In that case a *compromise* may be reached. Both parent and school personnel agree to disagree on one or more issues but do so in the spirit of cooperation and together are able to work for what is best for the child. Compromise was the result of a problem-solving conference held with Mr. and Mrs. Stafford and their sixth-grade daughter Joanna. Joanna had a serious personality conflict with a newly assigned teacher and the situation had gone from bad to worse. The new teacher felt that Joanna was an indulged and spoiled adolescent. Her parents felt the new teacher was incompetent. The principal was caught in the middle. The Staffords wanted an immediate change in her placement but agreed to a temporary plan designed by the teacher, the principal, and Joanna. There wasn't complete support from home, but the Staffords agreed to "wait and see" before pressing the transfer issue any further.

Confrontation/capitulation. When there is no agreement and little promise for consensus or even compromise, the result is *confrontation/capitulation*. If you as a parent want a course of action to be taken that school personnel do not find acceptable, or school personnel want a course of action to be taken that you as a parent do not find acceptable, an impasse can be reached. Effective administrators and teachers always keep looking for ways to solve problems, but if an administrator is unwilling to talk or listen, or a parent is intractable, capitulation is the only answer. While this is clearly the court of last resort, if you cannot solve the problem in a way that is satisfactory to all parties, it may be necessary to look for another schooling option for your child. It is important to remember, however, that **the goal of problem solving is not to get your own way, but to help your child be successful in the academic, behavioral, and social arenas.**

Three Critical Aids to Successful Problem Solving

There are three things that you as a parent can do that will greatly increase your chances of successfully solving most of the schooling problems your child will encounter in the course of his or her passage from kindergarten through middle school: 1) set the stage for effective problem solving before you have a problem, 2) know and believe in your child, and 3) know how to participate in and manage a parent-teacher conference.

☐ *SET THE STAGE FOR EFFECTIVE PROBLEM SOLVING BEFORE YOU HAVE A PROBLEM.* Setting the stage for effective problem solving at school takes place when you first enroll your child in school. Terry Frith, author of *Secrets Parents Should Know about Public Schools,* suggests that all parents do the following things when enrolling their children in school for the first time or when transferring to a new school. Although her comments are specifically directed to parents of public school students, the suggestions will work well in any school setting.

- Make a pre-enrollment appointment with the school's administrator several days before you plan to officially enroll your child.
- When you call for the appointment, begin to build a positive relationship with the school secretary(ies).
- Dress in a businesslike manner.
- Demonstrate a sincere interest in the school's concerns.
- Communicate an appreciation for school and administrative issues and your ability to assimilate new data by offering supportive comments and succinctly paraphrasing the new information.
- Make brief and positive comments about your child.
- Give notice that you will be on the scene.
- Notify appropriate school personnel orally and in writing of all health concerns and/or other critical or potential problems.
- Cultivate an "ally" relationship with the school personnel involved with your child.[4]

You might think it's impossible to do all of these things, but I've met one person who's done them all and more. To make the story even more unbelievable, she was a single parent who worked full-time. Her son entered my school in kindergarten, and she knew that without some hard work on her part, we wouldn't understand and appreciate Josh. He was a problem just waiting to happen in school, but because she did everything "right" there wasn't a teacher in the building who didn't move mountains to make sure that school went smoothly for Josh. She believed in her child and was willing to do anything to help him be successful.

☐ *KNOW AND BELIEVE IN YOUR CHILD.* It's essential to maintain a level of confidence about your child that enables you to confront the school at any time with any problem. Jeannie Oakes, a Harvard professor and researcher, encourages parents to approach their schools with the following set of convictions about their children firmly fixed in their minds:

> My child is a capable learner. Under the right conditions, he can accomplish almost anything the school expects him to. When he meets with difficulty, the least likely reason is that he is not smart enough.

> My child wants to do well at school, academically and socially. If her behavior seems otherwise, it's not because she wants to do poorly or get into trouble. Trust her wishes for success, even when she misjudges how to act on them.

> What is true of my own child is also true of others. Often actions that improve conditions for your child will benefit his classmates. Similarly, actions on behalf of other children will often benefit my child.[5]

Coming to the problem-solving table with a strong belief in your child will give you the courage you need to press for solutions that benefit your child and will give you the motivation and desire to help your child personally in the home setting as well. Abdicating all of the responsibility for your child's learning to the formal school structure means that you will be shortchanging your child's future.

☐ *KNOW HOW TO PARTICIPATE IN AND MANAGE A PARENT-TEACHER CONFERENCE.* Coming to the parent-teacher conference with confidence and skills is the third way you can help to insure speedy and successful resolution of school problems. It's safe to say that teachers and administrators are often as nervous as you are in anticipation of a difficult conference. If you enter the conference in the spirit of criticism and confrontation, there is the strong possibility that the conference will end without a suitable resolution to the problem. There is nothing wrong with permitting the teacher or administator to save face. Remember, your goal is to solve the problem your child is having, not to intimidate and offend everyone connected with the school. Remain calm. Be a good listener. Ask pertinent questions. Share information about your child in a positive way. Keep the conference focused on positive, action-oriented solutions. If you are apprehensive about the conference, solicit the help of a friend to rehearse the key points that you wish to make. If you know you have a short fuse and are likely to lose your temper or get angry, role-play the situation with a spouse or friend to reduce the likelihood of an explosive encounter. Continually focus on the positives— both as they relate to your child and as they relate to the teacher and the school.

Looking Ahead

Let's do a bit of reviewing before we move on to Chapter Two. We've identified the major kinds of schooling problems, looked at a seven-step problem-solving model and ways to achieve solutions, and explored some of the barriers that can arise along the way. Inherent in the identification of a schooling problem is often the assignment of blame or causation. While it is often helpful to know what's at the root of any given problem, assigning blame can often stand in the way of creative solutions to problems. Blaming the school/teacher/administrator for a problem your child is having can be a dangerous game. You can get caught up in pointing the finger and fail to recognize your child's need for help. Sometimes parents have to experience several different teachers in various schools and waste much valuable time before they finally realize that their child needs help desperately. Therefore, the majority of this book (Chapters Two through Nine) is based on the assumption that you recognize the schooling problem your child is having and want to do everything you can to solve it by supporting your child at home and by working with the teacher at school.

There are, however, some schooling problems that are larger and more generic. They can directly impact your child's success in school and need to be addressed by anyone who is serious about solving schooling problems. In Chapter Two we'll look at the kinds of problems that exist in individual schools or in districts and what you can do to solve these problems.

❖ Resources

If you would like more information on the topics covered in this chapter, the following books will be helpful to you.

Barth, Roland. *Improving Schools from Within*. San Francisco: Jossey-Bass Inc., Publishers, 1990.

Frith, Terry. *Secrets Parents Should Know about the Public Schools*. New York: Simon & Schuster, 1986.

Laughy, Linwood. *The Interactive Parent: How to Help Your Child Survive and Succeed in the Public Schools.* Kooska, Idaho: Mountain Meadow Press, 1988.

Oakes, Jeannie, and Martin Lipton. *Making the Best of Schools.* New Haven, Conn.: Yale University Press, 1990.

Oppenheim, Joanne. *The Elementary School Handbook: Making the Most of Your Child's Education.* New York: Pantheon Books, 1989.

2

IT'S ALL THEIR FAULT

When Schools Aren't Working

If you're looking for data to support the argument that the schools of this country are in bad shape, you won't have any trouble finding plenty of it. Books, magazines, and newspapers are full of finger-pointing and criticism. The reports document low test scores, poorly prepared teachers, watered-down curriculums, and lazy students. Interestingly enough, while these opinions are frequently held by Americans about schools in general, when asked about the specific schools that their own children attend, parents are much more positive and optimistic. But even in the best of schools and systems, you can encounter serious school problems. Administrators can be unresponsive. Teachers can be incompetent. The curriculum can be outdated or weak. And students can test poorly on standardized tests. If these problems are encountered in your specific school, they are worth investigating and doing something about, especially if you are limited in terms of pursuing other schooling options.

What Can I Do about an Unresponsive Administrator?

Even in the best of school districts, there are principals and administrators who were trained to believe that parents should be seen and not heard. These officials are resentful and defensive when confronted with knowledgeable and assertive parents, and they can make positive problem solving in the school setting very difficult. Faced with an individual like this, you will need to strategize and plan very carefully to get problems solved productively.

Being highly visible in the school environment is one way to insure that an unresponsive administrator will take you seriously. There are dozens of ways that you can increase your visibility at school (even if you work full-time). Arrange for at least one informal conference a year to chat about what is happening at school, your child's progress in his or her classroom, and any other issues you have on your agenda. This conference should have no real purpose other than to establish a good working relationship with the administrator. Follow up your visit with a brief thank-you note of appreciation for the time he or she devoted to talking with you. If you can't volunteer at school on a regularly scheduled basis, perhaps you can make instructional materials at home or talk about your job during a career day. By all means, join and become active in the parent-teacher organization at either the school, the district level, or both. If you can only be at school occasionally, volunteer to help with class parties or field trips whenever you have the opportunity. Every exposure you have to the school and its personnel is "money in the bank" when it comes time to dealing with an unresponsive administrator. The unresponsive administrator respects and understands political influence and power, and through your involvement you're sending the message that you know how to use power. Naturally, throughout your school involvement you're working to develop trust with all school personnel by keeping your promises, being punctual, being thorough and conscientious, and dealing with problems rationally rather than emotionally.[1]

Of course there are also dozens of positive side effects for your child when he or she knows that you're involved at school. At issue here, however, is how to work around a system that is sometimes unresponsive to the needs of individual students and parents. "When teachers and administrators 'slip' and behave in less than a professional manner, these 'slips' are far less likely to involve children whose parents are positively visible at school and are more likely to involve those children whose parents are extremely negative or who are totally uninvolved."[2] When faced with an administrator who refuses to offer any help whatever on a *school problem,* the option of seeking out his or her superior and ultimately carrying the problem to the school board always exists. There is a price to pay for escalating the problem to this level, however. You will lose any credibility and support in the local school if you do so. Even teachers who know you are right in what you are doing may "gather the wagons round the campfire" and defend their fellow educators.

What Can I Do about Incompetent Teachers?

You'll seldom get your principal to admit that there are any incompetent teachers on his or her staff, but the fact remains that some teachers are much better than others, and some are downright harmful to your child's health. The most important thing that you can do is to discover through your own personal research who the best teachers are and then do everything in your power to make sure your child gets assigned to a good one.

Each school works a bit differently with regard to class assignments. Once you've figured out how the game is played in your school you will know how to strategize to get what you want. The worst thing to do (and I discovered this from personal experience) is to demand that a placement be changed after the decision has already been made. Find out when teacher assignments are typically made, and well in advance of that time make an appointment to see the principal. The strategy that focuses on the positive aspects of one classroom teacher and the educational needs of your child will be far more effective than making negative statements about a specific teacher or veiled threats about what you will do if you don't get your way. Put your request in the form of a letter that details your thinking and offers supporting data. Don't wait until the class list has been posted or school has started and then demand a change. The administrator will be loathe to reverse a decision he or she has already made and thus be made to appear to the teaching staff as if he or she has "given in" to "pushy" parents. If the teacher is truly incompetent, you will probably get what you want if you plan ahead and act in a rational manner.

What Can I Do about Tracking?

Another issue of importance with regard to student placement involves tracking. Tracking is the placement of students in classes on the basis of their abilities. This practice often begins as low as first or second grade. The unfortunate part of tracking is that once a student is assigned to a "low" group or track, he or she rarely moves out of it. Placement in a "low" reading group in second grade can often mean a child is destined for a vocational track in high school. The idea of tracking is based on some assumptions that at first seem quite logical and sensible. After all, don't children learn better if they are grouped with those who have similar abilities? Won't children who learn more slowly be embarrassed and suffer emotional and educational damage if they are placed with brighter classmates? Don't teachers and administrators with their years of training and experience know what is best for students with regard to class placement? And can't teachers do a better job of teaching if all of their students are on a similar level? The answer to these questions is not necessarily yes.

One of the most outspoken contemporary critics of tracking is Jeannie Oakes. On the basis of her research, my teachers and I totally changed our grouping practices. We had previously put all of our "gifted and talented" students in one classroom with a teacher who was trained to meet their needs. All of the other students were placed in a second classroom with a teacher who was trained to meet the needs of students who needed extra help. But Oakes' research convinced us that tracking does not promote achievement for the average and lower-ability students, and it may not even bring benefits to the smartest kids in the class. If your child is in the top group you probably haven't done much thinking or worrying about tracking. But the practice should give you much cause for concern if your child has been placed in a lower group. This placement could already be closing the doors to college for him or her. In addition to not having a positive effect on student achievement, tracking does not help slower children feel better about themselves. In fact, it was the attitudes and discipline problems that developed in our "low" class that forced us to look at exactly what messages we were sending to these students by labeling them in such a fashion. Being in a low class "fosters poor self-concepts, lowered aspirations, and negative attitudes toward school."[3]

While administrators and teachers usually feel that their placements are fair and accurate, the truth of the matter is that tracking of students results in a self-fulfilling prophecy. We found in our mini-experiment that the low motivation, poor effort, and discipline problems found in students in the "low" class were more a result of having been placed in that class than the result of any inherent learning problems the students had. While teachers who have never had the opportunity to work with classes made up of students from all ability levels may feel that tracking makes teaching easier, the fact is that no matter how homogeneous a class may start out to be, there are vast differences in learning speed, learning style, interest, effort, and aptitude for various tasks. Every teacher needs to accommodate for individual differences, and the benefits that accrue to all students when tracking is abolished more than make up for any extra inconvenience the teacher may have to experience.

Your efforts to minimize or abolish tracking should focus on information gathering.[4] The following questions should be discussed in public forums: How does the school make tracking decisions? How are teachers assigned? How many classes are tracked? How many children assigned to low tracks ever move into higher ones? What is the distribution of track enrollments according to children's race and gender? A school should operate on the premise that all students can learn, and tracking assumes that some students are not capable of learning major portions of the curriculum. My own small experiment with abolishing tracking resulted in no change or an increase in achievement for gifted students and a major jump in achievement for students formerly grouped in the "low" class. Do all you can to see that your child has as much of his or her classroom experience in a heterogeneous group. The more severe his or her learning problems or deficits, the more important is his or her placement with average to above average children.

What Can I Do about Outdated, Weak, or Inappropriate Curriculum?

What can you do if you feel your children aren't learning enough or are learning the wrong things? There are several approaches to take, and they should probably be taken simultaneously. The first thing to do is to institute some type of home-learning program that makes up for the deficits you find at school. Some parents feel so strongly about the watered-down curriculum they find in their schools that they opt for home schooling.[5] But at the very least, provide plenty of books, encyclopedias, magazines, and learning materials at home in areas that you think are being missed. You can purchase commercial home-schooling materials as well if needed.

The second thing that can be done is to determine how much flexibility the local school has to change its own curriculum. In many areas, school-based or site-based management exists, and teachers and principals have the power to make decisions about what will happen in their individual schools. If that is the case, parent-teacher organizations can exert influence and supply funds to purchase materials. If curriculum decisions are made at a district level, then you'll have to get involved through a citizens group or the school board to effect change.

A third possibility is to volunteer to "teach" the areas that you feel are missing. Parents in our community felt that art appreciation was being neglected. The school board wasn't able to fund any extra teachers or purchase materials, but a group banded together and began a "Picture Lady Program." Parents have also begun reading-incentive contests, purchased books and computers for school libraries, and established math and science labs that were desperately needed.

What Can I Do about Poor Test Scores?

If your school is at the bottom of the barrel with regard to test scores, everyone should be concerned. While tests measure only a small portion of what students should be learning in school, if the scores are very low, it's time to look for ways to improve. Poor test scores give parents a perfect opportunity to turn the spotlight on what needs to be changed. In the state of Illinois, each school issues a yearly report card, and when scores aren't where they should be, we are required to write school improvement plans. This mandate came from the state legislature and was part of the political process that preceded a massive school-reform package.

What Can I Do about Poor Discipline?

Poor discipline is one of the most serious problems that can be found in a school. Student and teacher safety, ability to learn in a relaxed environment, and respect for property and individuals are all important characteristics of an effective school. If they are not present, volunteer to begin working on the problem immediately. Volunteer to chair a discipline task force with representatives from the teachers, administrators, students, and parents. Use the problem-solving approach laid out in the first chapter. There are dozens of schools across the country that have improved their test scores, dramatically increased student and teacher morale, and beautified their buildings. And it all began with a school-wide discipline plan that everyone had a role in developing. Seek out the individuals who believe as you do that students will learn better in a structured and well-disciplined environment and band together with them to bring about change.

How Effective Is Your School?

If you're intrigued by the idea of learning more about how your school functions and whether it is doing a good job for all children and not just yours, then the following checklist will help you evaluate your school. It was developed by the Council for Basic Education,[6] and the focus is on learning for all students. This questionnaire could be the basis for a discussion at a parent-teacher meeting or a conversation with an individual teacher or principal. Those individuals who are doing their jobs well will welcome the opportunity for such dialogue.

School Questionnaire

If a school can answer YES to the following questions, all students in the school are probably learning at capacity. A NO answer indicates that the school should take corrective action to become more effective.

Leadership by the Principal and Senior Staff

Yes No Does the school have a clear, well-written, concise statement of instructional goals?

Yes No Do the school's leaders have the freedom and authority needed to carry out programs that will achieve the stated goals?

Yes No Is the principal decisive and firm?

Yes No Does the principal confer regularly with senior teachers and administrators?

Yes No Does the principal seek ideas and suggestions from the rest of the staff?

Yes No Does the principal fairly enforce rules and decisions for everyone?

Yes No Does the principal effectively allocate resources according to stated priorities?

Yes No Is much of the principal's time devoted to supervising instruction, visiting classes, and responding to such visits?

Yes No Does the principal hold high expectations of academic achievement for the staff and students?

Yes No Are the principal and other senior staff members well-grounded in the basic subjects?

Climate of Orderliness

Yes No Has the school published a statement of expectations and standards for the conduct of staff and students?

Yes No Are such statements widely understood and accepted?

Yes No Does the school have a strong sense of community?

Yes No Does the school cooperate with parents and civic agencies on disciplinary matters?

Yes No Do students have positions of responsibility for student activities, conduct, and school property?

Yes	No	Do students and staff members have numerous opportunities to work jointly on school projects?
Yes	No	Do staff members have consistent disciplinary values and practices throughout the school, as opposed to having different standards in each classroom?
Yes	No	Are students praised for good performance?
Yes	No	Do students believe that staff members genuinely care about their well-being?
Yes	No	Is the tone of the staff businesslike and professional yet interested in the students?
Yes	No	Do staff members spot disorders early and respond quickly and firmly?
Yes	No	Are reprimands delivered quietly, without disrupting the class?
Yes	No	Are parents notified of discipline problems with their children?
Yes	No	Does the school keep useful records of delinquency, truancy, disruption, vandalism, tardiness, absences, and other kinds of anti-school behavior?
Yes	No	Is the school clean and well maintained; are needed repairs made promptly?

Emphasis on Academic Achievement in Basic Subjects

Yes	No	Does the curriculum include requirements in all the basic subjects: English (reading and literature, writing and reasoning, speaking and listening), mathematics, science, history, government, geography, foreign languages, and the arts?
Yes	No	Are elective subjects supplements to, rather than substitutes for, basic subjects?
Yes	No	Are academic priorities clearly understood by staff, students, and parents?
Yes	No	Is homework regularly assigned and checked?
Yes	No	Are academic problems diagnosed early and dealt with promptly?
Yes	No	Is student mastery of basic skills and knowledge stressed over teaching methods?
Yes	No	Are the standards for promotion and graduation understood by all?
Yes	No	Is promotion based on scholastic achievement rather than time spent at a grade level?
Yes	No	Is the curriculum flexible enough for students to achieve common objectives through differing means or at different rates?
Yes	No	Are curricular and classroom distractions from academic achievement recognized and minimized?
Yes	No	Does the first year of instruction in reading stress the rapid and systematic mastery of phonics?
Yes	No	Do all courses require students to write?

Yes   No   Are textbooks selected to meet predetermined and stated curricular objectives?

Yes   No   Does the faculty coordinate instruction grade-to-grade and plan the curriculum sequentially?

Yes   No   Does the school give public recognition to the academic accomplishments of students and staff members?

Assessment of Student Progress and Academic Programs

Yes   No   Is there a coherent plan for regular assessment of students, individually and collectively, especially in the basic subjects?

Yes   No   Are group averages of critical performance indicators (e.g. test scores, course grades, course enrollments, and attendance) similar for various students, regardless of race or family income?

Yes   No   Does the system of records make it possible to analyze group averages and performance indicators by race and family income?

Yes   No   Are the purposes of testing clearly understood?

Yes   No   Do test results tell all concerned what they want to know?

Yes   No   Are students tested on what is actually taught, even though it is not always identical to the published curriculm?

Yes   No   Are several criteria, such as multiple test scores and teacher recommendations, used in making important decisions about students (e.g., for promotion, remediation, and graduation)?

Yes   No   Does the school seek valid and useful comparisons with other schools?

Yes   No   Are impartial outsiders asked to evaluate the school periodically?

Yes   No   Are students, parents, teachers, board members, and citizens satisfied with academic achievement in the school?

Teachers' Values and Expectations

Yes   No   Are teachers confident that all children can learn?

Yes   No   Are teachers enthusiastic about teaching the basic subjects?

Yes   No   Do teachers know and support the educational philosophy, academic policies, and priorities of the school?

Yes   No   Are teachers good models of conduct and academic commitment?

Yes   No   Are teachers well-educated in general and in the subjects they teach?

Yes   No   Are teachers available to students for special help on academic or personal problems?

Yes   No   Are teachers well-prepared for class? Do they start and end class promptly?

Yes   No   Do teachers speak and write well?

Yes   No   Does staff development seek to improve the academic background of teachers?

Yes   No   Are teachers cooperative and supportive of each other?

Yes   No   Do senior teachers act as mentors for less experienced teachers?

Support from Parents and Other Citizens

Yes   No   Do parents, school board members, and other citizens have access, as
            appropriate, to teachers, administrators, classes, and school records?

Yes   No   Do parents receive a handbook of school policies?

Yes   No   Does the school explain the uses of standardized testing and caution about
            abuses?

Yes   No   Do parents receive timely information from the school and from the school
            board?

Yes   No   Does local news coverage of the school stress academic achievement?

Yes   No   Does the school inform parents about their children's placement in ability
            groups and the consequences of such placement, choice of courses, perfor-
            mance on homework, and academic progress?

Yes   No   Does the school urge the importance of reading aloud to young children and
            of having home study time free from TV, phone calls, and other distractions?

Yes   No   Does the school encourage constructive citizen participation in academic
            programs and support of policies on homework, attendance, and discipline?

Yes   No   Does the school cooperate with parents and civic agencies to achieve
            concerted action by the entire community in the education of youth?

The Council for Basic Education that authored the above checklist is a nationwide association of policymakers, educators, parents, and other citizens who are committed through a
combination of services and programs to advise and inform members of education, business,
and civic groups about educational development and trends. They publish a variety of helpful
books and pamphlets that can assist you in any school improvement efforts you wish to begin
in your local school.

❖ Resources

If you would like more information on the topics covered in this chapter, the following books will be helpful to you.

Barth, Roland S. *Improving Schools from Within.* San Francisco: Jossey-Bass Inc., Publishers, 1990.

Frith, Terry. *Secrets Parents Should Know about Public Schools.* New York: Simon and Schuster, 1986.

Oakes, Jeannie, and Martin Lipton. *Making the Best of Schools.* New Haven, Conn.: Yale University Press, 1990.

Parsons, Cynthia. *Seeds: Some Good Ways to Improve Our Schools.* Santa Barbara, Calif.: Woodbridge Press, 1985.

Rioux, William. *You Can Improve Your Child's School: Practical Answers to Questions Parents Ask Most about Their Public Schools.* New York: Simon and Schuster, 1980.

Unger, Harlow G. *"What Did You Learn in School Today?" A New Parent's Guide for Evaluating Your Child's School.* New York: Facts on File, 1991.

3

READING AND WRITING

When Kids Haven't Got the Basics

One of the most serious and debilitating of all school problems is the inability to read and write at an acceptable grade-level standard. I have chosen the words "grade-level standard" to describe a basic level of competency that we want all students to reach. The feelings of despair, frustration, and lack of self-worth that your child feels at his or her inability to read and write like his classmates will only increase as he or she advances through the grades, so it is imperative to give your child all the help you can as early as possible.

I was reminded of the impact that poor reading and writing skills can have throughout a person's life in a poignant way during a recent conversation with a young woman in her early thirties. Although Sonia is an attractive and successful nail technician earning plenty of money, her lack of a high-school diploma has been a constant source of embarrassment and humiliation to her. She was agonizing over a decision to sign up for an adult education class to prepare her to pass the test she needed in order to receive the degree. She shared the frustration that had dogged her throughout elementary and junior high school until in rebellion she dropped out of high school after one year. With tears in her eyes, she recounted the story of the teasing to which her father subjected her as a result of her poor reading skills. She is still terrified of failure. What has happened to Sonia needn't happen to anyone.

Reading and Writing: Questions and Answers to Help You Understand the Basics

In this chapter we'll first look at some basic definitions, ideas, and philosophies about reading and writing. This information will be shared in a question-and-answer format to help you find just what you need to know. Then we'll look at what you might do to help your child. You don't need an advanced degree in remedial reading to help your child, but you do need to understand the "why" behind the problems your child is having as well as the underlying reasons for the "what" you'll be doing. Over and over again I have seen amazing academic gains when parents, teachers, and students work hand-in-hand to solve a schooling problem.

What is reading? Some people think that once a child has pronounced a word, either silently or orally, he or she is reading. But pronouncing the word is only word identification. Of course, that's a basic prerequisite to reading. But mere word identification is not reading. It's word calling. What a child needs to experience in order to be reading is meaning or comprehension. The child needs to understand, react, and learn from the printed page in order to be reading. One formal definition of reading I've encountered says: "Reading is the meaningful interpretation of printed or written symbols."[1] The key words in this definition are *meaningful interpretation*. For reading to take place, the reader must gain meaning. The reader must think and understand. Reading takes place only when an individual interacts with symbolic information. The process of reading involves the following seven steps:

1. *Recognition: the reader's knowledge of the alphabetic symbols.* This step takes place almost before the physical aspect of reading begins.

2. *Assimilation: the physical process by which light is reflected from the word and is received by the eye, then transmitted via the optic nerve to the brain.*

3. *Intra-integration: the equivalent to basic understanding, referring to the linking of all parts of the information being read with all other appropriate parts.*

4. *Extra-integration: the process in which the reader brings the whole body of his previous knowledge to the new knowledge he is reading, making the appropriate connections.* This includes analysis, criticism, appreciation, selection, and rejection.

5. *Retention: the basic storage of information.* Storage can itself become a problem. Most readers will have experienced entering an examination room having stored most of their information in preparation for the two-hour exam period. Storage, however, is not enough in itself, and must be accompanied by recall.

6. *Recall: the ability to get back out of storage that which is needed, preferably when it is needed.*

7. *Communication: the use to which the information is immediately or eventually put.* Includes the very important subdivision, thinking.[2]

Why is reading so important? I asked a group of kindergarten parents at orientation what they wanted their children to learn at school this year. The majority answered, "To learn how to read." Success in any school system is based on reading ability. A child's concept of herself as a student is frequently based on her earliest experiences with learning to read. Our testing programs are based on the ability to read. But, most importantly, reading is our link with the world. It lets us share ideas, travel, learn, experience the pain and joys of others, and enrich our lives.

Illiteracy is one of our country's biggest social problems. The U.S. Department of Education estimates that twenty-seven million Americans can't decipher a street sign or the number on a bus, and forty-five million have never read a book or newspaper. These people are cut off from the things that you and I take for granted. More importantly, they are unable to function effectively in our society.

How do children learn to read? Thousands of volumes have been written on the teaching of reading. Professors and teachers by the score have learned to teach reading. Or at least they think they have. Reflect for a moment about how many courses are offered on the teaching of talking. We don't *teach* our children how to talk. We *talk* to them. Many children learn to read in the very same way—when we *read* to them. A child can only learn to talk by talking. That same child can only become a skilled and fluent reader by reading.

What happens when a small child utters an incomprehensible phrase? We attempt to understand what was said and restate what we thought was said. We engage in conversation. We give feedback to the child. Meanwhile, the child is constantly figuring out the rules for this "talking game" and trying out new variations all the time. By three years of age, the child who has engaged in constant face-to-face interaction and communication with caring adults understands most of the language that he will use in ordinary conversation for the rest of his life.[3]

The same patterns hold true for the printed word as for the spoken word. If a child hears the printed word read aloud from birth, he is more likely to develop a curiosity to figure out the rules for reading, just as he figured out the rules for talking. Children begin learning to read when adults make sense out of the printed page for them. They learn something more about reading every time we read aloud to them.

Children learn that individual letters have different names, that certain letters make certain sounds, and that combinations of letters stand for words. They read their names, the street signs, simple words like *ball* and *cat*, and soon they are deciphering all kinds of words and bringing meaning to the printed page. Older children and adults can learn to read in the very same way once they overcome the self-doubt and failure that may have accompanied their first attempts at learning to read.

Does everyone learn to read the same way? My own children, one a girl, the other a boy, are perfect examples of how each child learns to read in a slightly different way. My daughter learned to read quite independently and unbeknownst to me. She arrived home in early October from kindergarten and announced that she had learned to read.

She needed no formal instruction in phonics or word-attack skills. The whole process simply fell into place for her. My son, who had been exposed to the same amount of reading aloud and language development activities at home, needed much more formal instruction in phonics under the tutelage of a classroom teacher. Today, their IQs are nearly equal and their grade-point averages in college are the same. They even graduated from high school with the same class rank. But they learned to read at very different rates and in very different ways. Children need exposure to a variety of instructional methodologies in the beginning. Some will catch on right away to the idea of whole words, and others will need a structured phonetic approach. A reading program that combines several approaches is the best one for all children.

Many educators are engaged in debate about a phonics approach to early reading instruction versus a whole-language approach. They seem to have no argument about their ultimate goals—both groups want kids to learn to read and understand. An educator who has worked extensively with learning-disabled children, Priscilla Vail, has made some especially insightful observations about these two approaches to instruction. She calls the phonics approach the "structure" of language. "Structure refers to the nuts and bolts used in assembling (spelling) or decoding (figuring out what it actually says) written language."[4] She further makes the point that most children don't figure out the structure of our language on their own. They need direct, multi-sensory instruction. When a child looks at a word like "money" and thinks that it says "morning," he needs instruction in some very specific skills for figuring out how to break the code. Author Rudolph Flesch first drew attention to the problems children have learning to read without phonics in his book *Why Johnny Can't Read,* published in 1955. In 1981, he still felt that little progress had been made by education when he wrote *Why Johnny Still Can't Read: A New Look at the Scandal of Our Schools.*

In her comprehensive study of the best instructional practices in reading, Marilyn Adams says:

> The question of how best to teach beginning reading may be the most politicized topic in the field of education. To the uninitiated, the irrepressible question is: Why? One reason is that we care universally and passionately about the success of beginning reading instruction. It is the key to education, and education is the key to success for both individuals and a democracy.[5]

But another reason, in my opinion, is the business that revolves around training teachers, selling textbooks and programs, and making a name for oneself in the research and development circuit. Everyone wants to have "the right answer," and they want school districts to buy it from them. Professors want to have the ultimate staff development program and use it to pave their road to fame and fortune. I have exaggerated the true state of affairs just slightly, but the great debate that rages in educational circles can often yield devastating results for students and their parents. If you encounter a teacher or administrator who doesn't believe that phonics should be a key part of your child's instructional program, point that individual to Adams' work. Regarding the importance of teaching phonics, Adams says:

> Deep and thorough knowledge of letters, spelling patterns, and words, and of the phonological translations of

all three, are of inescapable importance to both skillful reading and its acquisition. By extension, instruction designed to develop children's sensitivity to spelling and their relations to pronunciations should be of paramount importance in the development of reading skills. This is, of course, precisely what is intended of good phonics instruction.[6]

But if you encounter a teacher who believes that phonics first and only is the way to developing strong readers, then also point *that* individual to Adams' work. For she has also made an excellent case for the thoughtful integration of another aspect of instruction—the aspect that Priscilla Vail calls the "texture" of language. "If phonics is the structure, 'texture' refers to the ornamentation which gives language its color, intensity, rhythm, and beauty."[7] Integrated instruction blends both structure and texture and goes beyond the simplistic approach that promises your child will learn to read in sixty days if only you'll invest four hundred dollars in a set of cassette tapes. However, if students are exposed to only the texture (a total whole-language approach without a strong phonetic component), they will "watch, listen, mimic, and recite." They'll be able to "recite a story refrain along with the class, but won't be able to decipher a cereal box."[8]

Is there any way of predicting that a child will have a reading problem? While there are many variables that affect a child's success as a reader, there probably isn't any single one that researchers can point to with certainty. An understanding of each of the "problem variables," however, can help you spot them in your child's profile so that you can be alert for how they might combine and interact to create the possibility of reading problems for your child.

Chronological age and *sex* are two such variables. Researchers have found that younger students in a classroom are often less ready and able to work, and that this characteristic is especially prevalent in boys. One researcher found that at around the age of six (when most schools are teaching beginning reading) boys lag twelve months behind girls in skeletal age. While these findings certainly cannot be generalized to all children, there is a strong likelihood that the youngest boys in any given classroom will be the least ready for any kind of formal instruction in reading.

A third critical variable that researchers have identified as a strong predictor of how children will achieve in school is *the educational level of the mother.* This variable can be, but is not necessarily related to, socioeconomic status as well. If you've struggled with school and have your own set of educational problems, then understanding and using the techniques in this book are doubly important for you. As I spoke with Sonia (whom we first encountered in the beginning of this chapter), one of the key reasons behind her decision to go back to school was how her educational level would influence her unborn children.

A child's *neurological status* can also impact her ability to be a successful reader. Problems during the prenatal period, birth, or early years of growth and development that may have impacted brain development must always be considered when looking at a potential reading difficulty.

Auditory perception is a critically important skill for success in reading. Being able to sequence events after hearing about them, being able to remember what one has heard, and finally, being able to discriminate between a wide range of sounds are very important to the beginning reader. If your child seems to have problems in these three areas, it will be important to make sure he has special training along with reading instruction.

While there was a time when teachers cited *emotional problems* as a cause of reading difficulties, there is now widespread agreement that emotional problems are usually the *result* rather than the *cause* of the problem.

If we know so much about what will cause reading problems, aren't there any programs that can prevent them? Marie Clay, the New Zealand educator who has done extensive research in the areas of reading problems, has developed a program called Reading Recovery that is being implemented in selected sites in the United States. Clay requires that the teachers involved in her program be trained in a year-long program and consequently the replication of her program is often difficult and costly for the average school. The program is used with first-grade students whose diagnostic tests indicate the possibility of reading problems. Clay's program is laid out in her book *The Early Detection of Reading Difficulties.*[9] Many schools have adapted their versions of Reading Recovery with great success. Other programs similar in nature to Reading Recovery that have been developed around the country include Jeanne Chall's Reading Laboratory at Harvard University and the program at the Benchmark School in Philadelphia. Encourage your child's teacher and principal to investigate the use of any of these models to help children who are having a problem learning to read.

What is writing? Writing is the mechanism that allows us to organize our ideas and express our thoughts in a permanent fashion. Before the advent of inexpensive telephone calls, people wrote letters to one another. Their thoughts and feelings became a lasting record of the communication that took place between two individuals. I have a friend who only lives a few miles away. She could easily pick up the telephone and call me. But during the past year as I have mourned the loss of my husband, she has written me cheery notes and words of inspiration and challenge. I cherish these tangible expressions of her love and care. They serve as a history of our relationship.

Why is writing important? You may mistakenly think that if your child isn't destined to become an author or journalist, writing skills are not that important. But there are three very important reasons for encouraging your child to polish his writing skills. First, *a person's writing conveys his innermost thoughts and feelings, who he really is as an individual.* When I left my elementary principalship after eight years, each student in my school contributed a page to my memory book. Even the kindergarten students wrote. But the most memorable page was written by a fifth grader who chose to take her own life several months ago. Upon learning of her tragic death, I immediately turned to the page she had contributed. It was a beautiful original poem full of poignancy and tenderness. I shared it with her mother. "This is really my daughter," she said, as her eyes filled with tears. I had the page enlarged and framed as a gift for her. This page in my book is a permanent reminder of how this young life touched mine. The enlargement for her mother is a reminder to all who will see it of how important the written word can be when we no longer have a loved one with whom to talk.

A second reason for writing has to do with *the psychological and emotional autonomy one experiences when one achieves power over the written word.* Through writing we grow as individuals. Students in our district's elementary schools keep private journals. If a student wishes to share what she has written with the class or her teacher, that is her prerogative. The purpose of writing is not only to practice the thinking and organizational skills that develop with daily writing, but to give students an opportunity to learn more about how they think and feel. During the past year I completed the writing of a book about mothers and daughters. I did not know when I began writing that the experience would be a form of therapy that would result in enormous breakthroughs in my own psychological, spiritual, and emotional well-being. Writing can help us grow as individuals. This is true for children as well as adults.

A third and very practical reason for becoming a good writer is that *no matter what vocation or career your child chooses, the ability to write will enhance his or her opportunities for success.*

Exactly what is journal writing? The daily journal that many students (even in kindergarten) now write in school is the modern version of the old-fashioned diary some of us used to keep. At the time we probably didn't realize that we were doing something far more important than recording the details of our latest crushes to be read and laughed about in adult years—we were practicing our writing and thinking skills. Just as students become better readers through reading, they only become better writers through writing. The emphasis in classrooms today is on providing daily opportunities to write. Some parents assign sinister meaning to the journal experience, feeling that the journal is an opportunity for teachers to invade the privacy of their students. Journal writing is, however, a widely respected practice. When I was an undergraduate at Wheaton College, everyone enrolled in any kind of creative writing course was required to keep a journal. If your child doesn't have the opportunity to write on a daily basis at school, buy him or her a special notebook in which to record something on a daily basis.

What is the relationship between reading and writing? Writing (and talking) are the flip side of reading (and listening). Educators and school psychologists use the terms *receptive* and *expressive* language to describe the two areas that we all need in order to be effective communicators. Receptive language develops before expressive language in a child. We've all experienced the wonder of realizing that our crawling baby is actually responding to a verbal request or question we have stated. We are amazed that she can understand even though she is not talking yet. Her receptive vocabulary is much larger at this point than her expressive vocabulary. In order to begin talking, she must have a large and rich receptive vocabulary. (This is much the same when an adult learns a foreign language; most people can understand what is spoken before they can generate speech themselves.)

Research indicates that children's achievements in reading and writing are generally quite strongly and positively related.[10] In many classrooms across the country today, children are encouraged to write before they receive any formal reading instruction. In homes where early readers develop, there is a strong emphasis on the provision of writing materials and written communication. In our own home, my children "wrote" stories on an old electric typewriter long before they were reading formally. Children learn to write by writing just as they learn to read by reading. Spelling, punctuation, and all of the mechanics that our English teachers found so important are secondary to the thinking processes that are taking place as the young child makes his first attempts at scribbling his thoughts.

In the most effective classrooms reading and writing are taught in an integrated way. Children respond in writing to the ideas they have encountered in their reading. Children write their own stories after they have explored the stories that others have written. Reading and writing are inseparable activities.

What is print awareness and how does it impact learning to read? One of the most exciting discoveries that reading researchers have known about for a long time but are just beginning to translate into meaning for teachers and parents is something called "print awareness." The work of Marie Clay and John Downing is particularly exciting.[11] While this topic may not seem relevant to you if you're faced with a middle-school child who has a reading problem, read on. More than likely, your child's early teachers weren't aware of this concept and tried to teach letter-sound relationships before your child even had any print awareness. They put the cart before the horse. Print awareness is something that many children acquire almost by osmosis through regular reading aloud in the early years. But other children, for a variety of reasons—not all of which we totally understand—take much longer to develop this awareness. Researchers are finding that a child's performance on tests that measure print awareness is found to predict future reading achievement[12] and also to be strongly correlated with other more traditional measures of reading readiness and achievement.[13]

What are these important print prerequisites that seem so simple as almost to be ignored by parents and teachers?

☐ *PRINT IS CATEGORICALLY DIFFERENT FROM OTHER KINDS OF VISUAL PATTERNS IN A CHILD'S ENVIRONMENT.* Children with print awareness somehow have a sense that these squiggly lines have special meaning to adults that is different from the meaning they get from photographs, works of art, and any other patterns in the environment.

☐ *PRINT IS PRINT ACROSS ANY OF A VARIETY OF PHYSICAL MEDIA.* It can be in ink, crayon, on the television screen, written on t-shirts, and even scratched in the dust on the side of a truck. A child with print awareness knows that print is print no matter how it appears.

☐ *PRINT SEEMS TO BE ALL OVER THE PLACE.* Consider the many different places we see the printed word—television, billboards, books and newspapers, neon signs. The child even sees print on his toys and clothing.

☐ *DIFFERENT SAMPLES OF PRINT ARE USED BY ADULTS IN DIFFERENT WAYS.* Parents read newspapers before breakfast, food labels to decide on grocery store purchases, and street signs to find their way.

☐ *PRINT SYMBOLIZES LANGUAGE.* In order to become a reader, a child must understand that the printed word is nothing more than symbols for the spoken word he uses everyday.

☐ *THERE ARE DIFFERENT CATEGORIES OF PRINTED MATERIALS, EACH WITH ITS OWN CHARACTERISTIC APPEARANCE AND USE.*

☐ *PRINT HOLDS INFORMATION.*

☐ *PRINT CAN BE PRODUCED BY ANYONE.*[14]

What is sustained silent reading? Sustained Silent Reading is just a fancy name for curling up with a good book and letting the rest of the world go by. It's a wonderful activity for a reluctant reader who needs encouragement and support for her recreational reading. In many schools, every class stops at the same time every day to read silently together. In some schools the program is called DER (Drop Everything and Read). No matter what it is called, it's one of the best things that any child can do to improve her reading skills. I always tell kids that good athletes don't win championships by thinking about practicing. They win by shooting baskets or running the track or kicking the football. Kids only get to be good readers by reading, reading, reading. You should have your own version of SSR at home whenever you can. Turn off the TV, stop doing chores, hang up the telephone, and read together as a family. You can read newspapers or novels. It doesn't matter what you read, just *read*.

What are reading groups and how do they impact my child's achievement in reading? You may recall from our discussion of tracking in Chapter Two that grouping students according to their achievement or ability levels can often have a detrimental effect on self-esteem and on opportunities to learn higher-level concepts. Researchers found when watching videotapes of reading lessons that teachers spent more time teaching comprehension to high-level reading groups and more time teaching phonics and basic skills to low-level groups.[15] Poor readers need as much or more instruction in comprehension strategies as good readers and yet they are often shortchanged.

Many educators can make a good case for reading groups—students receive instruction at their own level; students move along at their own pace. The advantages seem endless. I'm just not convinced that the reasons don't serve the interests of the teacher more than the student. I'm totally supportive of cluster groups to help students who are having problems or who need intense special help (such as those programs mentioned earlier like Reading Recovery or Project Read), but I haven't seen many children move from the low reading groups in which they started to a high reading group by the later elementary years. They just become locked into a low-achieving track, and frequently it has to do with teacher expectations as much as student achievement.

How can I find out about my child's grade level in reading? The place to begin is at your child's school. But even the information they share with you could be misleading and not tell the whole story. They might tell you that your fourth grader is reading in a fourth-grade book. That won't necessarily tell you what kind of success he's experiencing in reading that book, however. He may be having a difficult time pronouncing many of the words, be confused on what some of the words mean, or even be missing the meaning of what he is reading. They might tell you that he got a 4.2 grade equivalent score on the standardized reading test that was given. That means he scored as well as the average fourth grader two months into the school year. However, in many classes and schools, the majority of the students in the class perform well above grade level on nationally normed standardized tests. So your child could look average on the standardized tests and still be performing well below his peers at school. An important question to ask your child's teacher is how well he or she is performing in relation to the class. Is she an above-average, average, or poor reader? An individually administered test that measures word attack skills (phonic ability), vocabulary (word meaning), and comprehension (how well your child understands what he/she is reading) will give you the best indication of her actual grade equivalent score. The test should be given by a trained reading specialist who has worked with children who have reading difficulties. In the individualized test setting, the teacher can watch which strategies your child uses, what types of reading situations cause the most difficulty, and pinpoint specific problems. In a large group-administered standardized test, even a good guess will make a poor reader look better than she actually is.

How important are reading test scores and what do they mean? Here's a sample of one child's test scores. Sarah, a sixth grader, is in an average reading group and gets B's and C's on her report card. Let's see what the scores can tell us about her reading ability that her group placement and school grades don't.

	Stanine	Percentile	Grade Equivalent
Reading Comprehension	4	38	5.9
Vocabulary	7	85	7.4
Total Reading	6	67	6.5

Test scores can be reported in any of three ways: stanines, percentile rank, or grade equivalent. Remember that we are looking at a standardized test score. That means the test has been given to tens of thousands of children. All of the scores of all of the students in the "norming" group were ranked and subdivided into nine different groups—stanines. The lowest 10% of the scores fall into the first stanine and the highest 10% of the scores fall into the ninth stanine. Educators consider scores in stanines 1, 2, and 3 to be very low, scores in stanines 4, 5, and 6 to be average, and scores in stanines 7, 8, and 9 to be high.

Another way of looking at test scores is by percentile ranking. This score tells us that on the Reading Comprehension subtest 62% of the students who took the test did better than Sarah did.

A third way of looking at scores is by grade equivalent. This tells us how well Sarah did compared to students at her grade level. She scored about as well as students who had been in the sixth grade for two months. If Sarah's test was taken at the end of sixth grade, her grade equivalent tells us she is behind sixth graders across the country. It's important to remember, however, that she may be significantly behind or ahead of other students in her actual class depending on the overall achievement picture in her classroom and school.

To me as an educator, the most worrisome thing about Sarah's testing profile, although it is average overall (Total Reading), is her weak comprehension score. She is not understanding the "big picture" about what she is reading with the same level of skill with which she can understand word meanings. She needs instruction in comprehension strategies to increase her level of comprehension.

Are there any tests to measure my child's grade level in writing? If you suspect that your child's writing skills do not measure up to those of his classmates, there are two excellent tests that will give a standardized score. They are the Test of Written Language (TOWL) and the writing subtest of the Woodcock Johnson Achievement Battery. Both of these tests should be administered by a licensed psychologist or school psychologist.

What are the major writing problems? If you've tried to read an essay or story your child has written only to be confronted with a page of unintelligible gibberish, you may feel you already understand the nature of his or her writing problem. He's illiterate. You shouldn't, however, jump to the wrong conclusion until you've attempted to understand the specific nature of the problem. There are problems of mechanics, content, organization/motivation, and language disability. All problems can be addressed with proper instruction, but children with language disabilities need to understand and learn to compensate for what may be happening in their brains when they try to produce written language from their thoughts (more on this topic in Chapter Nine).

Some children have wonderful ideas but can't get them into an acceptable written format. They have problems with spelling, handwriting, punctuation, and grammar. Teachers frequently can't get past all the errors to discover and appreciate the creative ideas.

Some children have beautiful handwriting and superb punctuation but don't know enough about the subject to write about it, or they write about everything but the subject. I recently read an essay submitted as part of our state writing assessment. The student had written four beautiful pages that were a model of form. She just hadn't written anything about the topic that was assigned.

Some children have problems of organization and motivation. They just don't want to write because they have a mental block. Most adults can relate to this feeling. They didn't have proper instruction in writing when they were in school and only remember the papers they received back from their teachers sprinkled with red marks and large F's. Some children want to write and even get lots down on paper, but it is so muddled and disorganized that only a private detective could uncover the topic sentence. Still others think that quantity will always make up for quality and write forever, hoping you'll be impressed with their ramblings. There are ways to help your child with all of the above problems.

What are the most important things to remember as I try to help my child with reading and writing at home? Helping your child at home to overcome a reading and writing problem can be one of the most rewarding things you'll ever do. But it can also be one of the most frustrating experiences you'll ever have unless you keep some important guidelines in mind. Among many good ones suggested in Barbara Fox's helpful volume, *RX for Reading,* are the following:[16]

- *Pace your learning sessions carefully.* Don't push your child beyond his time limits. Younger children can usually work for about ten to fifteen minutes at one sitting. Children in the intermediate grades (3-5) and middle-school grades (6-8) can usually work for at least 30 minutes.
- *Be generous with encouragement and praise when your child is correct or does something particularly well.*

- *While you should always give your child a chance to correct herself when she makes a mistake, don't waste a lot of instructional time putting your child on the spot.*
- *Provide lots of variety in your choice of materials, activities, and work location.* Your child will be more interested if you keep him guessing about what's going to happen next.
- *Get everybody in on the act.* You don't have to be the only one to provide help. Moms, dads, older siblings, grandparents, aunts, uncles, and baby sitters can all be used to help children with learning activities.
- *Enlist the help of as many professionals as you can.* Get suggestions for activities and materials from teachers, books, and specialists in the field.
- *Use your own good judgment about what is best for your child.* You know him better than his teacher, the school psychologist, or your pediatrician.
- *Make sure you have a special spot in your home for your child to keep all of her learning materials.* Most of the home schoolers I know have set aside either a room or a corner of one as a learning center. They have dictionaries, atlases, a small set of reference books, flash cards, and learning games arranged for easy access. There are all kinds of colorful storage containers that can house pens, pencils, markers, and paper. Make this learning center as attractive as possible.
- *Talk openly about what you are doing.* Encourage your child to share both positive and negative feelings. It is a good sign when your child can verbalize what he is thinking about the learning experience. Just remember to be a good listener who is as nonjudgmental as possible.

***What are the major pitfalls of working one-on-one
with my child to improve his reading and writing
skills?*** It's easy to get discouraged by the enormity of the
goal when you begin working one-on-one with your child to
improve his reading and writing skills. Both of you can
become frustrated. But your job will be easier if you remember these simple hints. Many of them were suggested by
Barbara Fox.[17]

- *Don't compare your child to others.* Comparing your
  child to others who may be sailing through school will
  only discourage and frustrate you. Each child has her
  own unique set of strengths and weaknesses. You must
  focus on your child's strengths and build her up.
- *Don't ever substitute your learning sessions for playing
  outdoors, going to the movies, or other recreational activities.* If your child ever feels that he is being penal-
  ized for his school problems, you can forget about
  achieving any positive results from your work
  together. Also be aware of what other children in the
  family are doing when you and your child are working
  together. If everyone else is having a party, don't expect your child to enjoy learning.
- *Don't interrogate your child.* The worst possible thing
  you can do is to start questioning your child about
  everything that happened at school the minute she
  walks through the door. Wait for her to share good (or
  bad) news when she's ready.
- *If you're devoting time to solving a serious schooling
  problem, then scale back other outside activities.* It's
  long been my contention that children today are over-
  booked and don't have enough time to be children. If

you've got Scouts, piano lessons, a church activity, and sports, then learning will come last. Your commitment to learning will have to be first if you're dedicated to solving the problem.

- *Just remember that every day won't be wonderful.* Talk to a classroom teacher and you'll discover that they have down days in the classroom as well. Put things aside and come back fresh tomorrow.

Things You Can Do at Home to Improve Your Child's Reading and Writing

Kindergarten through second grade. Helping your kindergarten through second-grade child if he or she has a reading and writing problem is best done daily in the following four ways: 1) "sponge activities" that you organize and direct; 2) parent reading aloud of stories; 3) reading together of easy and predictable books that your child can often "read"; and 4) a writing activity associated with one of the reading activities.

1. Sponge activities are learning experiences that take place in a five- to ten-minute period of time. Children usually think of them as games. But the key is constant repetition in a context of fun. You don't need to focus on "teaching" specific skills as much as encouraging practice and giving positive feedback.

There are hundreds of sponge activities that will serve your purpose. I couldn't possibly provide a comprehensive, all-inclusive list. But I'll give you some good examples (see Appendix A for a list of some excellent resource books). Just get started and let your imagination flow. Work closely with your child's classroom teacher to review the sounds your child is learning in school. The speech pathologist in your school is also a wonderful source of language development "sponge activities." He or she usually has only about 15-20 minutes per day to work with a child and uses dozens of "games" to practice correct speech. These same games are wonderful to help in learning letter sounds.

Phonics Sponge Activities

Tic-Tac-Toe. Instead of filling the empty squares of your tic-tac-toe game with x's and o's, you and your child each can choose a different beginning consonant or blend. Here's how the game works: You choose the letter "b" and your child chooses "f." When it's your turn, you write a word beginning with the letter b in the empty square (boy or ball). Your child writes a word beginning with the letter "f" in his empty square (fur or fun). As your child gains more skill you can move to ending or middle sounds as well. This game can be played while you wait at the doctor's office, in the car, or just about anywhere you've got a few minutes on your hands.

Sound Sort. Collect all of the interesting pictures you can from magazines (your child can help). To play sound sort ask your child to put all of the pictures of objects beginning with a certain letter in a large envelope.

Rhymes and Chants. These wonderful verbal playthings teach concentration, memorization, sensitivity to sounds, rhyme, and rhythm. Check out several books that include nursery rhymes, jump rope chants, and silly poetry. Play with language at every opportunity.

Consonant Box. Use a recipe box and put in alphabet dividers for all of the consonants. Use 3x5 cards to write words for every consonant and file them under the appropriate letter. This collection of word cards can be illustrated, and dozens of games can then be played (e.g. sorting cards into categories like animals, flowers, sounds). Since some letters make more than one sound (cat and cent), you child will also learn this important phonetic principle.

Sound Hop Scotch. This is a great game for an active child. Put the sounds you're trying to learn (work with the teacher at school on the sounds they are using there) on any hard floor or outside pavement. Each playing square should have a letter written in its center. Give the child directions on which lettered square to jump to, but use clues like: "Jump to the first sound in baby," or "Jump to the letter that makes the 'buh' sound."

Vocabulary Sponge Activities

The sponge activities for vocabulary focus on teaching your child to recognize words at a glance rather than sounding them out. This is usually called developing a "sight-word" vocabulary and good readers use both the sight word and the phonetic approach. In fact, the English language is filled with many words that defy all phonetic rules and must simply be learned. Words like *one*, *here*, and *only* are perfect examples. Some well-meaning parents (and teachers) buy or make flash cards with the most common words on them and then simply drill. This can kill anyone's interest in learning new words. Make sure that your work with vocabulary is fun and takes the form of a game.

Word Hunt. Write several words that you want your child to learn on a 3x5 card. Then give her a newspaper or magazine and ask her to hunt for the words and circle them. After she's circled them all, count them and then ask her to read the word in every location in which she has found it.

Word Concentration. The popular children's game of Concentration can be adapted to teach any set of fifteen words you want to use. Write the fifteen words on two cards each. The goal of the game is to find as many word pairs as possible. If a player turns over a matching pair of words, he gets to keep both cards.

Bingo. Play Bingo with your child in the time-honored way but use words instead of letters and numbers. Make a number of different bingo cards with a variety of combinations and everyone in the family can play after dinner.

Classifying. This is a wonderful game to develop higher-level thinking skills as well as vocabulary. Decide on the categories you want to use (be sure to choose ones that especially interest your child) and write words that are examples of each category on three-by-five cards. Your child can mix and then organize the cards by categories.

Comprehension Sponge Activities

While phonics and vocabulary are important in the reading process, they are only tools to access meaning, the real heart of reading. There are many students who have wonderful decoding skills and can pronounce any word you give them. They just can't figure out what all the words put together actually mean. Teaching students strategies that will help them with comprehension is much more challenging than teaching phonics and vocabulary. All of the sponge activities you use to improve comprehension should focus on *getting your child to think!*

The Main Point. This game is a younger version of a time-honored school activity—finding the main idea in a short article or paragraph. Find pictures that tell a story (you may wish to purchase some from a teachers' store). Show your child the picture and then ask him what he thinks the picture is about. Choose a title together and then write it under the picture.

What's Missing? Write out simple directions for making or doing something and ask your child to tell you what step in the process is missing. Making a peanut butter sandwich, getting dressed in the morning, or taking a trip to the grocery store are all examples of activities you could use.

What Do You Think Is Happening? I still play this game myself when I'm in an airport or restaurant. But you can play it with your child. Choose an individual or a scenario you encounter in your daily life and begin to speculate about the personality, habits, and life story of someone you see. Or make up a story that could explain something you see in a store or on the street. This game is loads of fun, stimulates the imagination and helps children make predictions (a comprehension skill that is vital for success in reading).

Comic Lineup. Play this game every Monday with a good comic strip from the Sunday comics. Cut up the frames and scramble them. Then ask your child to put them in correct order. You will be able to see how she thinks and which sequencing activities give her the most difficulty.

What's Next? Before playing the game, make a deck of twenty-four cards—twelve cards with a cause and twelve with the effects that result. Write the causes in one color of marker and the effects with another. Shuffle the cards and deal six to each player. Put the rest on the table and turn the first card face up. Take turns trying to match the face-up card with one in your hand.

2. Hearing parents read aloud daily is critically important for the child who is experiencing difficulty with reading. Choose stories that are rich in language and plot. Choose non-fiction books that share facts and information about interesting topics. You need to give your child every opportunity for enlarging his language and experience base, and the daily reading of quality children's literature is the best way to do this. You should read at least two or three good books each day. (See Appendix A, Parent Read-Aloud Resources, for titles of books that contain read-aloud suggestions for kindergarten through second-grade level, or consult your school and public librarians.)

3. Reading *together* every day is different in some very important ways from the reading-aloud experience mentioned earlier. This read-together experience will attempt to engage the child in "reading" and the choice of books for this experience will be totally different from the parent read-aloud books mentioned in the preceding section. Choose easy, predictable books with patterns of rhyme and repetition that your child can begin to "read" on her own. In the beginning choose books that are very simple and then gradually increase the amount and complexity of the language when your child seems ready. Choosing the books for this read-together portion of your day can be very time-consuming. In Appendix A I have included a list of Parent-Child Read Together Resources that Marie Clay uses for her Reading Recovery program, as well as a list of publishers where these types of titles can be obtained. If your child is having trouble with reading and your school has no such program to help him or her, purchasing your own books, though expensive, will be worth it.

4. Doing a daily writing activity associated with one of the reading activities is a fourth and final component of your program to help your child with reading and writing problems. If your child doesn't keep a journal at school, then keep one at home.

The following writing activities can be done on a daily basis three or four times a week depending on your and your child's schedule.

Daily Journal. Keep a record of each day. Start with pictures and add writing as you feel comfortable. Describe what has happened each day, what the weather is like, or how you feel. Don't worry about spelling or punctuation. Use invented spelling (writing out how it sounds, using only beginning and ending sounds).

Lists, Lists, Lists. Make lists of people you need to pray for, what supplies you need for school, or groceries you need to buy. Making lists is a great way to get organized. Make a list of all of your favorites—food, pet, game, TV show, movie, color, etc. Make an inventory of all your toys by writing them down. Read the story called "The List" in the book *Frog and Toad* by Arnold Lobel. It's a great way to introduce the concept of making lists.

How Do We Do It? Write the directions for doing things. Write down how to make a peanut butter sandwich, how to make your bed, or how to play hop-scotch. Anything will do.

Notes and Letters. Write thank-you notes and letters to relatives. Write a note to your teacher or best friend. Find a pen pal and exchange letters with him or her. Write notes to put in Daddy's or Mommy's lunchbox or briefcase each day. Use sticky notes to leave messages for siblings on the bathroom mirror.

Labels and Signs. Make a sign for the door of your room. Make labels for furniture and objects in the house.

Place Cards. Make name cards for the dinner table or parties.

Scrapbooks and Notebooks. Make scrapbooks of trips and excursions. Write descriptions under the brochures or photographs in the scrapbook.

Third grade through fifth grade. You will need to use a slightly different approach to helping your third- through fifth-grade child with a reading and/or writing problem. The program may need to be more remedial in nature because the "failure-discouragement" syndrome may already have taken hold. At this point it will be important for you (if you can) to find out what is keeping your child from being a successful reader. There are many reading restrictors— health, school, home, learning ability, language development, and social and emotional development. Figuring out why your child is having a reading problem may be a little like solving a mystery. You will need to be a detective to see if any of these "reading restrictors" is having a negative impact on your child's learning.

☐ *HEALTH.* Children must be able both to see and hear to be successful readers. You've probably already investigated this as a possible cause of problems when your child began school, but health status can change dramatically overnight. Rule out any problems with hearing and vision.

Other health problems such as severe allergies or infections that cause a child to miss a great deal of school can impact learning. Regular attendance is very important, especially during instruction. Many children who do poorly in reading have simply missed large chunks of instruction and do not have a good foundation on which to base new learnings.

☐ *SCHOOL*. How can school be a reading restrictor? Unfortunately, in the hands of a poor teacher, even the most dedicated student can have learning problems. Talk with your child regularly about what is happening at school. Look over his or her papers, go to all scheduled parent conferences, and become an educated consumer of your school system, whether it be Christian or public.

☐ *MOBILITY.* Children who move frequently may miss out on important skills. Make sure when you move that all records are transferred and that you are aware of the reading levels and abilities of your child.

☐ *HOME*. Are there emotional factors in your family that cause your child to lie awake at night with worry? Are school attendance and achievement a low priority in your family? Or are you putting so much pressure on your child that she is responding with nervousness and failure? Do you neglect reading aloud with your children?

Affixing blame is not nearly as important as solving the problem. However, if there are home patterns that should be changed, neglecting to address them will only cause the problem to grow worse.

☐ *LEARNING ABILITY.* The child who appears to have average or above-average intelligence but still has problems learning to read may well have a learning disability. The learning-disabled child may have a short attention span, problems organizing himself and his homework, difficulty remembering spelling words, and problems controlling his behavior. Public schools are required by law to evaluate and offer services to children who have diagnosed learning disabilities. Search out help.

☐ *SOCIAL AND EMOTIONAL DEVELOPMENT.* The last restrictor of reading achievement is most often seen in older children and adolescents. Problems that were evident in preschool and early elementary years may have been allowed to go untended. Layers of failure and discouragement often result in students with poor attitudes or severe discipline problems. Most adolescents would rather be thought of as "smart-alecky" or "troublesome" than "dumb." Their feelings of self-defeat come out in antisocial ways, and we often fail to connect them with the obvious academic problems.

Now that you have determined if any of the reading restrictors are keeping your child from being a successful reader, you will need to take steps to remediate the problem. But you must also take steps at home to make up for lost time.

Helping your third- through fifth-grade child if he or she has a reading and writing problem is best done daily in five ways: 1) twenty minutes of the parent reading aloud selections that are much more challenging than the child could read independently; 2) fifteen minutes of silent reading by the student of material that is highly interesting and easy enough to be fun; 3) direct instruction from a trained tutor or teacher for both parent and child together in one or several of the five basic reading strategies; 4) use of one or more of the strategies during homework/study sessions; and 5) a writing activity.

1. Parent reading aloud. It's never too late to begin reading aloud. Along with more challenging books, choose a book of high interest that your child will be able to later read on his own. I personally felt the need to have this kind of book in a Christian format and have begun writing a series for young people that many parents are enjoying as much as their kids.[18] The bibliography of read-aloud resources listed in Appendix A (Kindergarten through Second Grades) is appropriate for use with this age level as well. Most of the books contain age-graded recommendations.

2. Sustained silent reading by the student. The trick to helping your child choose a book for independent reading is to find one that catches her interest and then to have several more like it, ready to thrust into her hands when she's finished the first. The book needs to be fairly easy to read, have a predictable plot, and have characters to whom children can easily relate. (See Independent Reading Resources in Appendix B for further information.)

3. Five basic strategies to improve reading comprehension. The purpose for teaching reading strategies to students is to get them to think while they're reading. Research has shown that children with poor comprehension do little "talking to themselves" or thinking while reading. Strategies are most helpful for children who are having problems with comprehension. However, if the strategy becomes the end rather than the means to an end, then the purpose has not been served. Hiring a trained reading teacher/tutor to teach one or more of these strategies to your child over a several-week period could result in a marked improvement in your child's comprehension abilities and be well worth the investment. Just make sure the tutor understands the importance of modeling for the child. If you plan to teach your own child, practice using the strategy several times on your own to make sure you have a clear understanding of how it works. Remember not to overload your child with too many strategies all at once. It is far better to master one strategy and use it consistently than to become totally frustrated and confused.

☐ *STRATEGY ONE: SELF-QUESTIONING.* The critical attribute of this strategy is teaching the reader how to ask good questions. The tutor/teacher must model the process of asking questions and then give the student the opportunity to practice and evaluate good questions as together they read a section from a social studies or science book. Students need to ask both content and process questions as they read. Content questions relate to the content of the reading material (e.g., What are some of the causes of the Civil War?). Process questions relate to how well the student is understanding what he or she is reading. Examples of process questions that students might ask before, during, and after reading are given below. In teaching this strategy, it is absolutely critical that the tutor/teacher model the strategy (say the questions out loud and give answers that the teacher is thinking) and then work closely with the student while he or she tries it independently. The student who is having a difficult time with reading comprehension needs to hear tutors, teachers, or other students thinking aloud so he gets the idea of what should be going on in his head while he is reading. The student with poor comprehension generally has nothing going on in his head while he is reading.

Process Questions to Ask Prior to Reading
What is my purpose for reading?

What task will I be asked to perform? (test, paper, speech)

What do I know about the topic?

Do I know enough to skim the material or should I read slowly and carefully, perhaps taking notes?

What is the organization of the text?

What signal words might help me understand the text?

What might I learn about from this reading?

Process Questions to Ask During Reading

Do I understand what I am reading? Does it make sense to me?

What did I just read? (summary)

How are the ideas in one paragraph (section) related to another paragraph (section)?

What will I learn about next?

Process Questions to Ask After Reading

What were the major ideas in what I just read?

What did I learn that was new to me?

What will I do with this information now?

☐ *STRATEGY TWO: GRAPHIC REPRESENTATIONS (MAPPING/PATTERNING/WEBBING).* The terms mapping, patterning, and webbing all refer to similar activities in which students construct a visual organizer or graphic representation to help categorize and remember information. These visual illustrations of verbal statements are similar to ones we encounter frequently in adult life such as flow charts, pie charts, and family trees. Graphic representations are good learning tools for students who are visual learners and are confused by an overabundance of text. This technique can be used by children of any age and is particularly helpful for students reading science and social studies textbooks or studying for tests in the content areas. (See Graphic Representations in Appendix B for further information.)

☐ *STRATEGY THREE: SQ3R.* SQ3R stands for Survey, Question, Read, Recite, Review. The technique incorporates self-questioning and self-monitoring. The student first surveys the section to be read, noting titles, subtitles, key words, graphs, and pictures. Secondly the student makes up questions he thinks might be answered in the text. These two steps happen before the student begins to read. The last three steps involve the actual reading, stopping periodically along the way to recite (either out loud or by taking notes), and finally reviewing or summarizing what was read. The only problem with this strategy is that many students who are having problems with comprehension to begin with have a hard time asking the right questions and summarizing the text. They need to see someone else "thinking aloud" or modeling for them before they get the idea.

☐ *STRATEGY FOUR: PAIRED READINGS.* This strategy can be used by you and your child working together or by two children working together. I am a great advocate of having children study together for tests. If the study session is structured properly, they will do an excellent job of teaching each other. Two students silently read a short part of a longer assignment. If one finishes first, she goes back and rereads the material for any key points she may have missed. After they've finished, both students close their books and put them away. One of the students is designated the Recaller and one the Listener. The Recaller orally relates what was read to the Listener. She cannot refer to the text at all. The Listener can only interrupt to clarify something that was said. After the Recaller has finished, the Listener does two things: 1) points out and corrects any ideas that were summarized incorrectly, and 2) adds any ideas that were omitted. The two students alternate roles as they move from section to section in the reading.

☐ *STRATEGY FIVE: INSERT.* This strategy is a way of helping students become more involved in their reading. Its only drawback is the need to mark in the text which the student is reading. Some recommend supplying the student with strips of paper to place alongside the text, but I have found that to be impractical. Students use the following code to mark sections of their text: a check mark (✓) for understanding; a plus mark (+) for new information; a question mark (?) for confusing places; an asterisk (*) for important information.

4. A plan for individualized guided reading using school textbooks (science, social studies, reading, health). After your child has mastered one or more of the reading strategies, he or she should practice using them when doing school assignments on a regular basis. The poor reader will need to see someone else use the strategies effectively and model "thinking aloud" on many occasions before he or she is ready to use a strategy independently.

5. Daily writing activities. If your child is writing in a journal at school each day, then you can consider omitting this activity at home. If your child is not writing daily at school, then buy him a diary or journal and ask him to write in it each day. Promise him complete privacy and don't ever violate that pledge. The purpose of journal writing is to encourage your child to think and to then record his thoughts. The journal should never be graded or corrected.

Sixth through eighth grade. If your child in sixth through eighth grade has a reading and writing problem, you'll need to get professional help to solve the problem. And not just any professional will be able to relate to your adolescent. You'll need an individual who gets along well with adolescents and understands how they think and feel. Your child is caught in a vicious cycle. The only way to get good at reading is to read. And if your child has been defeated by reading and won't read, that means she never will get good at it. You will have to find a way to break that cycle.

The first step is getting your child to admit that he or she has a problem. After a child has actually admitted she has a problem, you are one step closer to getting her support and active participation in a remediation program. Begin by getting a good idea of your child's strengths and weaknesses through testing. Hire a professional or see if you can get the school to administer a test battery. Then engage a tutor to help your child. Study with the tutor is best done daily (at least three times per week) in four ways: 1) twenty minutes of the tutor (or parent) reading aloud challenging material; 2) twenty-five to forty-five minutes of silent reading by the student that is of high interest; 3) direct instruction in one of the five basic reading strategies (see pages 67-70); and 4) daily writing activities.

1. Parent reading aloud. I have a friend who read aloud to her son until he left for college. His reading disability slowed down his reading of difficult literature assignments in high school and she found that when they read together his comprehension increased dramatically. If you can do this in the spirit of help and support rather than criticism and negativity, do it.

2. Sustained silent reading by the student. Encourage your child to read independently for recreation. One of the best books I have found to use as a resource for teens and preteens is *Comics to Classics* by Arthea J. S. Reed.[19] This volume addresses the unique problems of the adolescent reader and has hundreds of suggestions for high-interest books. The New York Public Library Office of Young Adult Services has also published a list of Easy-to-Read books for Young Adults. You can write to them for a copy. (See Independent Reading Resources in Appendix C for further information.)

3. Reading strategies for adolescent readers. It is critically important that your child begin to understand and apply many of the reading strategies discussed in the previous section. Once the strategies have been taught, they should be used with homework assignments and to study for tests on a regular basis. Either you or the tutor can help your child do this.

4. Daily writing activities. By this time in your child's academic career, the homework assignments are piling up. While it would be wonderful if you could encourage sixth-through eighth-graders to keep a journal, the likelihood of establishing that habit at home with all of the other demands on his/her time is almost nonexistent. Concentrate on the homework assignments that will contain plenty of opportunities for writing. The graphic representation strategies mentioned earlier and detailed in Appendix B are wonderful aids to helping kids get organized in their writing. Use any of the graphic representations as prewriting activities to help your child begin.

❖ Resources

See Appendices A, B, C for further resources for helping your child develop reading and writing skills.

4

TWO PLUS TWO
EQUALS FIVE
Math Illiteracy

There is no other area of school that causes more anxiety for parents than mathematics. They aren't surprised when their children are having problems with math, because they did, too. And when asked to help their child with math at home, they develop sweaty palms and nervous twitches. Actually, if the truth were known, there are quite a few teachers (especially at the K-6 level) who have the same symptoms. And that may account for the wave of reports in the early 90s that gave increasingly negative findings on student achievement in mathematics. We haven't been doing a very good job of teaching math, particularly at the elementary level. And that has resulted in kids who don't like math. Marilyn Burns, a gifted math educator, shares some of those feelings in her book *The I*

Hate Mathematics! Book[1] (the book would make a wonderful gift for your child).

"I hate mathematics so much it makes me sick."
"Mathematics is for sissies."
"People who like mathematics are really gross."
"What good is it anyway?"

Children have come to equate mathematics with the computational drudgery of arithmetic or with weird students who wear pocket protectors and carry calculators. The Second International Mathematics Study (SIMS) that compared the United States with other industrialized countries (excluding cultural and historical differences) indicated that the mathematics curriculum in this country is "one of minimum expectations that resists the changes necessary to keep pace with the demands of preparing students for contemporary life." The report found that today's mathematics curriculum is weighted down with the rudimentary skills of the nineteenth century and that although students learn to compute, they lack the knowledge and skills to apply those computing skills and solve problems. We all know how critical reading skills are to success in both school and later life, but many parents don't realize the important role that high-school algebra and geometry play as gatekeepers in their child's educational journey. Mastery of these two courses will enable your child to do better on standardized tests, go to college, and get a better-paying, upwardly mobile job. If a child doesn't take algebra and geometry, most post-high-school educational doors are automatically shut. Success in mathematics at the lower levels is essential for success in algebra and geometry.

Mathematics: Questions and Answers to Help You Understand the Basics

If you have turned to this chapter because your child is having a problem with mathematics, you will find more here than just ways to help him learn his math facts, although I've included some excellent strategies for doing that as well. In the questions and answers that follow, you'll find out just how mathematics *should* be taught by your child's teacher, what the curriculum in your local school *should* look like, and what you *should* be doing at home to help your child not only do well in math but like it! These "shoulds" may not be happening now, but they *should* be on the drawing board for the future. You'll read about resources that can help you structure a mathematically literate home, in much the same way that you structure a home rich with print materials and reading to encourage reading literacy. And hopefully, you'll come to the conclusion that math is something all kids need to live productive lives.

What is mathematics? Mathematics is the group of sciences (arithmetic, geometry, algebra, calculus) that deals with quantities, magnitudes, and forms, and their relationships and attributes. Unfortunately, many of us think of mathematics, especially at the elementary school level, only in terms of arithmetic. But as you will see in the sections ahead, mathematics in grades kindergarten through middle school is beginning to change. And *you* can help your child survive and succeed. In fact, the changes will help all children (and parents) be more literate mathematically.

What is the most important prerequisite skill that a child needs to think mathematically? Some researchers and theorists believe that the most important landmark in logical and mathematical reasoning is a concept that most children arrive at between the ages of five and eight. This concept was identified by Piaget as conservation and means that a "child recognizes a quantity stays the same unless you add to or subtract something from it, no matter how much you change it around or split it up."[2] You can see this concept at work in younger children by performing this simple experiment with them: Take a cup of water and pour it into a tall, narrow container. Show it to the child. Then pour the same amount of water into a wide flat one. If a child can conserve, he will say that the amount of water stays the same. If he cannot, he will insist that one or the other of the jars has more water. One theorist says that "until a child has this concept, he is not capable of any truly quantitative reasoning, nor of performing any mathematical operations with real understanding."[3]

There is another group of theorists, however, that questions Piaget's simplistic view of the child's mind. Piaget's view that learning mathematics can only take place after a child is "ready" and that mathematical concepts cannot be "taught" is being challenged by many. These researchers are beginning to look at the acquisition of "math readiness" much the way we have looked at reading readiness. In order to learn to read, children must be ready to associate the printed word with the spoken word and be able to handle the writing of symbols to represent individual sounds and words. In mathematics, children must link their concrete understanding of number statements (if I have two blocks in this hand and two blocks in this hand, then I have four blocks) to the abstract language of arithmetic (two and two makes four). They must then take it one step further and connect to a formal written symbolism ($2 + 2 = 4$).

Why do some children get off to such a bad start in math? One of the most critical aspects of our own number system that children find extraordinarily difficult to comprehend is the use of operator signs (+, -, =). If a child's only experiences with mathematics in school involve an immediate immersion in doing paper and pencil sums, then for many children, mathematics will be a dull and dismal world of attempting to decipher squiggles that don't make sense. The corrollary is having a child immediately begin to learn sounds without ever hearing wonderful stories and poems read aloud.

While children encounter numerals everywhere in their environment prior to attending school, the operator signs are not a part of the child's environment as are words and numerals. Children associate these signs only with doing "math facts" and do not connect them with representations of events or relationships involving concrete objects. In similar studies done in Britain and the United States, children were asked about what the equals sign (=) means. The researcher presented children aged 6 to 12 with various written and spoken sentences (including the forms $2 + 4 = $; $q = 4 + 5$ and $2 + 3 = 3 + 2$) and asked them to explain what these "sentences" meant. The children thought that $2 + 4$ was a stimulus for an answer that needed to be placed on the right. They tended to reject the form of sentences like $q = 4 + 5$ and change it to $4 + 5 = q$ or $q + 4 = 5$. One child thought the sentence presented was backwards. Children showed a strong tendency to reject statements like $3 + 2 = 2 + 3$. One child said the sentence should be changed to read $3 + 2 + 2 + 3 = 10$. The researcher and his colleagues concluded that children consider the symbol = as a "do something signal." There is a strong tendency among all of the children to view the = symbol as being acceptable in a sentence only when one (or more) operation signs (+, -, etc.) precede it. Some children, in fact, tell us that the answer must come after the equal sign. We observe in the children's behavior an extreme rigidity about the written sentence, an insistence that statements be written in a particular form, and a tendency to perform actions (e.g., add) rather than to reflect, make judgments, and infer meanings.[4]

The confusion that many of us still feel when confronted with a mathematical problem has its roots in the fact that we failed to make the connection between the written symbols and what they really mean in concrete terms. Our children are having the same problem.

What are the most important things I as a parent can do to develop a mathematically literate child? Many of the same things you will be doing as a parent to develop a child who loves to read will also influence your child's mathematical abilities—reading aloud, talking to your child (choose books that contain mathematical concepts), and responding to her requests for assistance with her play. But there are a number of additional things you can do that will specifically contribute to developing mathematical literacy.

- *At the same time you point out words to your child, point out numbers and the ways we use math in daily life.*
- *Practice estimation with your child whenever possible.* "Estimation helps the thinking about a problem that precedes the doing and is one of the most useful and 'sense-making' tools available."[5]
- *Emphasize the fun of "doing mathematics" rather than coming up with one correct answer.* The counterpart to

the parent drilling his preschooler with flash cards instead of reading aloud from excellent children's literature is the parent quizzing his three-year-old on two plus two, and losing the opportunity to play supermarket classification (classify what you buy according to whether you eat it for breakfast, lunch, dinner, snacks, or at any meal; whether it's smooth or crunchy; whether it's healthy or junk food; whether it's liquid or solid; whether it's a fruit group, vegetable group, meat group, or bread group; whether it's packaged in paper, plastic, cardboard, aluminum, or tin; whether you can eat it or not eat it; whether it costs under a dollar or over a dollar; and whether it weighs under a pound or over a pound). Naturally you wouldn't do all of these classfications in one shopping trip.

- *Model learning about math yourself by consulting some of the resources found at the end of this chapter.* Don't be afraid. Make the plunge to become more mathematically literate yourself.

What about helping my child with math facts? While it is critical for a child to *understand* the concepts of addition, subtraction, multiplication, and division, being able to produce (write and/or say) the answers to all of these important facts quickly and accurately is a skill that teachers value very highly. Standardized tests also emphasize speed in computation. Many teachers give timed tests (Mad Minute or Math Masters) and students who cannot succeed on these tests may get the idea that they are stupid in math. This is hardly ever the case, but do all you can to get your child over the "math facts hump" and then both of you can relax in math and enjoy the sheer fun of it.

What are some important strategies for learning addition and subtraction facts? There are some important strategies that can help you teach your children his or her addition and subtraction facts. Work with one strategy at a time and give plenty of opportunities for practice using concrete objects as well. Never teach the strategies in a high-pressure, do-or-die manner. These are only strategies. If they don't help your child to learn/remember his math facts, then don't use them. They are the "means," not the "end."

Addition Math Fact Strategies

Counting On
Use when one addend is a 1, 2, or 3.
Prerequisite skills:
  Can identify the larger addend
  Can tell the number that comes next.
Example: 8 + 3 = . . . **Think . . . 8, 9, 10, 11, so 8 + 3 = 11.**

Adding Zero
Use when one addend is 0.
Example: 3 + 0 = . . . **Think . . . Any number plus zero equals number, so 3 + 0 = 3.**

Commutative Property
Use for families of facts.
Examples: 5 + 3 = 3 + 5 . . . **Think . . . I know the answer to 3 + 5, so I also know the answer to 5 + 3.**

Doubles Plus One
Use for facts with a sum 1 more than a double.
Examples: 5 + 6 . . . **Think 5 + 5 = 10 so 5 + 6 is 1 more: 5 + 6 = 11.**
8 + 7 = . . . **Think 7 + 7 = 14, so 8 + 7 is 1 more: 8 + 7 = 15.**

Adding Nine

Use when one addend is a 9.

Examples: 9 + 5 . . . **Think 10 + 5 = 15, so 9 + 5 is 1 less: 9 + 5 = 14.**
8 + 9 . . . Think 10 + 8 = 18, so 8 + 9 is 1 less: 8 + 9 = 17.

The Hard Facts: Doubles Plus Two and Make a Ten

The following are hard facts for kids to remember: 4 + 6; 4 + 7; 5 + 7; 4 + 8; 5 + 8; 6 + 8.

Doubles Plus Two Examples: 4 + 6 . . . **Think 4 + 4 = 8, so 4 + 6 is 2 more: 4 + 6 = 10.**
5 + 7 . . . **Think 5 + 5 = 10, so 5 + 7 is 2 more: 5 + 7 = 12.**
5 + 8 . . . **Think 5 + 5 = 10, so 5 + 8 is 3 more: 5 + 8 = 13.**
Make a Ten Examples: 4 + 8 . . . **Think 2 + 8 = 10, so 4 + 8 is 2 more: 4 + 8 = 12.**
4 + 7 . . . **Think 4 + 6 = 10, so 4 + 7 is 1 more: 4 + 7 = 11.**

Subtraction Math Fact Strategies

Counting Back

Use when the subtrahend is 1, 2, or 3.

Examples: 12 - 3 . . . **Think 12, 11, 10, 9. 12 - 3 = 9.**
9 - 2 . . . **Think 9, 8, 7. 9 - 2 = 7.**

Subtracting Zero

Use when the subtrahend is 0 (6 - 0 = 6).

Any number minus zero equals that number.

Same Number

Use when subtracting a number from itself (4 - 4 = 0).

Any number minus itself equals zero.

Zero Finger

Use with the teen minuends (13 - 9, 15 - 6).

Use the right-hand index finger to cover the ones digit of a problem. *(Note:* The fingernail resembles a zero.) This is your zero finger. Answer easy "10" problem. Remove the zero Finger and add in the extra ones.

Example: 17 - 9 . . . **Think cover "7" with zero finger. Answer the "10" problem.**

10 - 9 = 1. Remove the zero finger and add in the extra ones 1 + 7 = 8.

Example: 11 - 4 . . . **Think cover "1" with zero finger. Answer the "10" problem.**

10 - 4 = 6. Remove the zero finger and add in the extra ones 6 + 1 = 7.

Related Addition Facts

Use related addition facts to figure out the answer.

Example: 9 - 4 . . . **Think 4 + ? = 9. 4 + 5 = 9, so 9 - 4 must be 5.**

What are some important strategies for learning multiplication and division facts? There are also some excellent strategies that can help you teach your children multiplication and division facts. Again, I repeat the warning. Work with one strategy at a time and give plenty of opportunities for practice using concrete objects as well. Never teach the strategies in a high-pressure, do-or-die manner. These are only strategies. If they don't help your child to learn or remember math facts, then don't use them. They are the "means," not the "end." I recently observed one of the strategies at work in a third-grade classroom where they were beginning to study multiplication. There were large sheets of butcher paper tacked around the room, one for the twos, one for the threes, etc. The class had brainstormed all of the things they could think of that came in twos threes, nines, tens. Of course there were the obvious items for twos: eyes, ears, hands. And some similar items for the fours: wheels on a car and legs on a chair. But one particularly creative student had contributed the following items to the lists: the Ten Comandments, the Twelve Apostles, and the Seven Deadly Sins. The strategies are intended to be used in order of their presentation. Once one strategy has been mastered, move on to the next. Almost all math facts your child needs to learn are covered by the given strategies.

Multiplication Math Fact Strategies

Two as a Factor
Review doubles from addition and build in concrete examples: 1 x 2 (pair of shoes); 2 x 2 (front and back wheels of a car); 2 x 3 (six pack of juice). Use domino doubles also.

Zero and One as Factors
Review the concept of any number times one equals that number and any number times zero equals zero. Children frequently confuse addition of 0 and 1 combinations with multiplication of 0 and 1.

Nine as a Factor/One Less than Pattern
9 x 6 = fifty-something
9 x 8 = seventy-something
9 x 4 = thirty-something

Nine as a Factor/Sum of the Digits
3 x 9 = 27 and 2 + 7 = 9
9 x 8 = 72 and 7 + 2 = 9

Nine as a Factor/Finger Multiplication
Number the fingers (left to right from 1 to 10). Bend the numbered finger being multiplied by 9. The number of fingers left of the bent finger is the tens digit; and the number right of the bent finger is the ones digit of the product.

Example: To multiply 5 x 9 bend the thumb on the left hand. The product can be be read from the remaining fingers in this pattern: 4 fingers left of the thumb and 5 fingers to the right of the thumb shows the product is 45.

Perfect Squares

3 x 3; 4 x 4; 6 x 6; 7 x 7; 8 x 8.

Use centimeter graph paper. Draw a square using the lines of the graph paper. Count the number of little squares inside the big square. Keep a running table of the different results for squares with sides 1 through 9 centimeters long. Use rhymes or tricks to help as well.

7 x 7 = 49 (one less than 50)

6 x 6 = 36 (it rhymes)

8 x 8 = 64 (count backwards by 2's (8, 6, 4).

Last Ten Facts

3 x (4, 6, 7, 8); 4 x (6, 7, 8); 6 x (7, 8); 7 x 8

Use multiplication facts already known and add on to achieve the new fact.

Example: 3 x 4 . . . **Think 2 x 4 = 8, so 3 x 4 is 4 more 3 x 4 = 12.**

Division Math Fact Strategies

Two as the Divisor

Use the concept of half. Divide a set of objects into two equal piles.

Five as the Divisor

Use concept of dividing nickels equally. Use the 5-minute intervals of time on a clock.

Nine as the Divisor

Use finger multiplication. Show the dividend with the fingers. The bent finger is the quotient. Emphasize the related multiplication facts as the aid for division.

Perfect Squares

Use centimeter graph paper. Name the perfect square as a number of little squares. How could all these little squares form a big square. How long would each side be? (3 x 3; 4 x 4; 5 x 5; 6 x 6; etc.)

The Last Ten Facts

Review the associated multiplication facts. 3 x (4, 6, 7, 8); 4 x (6, 7, 8); 6 x (7, 8); 7 x 8.

What seems to be the cause of the problems many children have in math? The most common problems children have with math are no different than the ones we faced growing up. They include anxiety, lack of speed in basic operations, failure to memorize math facts and, most importantly, lack of understanding about what they are doing. Until recently, the emphasis in math has been on computation, and teachers have moved to the abstract symbols long before children really understood the conceptual basis of what they were doing. Kindergarten students have been doing worksheets with math facts rather than exploring and discovering mathematical patterns with manipulatives. I've had many classroom teachers tell me they never understood the concept of division until they had to teach it in their own classrooms.

One researcher had this to say about that problem:

Most children aged 11 to 13 years seem able to perform calculations involving the four basic arithmetical operations of addition, subtraction, multiplication and division. However, their understanding of these calculations frequently appears to be limited, and in many cases their performance consists entirely of the meaningless manipulation of symbols. Furthermore, their ability to apply these basic operations to new and unfamiliar problems seems severely restricted.[6]

Most children start school quite capable of adding and subtracting when we place these operations in contexts involving concrete objects, people, or events. It's when we move too quickly to the abstract numbers that children begin having problems with math.

What about calculators? Calculators should be used by children the same way they are used by adults, to take the drudgery out of calculating. I'm sure that very few of us balance our checkbooks or complete our income tax forms by hand anymore. We use the calculator to help us. We do, however, understand what we're doing and are able to estimate the approximate answer to check our calculator work. Once a child understands and can manually do long division, there is little to be gained from doing page after page of problems. His or her energy could better be used on problem solving, graphing, patterning, or doing dozens of other activities that challenge the mind.

What should my child be expected to know at each grade level? There is always a danger in providing checklists for parents to use as measuring sticks since not every child will have every skill at precisely the same point in time in his or her schooling career. But it's important to determine not only how your child is doing but how instruction in your child's school measures up. Appendix D lists benchmarks in math knowledge and skills taken from *Family Math*,[7] an excellent book to have in your resource library. Compare the outcomes with your school district's math learning outcomes. If your school is still emphasizing only paper and pencil drill and computation, begin to lobby for change in this important curricular area. Please notice the skills of estimation and problem solving that are included at every grade level as well as the section on probability and statistics. These are extremely important skills that are left out of many school curricula.

What are math manipulatives and how can they help my child learn math? Manipulatives are objects (they can be expensive and manufactured or collected junk) that help students gain concrete understandings of mathematics before moving to abstract symbols. Examples of manipulatives include: unifix cubes, pattern blocks, geoboards, group attribute blocks, hundred charts, balance, graphing mat, base ten blocks, and tanagrams. See Appendix E for a list of publishers and suppliers.

How can I make math fun? Mathematics is really nothing more than a game, and if you can turn math instruction at home into games, you'll overcome the frustration and anxiety that accompanies a great deal of math tutoring. Games involve repetition (something we frequently need when learning mathematics). We relax when we play games, and that's something we all need to do more of when we learn mathematics. Parents and kids can do games together without all of the tension that accompanies drill and practice with worksheets. I've included some typical math games in the following sections, but you may want to consult the resources in Appendix E for more ideas. If books are out of print, you can borrow them from your public library.

What are the NCTM standards and how will (and should) they influence mathematics instruction in my child's school? NCTM stands for the National Council of Teachers of Mathematics. Their standards, released in

1989, were the result of three years of planning, writing, and consensus-building among the membership of NCTM and the broader mathematics, science, engineering, and educational communities, the business community, parents, and school administrators. The document describes what a high-quality mathematics program should look like. Many schools and districts are just beginning to evaluate their mathematics curriculum in the light of these standards, but their implementation is critical, in my opinion, to developing mathematically literate students. The standards have five goals to promote student self-confidence in mathematics: becoming mathematical problem solvers, learning to communicate mathematically, learning to reason mathematically, learning to value mathematics, and becoming confident in one's own ability.[8]

What does good math instruction look like? Good math instruction will look different at different grade levels, but the following characteristics should be found in any classroom, kindergarten through middle school.

☐ *THE TEACHER EMPHASIZES A PROBLEM-SOLVING APPROACH TO MATHEMATICS AND STUDENTS APPLY THE SKILLS THEY LEARN TO SOLVING REAL-LIFE PROBLEMS.*

☐ *MATH IS INTEGRATED IN ALL AREAS OF THE CURRICULUM.* Students learn to view math as a tool for understanding and solving problems in art, music, social studies, science, and health.

☐ *THERE ARE LOADS OF MANIPULATIVES (BLOCKS, COUNTERS, RODS, GEOBOARDS) AND MEASUR-*

ING TOOLS (SCALES, THERMOMETERS, RULERS, GRAPHS) IN THE CLASSROOM.

☐ *STUDENTS ARE ACTIVELY INVOLVED IN DOING MATHEMATICS RATHER THAN JUST LISTENING OR FILLING OUT WORKSHEETS.*

☐ *THERE IS AN EMPHASIS ON FINDING MULTIPLE WAYS OF SOLVING A PROBLEM RATHER THAN LOOKING FOR THE "RIGHT" ANSWER.* Teachers should be asking questions like: "Does anyone have the same answer but a different way to explain it?"

☐ *THERE IS AN EMPHASIS ON HELPING STUDENTS WORK TOGETHER TO MAKE SENSE OF MATHEMA-TICS.* Teachers should be asking questions like: "Can you convince the rest of us that that makes sense?"

☐ *THERE IS AN EMPHASIS ON HELPING STUDENTS RELY MORE ON THEMSELVES TO DETERMINE WHETHER SOMETHING IS MATHEMATICALLY CORRECT.* Teachers should be asking questions like: "Why do you think that?" Or, "Does that make sense?"

☐ *THERE IS AN EMPHASIS ON HELPING STUDENTS LEARN TO CONJECTURE, INVENT, AND SOLVE PROBLEMS.* Teachers should be asking questions like: "Can you predict the next one?" Or, "Do you see a pattern?"[9]

What are the most effective problem-solving strategies that I can teach my child? Many children, and some adults as well, have the misconception that people who are good at math just automatically "know" the answer. There are, of course, those rare "math whizzes" who can solve any problem instantly. But children need to be taught the following problem-solving strategies by name and then encouraged to use them in real-life problem solving situations. Using these strategies is what "doing math" is all about. The following strategies are taken from an excellent problem-solving kit by Creative Publications.[10]

Guess and Check

When there is no logical way to solve a problem, sometimes you just have to guess an answer and if it isn't correct, then guess again. Most children don't ever think of guessing as an appropriate strategy and have to be taught to try this one. For example, if the question "What number is two times the sum of its digits?" is asked, encourage your child to "guess, check, and adjust." Start with a two digit number like 11 and see what happens. The sum of the digits is 2 and that number is not 2 x 2 so we need a larger number. Let's try 15. The sum of the digits is 6 but 2 x 6 =12. Maybe if we looked at all of the multiples of 2, we could figure something out. How about 16. 1 + 6 = 7. But 7 x 2 = 14. We need an even number so let's try 18. 1 + 8 = 9 and 9 x 2 = 18. So that's the answer. The important part of this strategy is to let your child know that he/she doesn't have to come up with the right answer out of his head. Guessing and checking is the strategy to use.

Looking for Patterns

Looking for patterns is trying to find the sequence or the relationship between things. Patterns can be numerical or pictorial. The following problem illustrates the use of this strategy. Find a rule that helps you find the missing numbers by looking for a pattern in the first two series.

8, 3, 11

9, 5, 14

4, 8, _

6, _, 20

_, 7, 19

You can see from doing some guessing and checking that the rule is to add the first two numbers to get the third.

Make an Organized List

This third helpful strategy requires making lists as a way of visualizing all of the possible alternatives that are likely in a given situation. Again, I remind you that children frequently approach problem solving with the thought that unless they can come up with answer "out of their head" it isn't fair. They need to be taught how to use each of these helpful strategies. The following problem illustrates the use of this strategy.

At camp, these are the choices for supper.

Meat	Potatoes	Vegetable
steak	mashed	corn
trout	baked	green beans
	french fries	

List the twelve different suppers a camper could choose if he eats one item from each group. Help your child to get organized as he makes his lists. Exhaust all the possibilities using one starting point before going on to a different one. Steak, mashed potatoes, corn; Steak, mashed potatoes, green beans; Steak, baked potatoes, corn; Steak, french fries, corn; etc.

Make a Picture/Diagram or Model

The visual learner will love this problem-solving approach. The following problem needs the drawing/model strategy to solve.

A fireman stood on the middle step of a ladder. As the smoke got less, he climbed up three steps. The fire got worse, so he had to climb down five steps. Then he climbed up the last six steps and was at the top of the ladder. How many steps were in the ladder? (9)

Eliminate Possibilities

This strategy is used by detectives, school principals, doctors, and auto mechanics to figure out the best solution to a problem. The game of Clue is based on this strategy. Here's a problem to practice the strategy.

> Jeff has less than 30 marbles. When he puts them in piles of three, he has no marbles left over. When he puts them in piles of two, he has one left. When he puts them in piles of five, he has one left. How many marbles does Jeff have? (21)

Other helpful problem-solving strategies include acting out or using objects; using or making a table, working backwards, using logical reasoning, making the problem simpler, and brainstorming (solving the problem in a group and pooling ideas).

Things You Can Do at Home to Improve Your Child's Math Skills

Kindergarten through second grade. Helping your child be a successful math student is much like helping your child be a successful reader. It can be done. It just takes commitment and energy. Use these approaches:

☐ *READ-ALOUDS USING MATHEMATICS.* Maximize your read-aloud time by reading books that feature mathematical topics and concepts. See the Read-Aloud Math Books for Kindergarten through Second Grades in Appendix E for a few of the very best. They are essential read-alouds to show your child (and you) that math can be fun! Your public and school librarians can help you find others.

☐ *SPONGE ACTIVITIES ARE LEARNING EXPERIEN-CES THAT TAKE PLACE IN A FIVE-TO-TEN MINUTE PERIOD OF TIME.* Children usually think of them as games. But the key is constant repetition in a context of fun. You don't need to focus on "teaching" specific skills as much as encouraging practice and giving positive feedback. Sponge activities can also be "long-term" proejcts your child is working on and takes out every now and then. I've included some examples of sponge activities below. Consult the Resources at the end of this chapter.

Number Posters

Write the numbers 1 to 10 down the left-hand side of a piece of poster board. Next to each number glue that many objects. You can use raisins, beans, nuts, buttons, sticks, cotton balls, gumdrops, lifesavers, or washers. If your child wants to go on to 20, make a new poster. You can also glue objects in groups of ten, which will help your child count in tens. But first master counting to ten. Hang the poster up in the kitchen and use it to count everyday.

Calendar

Use the calendar everyday to talk about what day of the week it is, what month it is, what happened yesterday, what will happen tomorrow.

String It Up

Cut out lengths of string that correspond to the length, width, and circumference of various objects around the house.

Math in the Kitchen

Whenever you're cooking, you'll have opportunities to teach math. Don't miss out on any of them.

Math at the Supermarket

A trip to the store is filled with opportunities for teaching math. Ask your child to get three bars of soap, two packages of cereal, or five cartons of yogurt. At the checkout, always give your child the pennies to count and put in his penny jar.

A Penny Saved

Every now and then let him count 100 pennies and exchange it for a dollar bill (if he's agreeable). Deposit the dollar bill in his savings account and make a written record of it.

Daily Problem Solving

Build in a daily problem for your child to solve. You will need to experiment with the type and complexity of problems, but in doing so, you will sharpen your own mathematical abilities as well. Examples: There are only three cookies left in the jar. How can we divide them so everyone (Mom, Dad, and little sister) gets the same amount? The recipe calls for three large potatoes and I only have little ones What should I do? I've lost my other brown sock. Where in the world could it possibly be?

☐ *CREATING A POSITIVE MENTAL ATTITUDE TOWARD MATH.* If you can purchase only one book about doing math in your home, then buy *Family Math* (Stenmark, Jean, et. al., Berkeley, Calif.: University of California, 1986). It is filled with wonderful suggestions for family activities and, in addition, offers these wonderful suggestions about helping your child at home. The remarks in italic are mine.

- Let your children know that you believe they can succeed. *This attitude is critical in all aspects of your child's life, but especially so in math.*
- Be ready to talk with your children about mathematics and to listen to what they are saying. *If you do a lot of negative "self-talk" with regard to math, e.g., "I never*

got good grades in math either; it must run in the family," start to program in some positive statements.

- Be more concerned with the processes of doing mathematics than with getting correct answers.
- Try not to tell children how to solve the problem.
- Practice estimation whenever possible.
- Provide a special place for study.
- Encourage group study. *Encourage your child to work with others to solve problems and study math. Whenever my children have encountered a problem with homework, the first thing I suggest is calling a friend for help.*
- Expect that homework will be done. *Most schools have homework beginning in kindergarten. Supplement the homework with "fun" math activities as well.*
- Don't expect that all homework will be easy.
- Ask the teacher to give you a list of what your child will be expected to know at his grade level.
- Sit in on your child's math class.
- Look carefully at standardized test results if they are available.
- Don't make math drill work into a battleground.[11]

☐ *CREATING A MATH ENVIRONMENT AT HOME.* As you purchase items for birthdays and Christmas, think about buying math-related items such as manipulatives or games. Visit a local teachers' store or write for catalogs from the resource companies I've listed in Appendix E. Games that develop problem-solving skills include Battleship, Checkers, Made for Trade, Chess, Parquetry Blocks, Chinese Checkers, Parcheesi, Tanagrams, Yahtzee, Tri-Ominos, any deck of cards, or Uno.

Consider purchasing a computer. There are dozens of excellent software programs that provide drill and practice of math facts (in a motivating and interesting way) and challenging problem-solving activities. Gertrude's Secrets (The Learning Company), Math Blasters (Davidson), and New Teasers by Tobbs (Sunburst) are a few excellent programs.

☐ *STRATEGIES TO LEARN MATH FACTS.* There are still many teachers who judge a child's math ability solely on the basis of her ability to write and say the math facts in an accurate and timely way. Assist your child in every possible way to be able to do this (and then make sure she gets the "fun" side of math at home). Use the strategies mentioned earlier in the chapter to help your child master the shortcuts. Use manipulatives to help her understand the concepts behind the facts.

Third through fifth grade. Helping your third- through fifth-grade child if he or she has a math problem is best done in the following ways:

☐ *READ-ALOUD MATH BOOKS FOR THE OLDER CHILD.* You may think of your child in third through fifth grade as too old for math read-alouds, but think again. The selection of Read-Aloud Math Books for Third through Fifth Grades in Appendix E will introduce math in new ways to your child. You can delight as Socrates the Wolf tries to decide in which of three houses he might find three little pigs. You and your child will discover the wonderful world of permutations, combinations, and probability.

☐ *SPONGE ACTIVITIES.* Sponge activities for your third-through fifth-grade child can take the form of story problems (Creative Publications and Midwest Publications have excellent books). Teach your child the problem-solving strategies mentioned earlier. In the beginning you may need to model the strategies, but you will be surprised at how good your child will get at solving the problems on his own. Your child will have an opportunity to practice his math skills solving "real" problems.

☐ *CREATING A POSITIVE MENTAL ATTITUDE ABOUT MATH.* If your child has experienced failure in math, then creating a positive attitude by the time she is older can be a real challenge. You will have to model a good attitude, be a learner along with your child, and build in plenty of opportunities for success. Consult the list of ideas in the Kindergarten through Second Grade section of this chapter.

☐ *CREATING A MATH ENVIRONMENT AT HOME.* Consult the Math Environment section in Kindergarten through Second Grade for game ideas. Add Monopoly to the list. In addition to the computer games mentioned earlier, consider purchasing Math Blaster (Davidson), Math Man (Scholastic), Apple Factory (Sunburst), Puzzle Tanks (Sunburst), The King's Rule (Sunburst) and Building Perspective (Sunburst).

Sixth through eighth grade. If your child is having a serious problem in math at this level, then you need to move into serious remediation of the difficulties. You should arrange to have your child tested to discover why he or she is not able to succeed in math. I would not attempt tutoring my own child at this level. I would hire the services of a professional teacher or a high-school or college student who is good at math. Make sure your child knows the math facts. Make sure your child knows all of the problem-solving strategies. At this point, you don't have time for sponge activities and read-alouds. The prospect of high-school math placement is looming, and you need to do everything you can quickly to make sure your child gets the needed skills to be successful in an algebra class. If you have to move mountains to do it, then by all means hire the crane operators and bulldozers immediately.

❖ Resources

Creative Publications
P.O. Box 10328
Palo Alto, CA 94303

> Windows of Mathematics Series (K-2)
> Contains over 650 developmentally sound math activities.
>
> Franco, Betsy, Joan Westley, and Randolph Micaella. Titles are: *Matching; Shapes; Counting and Numbers; Comparing; Classifying and Graphing; Patterns; Reading and Writing Numerals; Number Concepts (0-9); Number Concepts (10-100); Adding and Subtracting; Measuring; Money and Time; Management Guide.*

Dale Seymour Publications
Palo Alto, California
"Used Number Series" 1990

> Grades K-1
> Stone, Antonia, and Susan Jo Russell. *Used Numbers: Counting Ourselves and Our Families.*
>
> Grades 2-3
> Russell, Susan Jo, and Rebecca Corwin. *Used Numbers: Sorting: Groups and Graphs.*

Grades 4-6
Russell, Susan Jo, and Rebecca Corwin. *Used Numbers: Real Data in the Classroom.*

Grades 5-6
Corwin, Rebecca, and Susan Freil. *Used Numbers: Statistics: Prediction and Sampling.*

Holt, Michael, and Zoltan Dienes. *Let's Play Math.* New York: Walker and Company, 1973.

Kaye, Peggy. *Games for Math: Playful Ways to Help Your Child Learn Math from Kindergarten to Third Grade.* New York: Pantheon Books, 1987.

Rosenberg, Nancy. *How to Enjoy Mathematics with Your Child.* New York: Stein and Day, 1970.

Toole, Amy L., and Ellen Boehm. *Off to a Good Start: 464 Readiness Activities for Reading, Math, Social Studies, and Science.* New York: Walker and Company, 1983.

Zaslavsky, Claudia. *Preparing Young Children for Math: A Book of Games.* New York: Schocken Books, 1979.

5

HE WON'T DO IT
Motivation and Underachievement

Aaron was a charming child. Curly dark hair, sparkling brown eyes, and the ability to talk his way out of anything. If you didn't know better you'd think that Aaron was an outstanding fifth-grade student. He certainly had the intellectual ability to be one; and all the test scores said so, too. He'd been tested to see if he had a learning disability and found to be completely normal. But he was failing all of his subjects and giving his mother an ulcer and his teacher gray hair in the process. Oh, Aaron pretended to work once in a while. He would give the impression of organizing his desk in a flurry of activity or pretend to be reading or writing, but his assignments were never turned in and he failed most of the tests. All of us who knew him believed that Aaron could make A's and B's, except Aaron. Faced with a child like this, what's a parent (teacher or principal) to do? Some parents send kids like this to military school, hoping that the discipline and structure will turn them into students. And sometimes it does—but at great expense both financially for parents and emotionally and psychologically for both parent and child. Some parents give up totally and resign themselves to having a high-school dropout/failure, because that's what usually happens to kids like Aaron when the work becomes more difficult and they fall farther behind. As an elementary school principal, I've worked with dozens of kids like Aaron, and there are many things that you as a parent can do to turn around the "underachievement syndrome." It's a difficult problem to solve and requires the cooperation of every adult who works with the child.

Chapter Five will be organized in a similar fashion to each of the preceding chapters. First, we'll look at some basic information, definitions, ideas, and philosophies about the subjects of underachievement and motivation. Over and over again I have seen amazing academic, behavioral, and emotional changes occur in children when parents and teachers work hand-in-hand to solve a schooling problem. The key is cooperation between all of the parties involved that leaves no room for blame and recrimination but focuses solely on solving the problem at hand.

Underachievement: Questions and Answers to Help You Understand the Basics

What is an underachiever? "Students who rank in the top third in intellectual ability, but whose performance is dramatically below that level" is the definition given to underachievers by Benjamin Fine in his book *Under-*

achievers: How They Can Be Helped.[1] You no doubt can list
at least a half dozen of the behavioral characteristics of an
underachiever if you live with one. Lawrence Greene has
compiled a list of nineteen.[2] According to Greene, if your
child exhibits only a couple of these characteristics, you
have nothing to worry about. If you can pick out anywhere
from three to seven of them as being descriptive of your
child, you have some potential problems developing. You
should pay special heed if your child exhibits a large number of characteristics and is in kindergarten through third
grade. Any child with a score of eight to eighteen is well on
his way to underachievement, and a score of nineteen
means your child is at real risk of academic failure. Here is
Greene's list.

1. My child's schoolwork is sloppy and illegible.
2. My child's projects are often incomplete.
3. My child procrastinates.
4. My child is having difficulty keeping up with his or
   her class.
5. My child's work is not handed in on time.
6. My child is disorganized at home.
7. My child is disorganized at school.
8. My child is irresponsible.
9. My child is forgetful.
10. My child lacks pride in his or her work.
11. My child shows little motivation.
12. My child avoids academic work.
13. My child makes excuses for poor performance.
14. My child avoids challenges.
15. My child lacks self-confidence.
16. My child becomes easily discouraged.
17. My child abandons difficult projects.

18. My child is easily frustrated.
19. My child appears to be functioning below his or her potential.

What is motivation? Motivation to learn is the key to school success and achievement. The fascinating thing about this quality, missing in underachievers, is that every child is born with the motivation to learn.[3] He or she just loses it somewhere on the way to school. Raymond Wlodkowski, a psychologist and expert in the area of motivating children to learn, believes there are three reasons that motivation to learn diminishes in some children.[4] Once a child enters the formalized school setting, the possibility for learning and growing at his or her own rate practically disappears. Oh, perhaps in the best of kindergarten and first-grade classes that use developmentally appropriate teaching practices children would not be subjected to grades and formalized textbooks. But in too many schools, children are expected to move in a lock-step fashion, and the failure to achieve an arbitrary "grade-level standard" can weigh heavily against a child's record.

A second contributing factor for a diminishing supply of motivation in children as they grow older according to Wlodkowski is that "the acquisition of advanced knowledge and skill is complex, demanding, and time consuming, especially for the less talented."[5] Schoolwork gets harder and harder, and those who aren't experiencing the level of success they once did no longer feel able to cope. Consequently, they lose their "motivation" or willingness to put forth effort.

A third impediment to motivation is the number of distractions that arise in the course of human development to take learners "off course." For young children these distractions can be as simple as television. In older children, the distractions can take the form of cars, girls, or even jobs.

What factors contribute to a child's motivational level? There are four major aspects to each of our lives and particularly the lives of children that impact their motivational level: culture, family, school, and the child herself (her learning style/emotional stability).[6] Researchers have widely documented evidence of how the Japanese culture values academic achievement and encourages motivation to learn among its children.[7] While cultural expectations of a particular group or nationality cannot be generalized in all cases, these characteristics must be considered when evaluating your child's motivational level.

The family is a second major aspect in the development of motivation in children. (Much more will be said about this important factor later in the section "Is it all my fault? What part does the family play in the development of an underachiever?") The school, a third major factor in the development of motivation, will also be discussed in detail (see "Can the school environment contribute to underachievement?"). The child's personality and temperament also contribute to his motivational level (see "What are the characteristics of the child that may contribute to underachievement?").

Isn't all this emphasis on achievement a little unhealthy? Aren't we really pressuring kids too much? Achievement certainly isn't the complete answer to happiness. If it were, there wouldn't be so many successful sports and movie stars whose lives end in suicide, divorce, and substance abuse. On the other hand, people who don't achieve any goals or take pride in anything they do are plagued with low self-esteem and a constant feeling of failure that is just as debilitating. As in any human endeavor, the encouragement of motivation and achievement in children must be balanced with well-rounded development in all aspects of life.[8] However, ignoring a child who is on the unhealthy path to apathy and self-destruction falls into the category of child abuse.

Is it all my fault? What part does the family play in the development of an underachiever? As an elementary school principal, I've always been loathe to assign blame to the parents or families of children who are having difficulty in school. My focus has been on solving the problem in a spirit of cooperation and collaboration. The researchers and therapists who work in this field are not nearly as kind and forgiving as I have been. Dr. Linnus S. Pecaut, founder of the Institute for Motivational Development, an organization that specializes in working with underachieving children, has written a book entitled *The Making of an Underachiever: Growing Up in the Shadow of Success* that describes a specific underachievement pattern: the highly successful, perfectionist father who creates an environment where his son has literally not had permission to live his own life.[9] Dr. Sylvia Rimm, who founded the Family Achievement Clinic, approaches the underachievement problem more globally in her writings. But she, like Pecaut, is blunt in her descriptions of family patterns that foster and indeed create an "underachieving child."[10] Rimm suggests a number of dysfunctional family patterns that contribute to the development of underachievement by imitation.[11] My personal research and experience,[12] and the work of Christian psychiatrist Paul Meier[13] support Rimm's assertions.

The categories are Sylvia Rimm's,[14] but the examples that follow are drawn from my own experiences as a teacher and principal.

☐ *I HAD EXACTLY THE SAME PROBLEM IN SCHOOL.*
Every time I had a conference with the Harris family I
knew I'd have to listen to both Mom and Dad talk about
their own unfortunate experiences in school. And they
weren't about to lay them to rest. I didn't have to wonder
why James and Joanne didn't like school and weren't
willing to try. Their parents gave them a perfect excuse
for failing. It was part of the family tree!

☐ *I CAN'T SEEM TO GET ORGANIZED.* I could count on
seeing Burt Baron in the school office almost every morning. Some days he'd forgotten his lunch money, other
days it was his cello. But the biggest reason for phoning
home was to see if his mother could locate a missing
homework assignment. Burt just couldn't seem to get
organized, but it was no mystery as to why. His mother
seldom managed to make it anywhere on time or follow
through to completion any project she undertook either.
Visiting the Baron's home, under construction for over
five years, gave the casual observer a clue as to why Burt
was never quite on top of things. He lived his life in the
midst of total chaos.

☐ *HE'S JUST LIKE HIS FATHER. MY HUSBAND WON'T
DO ANYTHING EITHER.* Mrs. Crittenden would
literally wring her hands as she poured her heart out
to me. And I could feel her frustration when she
dragged her husband to my office for a conference. He
didn't want to take any ownership of his son's achievement problem. His wife nagged him from morning till
late at night and the only way to survive was to tune it
out. His son, Adam, was just like him. Mom was doing
all the worrying.

☐ *THERE ISN'T ENOUGH TIME.* I still suffer from this syndrome at times. Parents who are heavily involved in career development and many outside activities can totally overlook the havoc they are creating at home. I've had many two-career couples who wanted me to take all the responsibility for their child's achievement. They were too important and busy to be bothered. And their children were smart enough to know how to really get Mom and Dad's attention—stop doing their homework and start getting bad grades.

☐ *MY PARENTS ARE GETTING A DIVORCE.* Once the lawyers have been hired, there's little that can be done to stop the snowball effect that divorce can have on a child's achievement. To assign blame is counterproductive, but to send the message to kids that they have permission to stop working just because their parents are divorcing is a mistake on the part of either party.

☐ *GOTCHA.* It's obvious the minute that some families sit down in the chairs around the table for a conference that they won't be able to step out of the roles they play at home. Either parent can play what Sylvia Rimm calls "the ogre" while the opposite parent is seen as kind and caring. The ogre sets limits and rules while the kind and caring parent continually offers excuses and support for underachievement. This set of parents is constantly undermining and opposing each other while their "little darling" quietly falls through the cracks. Another variation of this theme is what Rimm calls the "Daddy Is a Dummy" or "Mother Is the Mouse of the House." Parents sabotage and undermine the credibility of the opposite parent, leaving the child without an appropriate achievement role model. In totally dysfunctional families all four "sabotage rituals," as Rimm describes them, can take place simultaneously. While parents may be quick to admit that their marriage isn't perfect, they often don't have a clue about how their family relationships impact the achievement status of their child.

If you're having a difficult time identifying any of Rimm's categories with what's going on in your family, perhaps you'll find this Family Problems Checklist helpful.[15] The comments in parentheses are my additions to Greene's very excellent compilation.

Family Problems Checklist

Questionnaire

YES NO   1. Family members rarely interact or share time, activities, or interests. *(Family members need to have some opportunity to get to "know" each other and have "fellowship" as a group.)*

YES NO   2. Family members prioritize their own interests and are not available to assist other family members. *(In this age of doing your own thing and splitting everything 50-50, there is a real danger that couples will not recognize the need for unselfish commitment to the needs of one another.)*

YES NO   3. Family members are unable to create trust, to share, or to establish intimacy. *(The qualities of trust and sharing are essential if children are to feel a sense of responsibility and commitment to the mutual goals of the family.)*

YES NO   4. Family members have difficulty addressing family problems until a crisis develops.

YES NO   5. Family members have difficulty recognizing or responding to each other's needs, thoughts, and feelings. *(Mutual responsibility for helping one another when needs arise is critical to emotional well-being.)*

YES   NO   6. Parents seek to satisfy their own emotional needs and disregard their children's emotional needs.

YES   NO   7. Parents have difficulty establishing consistent rules and consequences for misbehavior.

YES   NO   8. Family members are required to share everything: time, activities, and interests. *(While togetherness is important, there needs to be mutual respect for everyone's individuality. Don't expect everyone to love Saturday afternoon football just because you do.)*

YES   NO   9. Family members are required to participate and agree, or are considered disloyal. *(There has to be room for expressing individual opinions. When family members have to keep their feelings bottled up, they will eventually come out in unhealthy ways.)*

YES   NO   10. Family attempts to protect its members from all outsiders. *(Children need friends and older adult role models in the church, community, and school. Making them feel disloyal for these relationships is unhealthy.)*

YES   NO   11. Family discourages individualization, independence, and separation. *(The family that closes its doors to the outside world is asking for heartache.)*

YES   NO   12. Parents are unable to establish intimacy in relationships with nonfamily members. *(If you've marked yes to questions 8-12, you need to examine carefully your view of the family and its purposes. Yours is a very unhealthy one.)*

YES   NO   13. Family members cannot "read" the thoughts and feeling of others in the family. *(People who live together need empathy and sensitivity for each other.)*

YES   NO   14. Parents use "we" when referring to their child's actions. *(Your child is an individual and so are you. If you use "we," you are identifying too closely with your child.)*

YES   NO   15. Parents communicate that the child is helpless to meet his own needs. *(If you don't believe your child can do it, how can you expect him to believe he can do it?)*

YES   NO   16. Parents are unable to unite as a couple and cooperate. *(This is one of the most devastating situations for a child to live in. The lack of a united front will be addressed in a later question and answer also.)*

YES   NO   17. Parents cannot agree on parenting issues. *(Your child will be confused in the beginning and gradually become a master manipulator.)*

YES   NO   18. One parent aligns with child against other parent. *(You're on a very destructive path.)*

YES NO   19. Parents put child in double-bind, no-win situations. *(There's no way a child will put forth the effort needed for achievement if his or her own parent is working against him constantly.)*

YES NO   20. Parents continually fight about children. *(Another sure-fire way to create a nonachiever.)*

YES NO   21. Parents permit children to create distance between them. *(This will destroy your marriage along with your children.)*

YES NO   22. Father or mother is absent from the home. *(Of course you can't always be there, but if you're never there, look out.)*

YES NO   23. Parent places priority on "peace and quiet." *(Refusing to confront issues to keep things peaceful can be just as destructive as too much fighting.)*

YES NO   24. One parent places work above family commitment. *(The overachieving parent can be one of the first reasons a child will underachieve.)*

YES NO   25. Raising children is the mother's job exclusively. *(I'm afraid this scenario still exists in far too many homes.)*

YES NO   26. One parent becomes overly dependent on children and "over protects." *(This is a very hard quality to recognize and accept in oneself. We always feel like we're doing the "right thing" for our child. But it's a dangerous course to follow.)*

YES NO   27. One parent dramatizes and overreacts to minor events. *(Living in a household like this is like being on a rollercoaster.)*

YES NO   28. Separated parents use children to "get back" at each other. *(The child becomes a pawn in the "war" between two adults.)*

YES NO   29. Single parent is overworked and has little time for children's problems. *(This is a really tough problem for single parents to handle. I've agonized with many over it. But the alternatives are less acceptable.)*

YES NO   30. One parent abuses the other parent physically or emotionally. *(The long-term damage that can be done to children if items 30-34 are present in the home is just beginning to be discovered. If any of them exist in your home, take the first step toward getting help immediately.)*

YES NO   31. Parents abuse child physically or emotionally.

YES NO   32. One child in family is selected for family ridicule or abuse.

YES NO   33. Sexual abuse of child by adult family member.

YES NO   34. Sexual abuse of younger child by older sibling.

YES NO   35. Chronic fighting and disagreement. *(Living in this kind of environment is very debilitating for both adults and children.)*

YES NO   36. Stepchild or stepparents resent or fear one another. *(The problems created when families blend [Items 36-39] are difficult ones to handle. Get professional help if you can.)*

YES NO   37. Stepchildren refuse to relate to one another.

YES NO   38. Children relate only to natural parents and consider other blended family members as intruders.

YES NO   39. Stepparent never assumes parenting role.

YES NO   40. Drug or alcohol abuse has caused children to become fearful or distrustful. *(I've worked with a number of underachievers whose problems can be directly related to an alcoholic or drug-dependent parent.)*

YES NO   41. Parents have difficulty putting their own lives in order. *(Kids need a role model for healthy living.)*

YES NO   42. Parents avoid responsibility. *(I can't tell you the number of families I've counseled in my office who want to blame all of their child's under-achievement problems on the school. Usually the child is in middle school before they are willing to recognize the part they have played. Then it's twice as hard to solve the problem.)*

YES NO   43. Parents are highly critical. *(Parents who have problems with items 43 and 44 look like they're doing the right thing. After all, aren't we supposed to have high expectations and let children know when they aren't doing the right thing? These folks carry it to the extreme, however. Nothing is ever right!)*

YES NO   44. Parents have unreasonable expectations.

YES NO   45. Children have placed excessive demands on themselves.

YES NO   46. Parents are compelled to deny that the family has problems. *(If you've completed this questionnaire and don't see yourself anywhere, ask an honest outside observer for an opinion. Usually someone who knows your family well can spot the problem immediately.)*

I hope it has been obvious to you as you read through this list that the preferred answer in every case is NO. If you find a pattern of YES answers or even one or two YES answers, then you have a serious family problem that should be addressed before it damages your child's ability to achieve, if it hasn't already done so.

Can the school contribute to underachievement? Lest you think that parents must bear the sole responsibility for creating underachievers, let's look at how the school does its share. Aaron, the young man you met at the outset of the chapter, provides a perfect example of how the classroom environment can either hinder or help the under-achievement syndrome. There are four types of classroom teachers that spell disaster for the underachiever: the angry, bored, easily satisfied, or rigid teacher. In some cases a teacher can fall into more than one category and then the year might as well be over before it starts.

I encountered Aaron early in my administrative career, before I thoroughly understood the importance of matching the learning style and personality of the child with that of the teacher. I once believed that it was useful for a child to "learn to get along with all types of teachers." The more I watched the "fallout" from such decisions, the more care I began to take with classroom assignments. Aaron was already an underachiever when he arrived in fourth grade, but having a teacher whose definition of flexibility was having a washroom break at 10:06 rather than 10:05 didn't help his attitude one bit. She had decided before the first day of school was over that she would break his spirit—and unfortunately he broke hers. The power struggle in which the two of them engaged over the course of the school year rivaled any major world conflict during the past ten years. Neither of them learned anything during the year. Even as early as kindergarten or first grade, a child can begin to slip into underachievement when faced with a teacher whose profile contains any of those unfortunate characteristics listed above.

In addition to your child's teacher, there are several other aspects of school that can exacerbate underachievement. One is competition. One of the worst underachievers I've ever met in my experience was a hardened second grader.

Competition was his undoing. He wanted so desperately to be first and win in every single thing that happened at school that he spent most of his time cooling off from his temper tantrums when he lost. In Chapter Two we discussed the deleterious effects of labeling and tracking. The first thing we think of when a child begins to fail is getting some special help for her. We label her disabled, we pull her out of the classroom with a special teacher or we put her in a lower group where she won't have to work as hard to keep up. In some cases, we even work with her completely on her own. Now the underachiever feels she can't do anything unless she has her own private tutor.

I made an amazing discovery in the school in which I served as principal for eight years. When I looked at the grades of all of the students in the lower groups, I found that they usually were getting D's and F's in the subject concerned. This fact flew in the face of the very reason groups were formed in the first place—so that students would be able to succeed at their own achievement level. My reply to my faculty when they questioned my decision to get rid of all groups and tracking was this: "Well, they can get D's and F's in the higher reading group and learn more in the process." In actuality what happened was that lower-achieving students began getting better grades when groups and tracking were abolished.

What are the characteristics of the child that may contribute to underachievement? Priscilla Vail, a learning specialist, calls them "smart kids with school problems." Her work has focused largely on gifted children who aren't achieving in school. While all underachievers certainly can't be called gifted, there are a number of characteristics of gifted children that can be seen in a large portion of the underachieving population.[16] These characteristics are one of the reasons that the choice of teachers for the underachieving child is particularly important. The characteristics are usually evident in the child's early schooling experience. If left unrecognized or untreated they can often result in a downward spiral in achievement.

☐ *RAPID GRASP OF CONCEPTS.* While to some it seems a contradiction to think that an underachieving student grasps concepts rapidly, it is this very quality that seduces the student into doing nothing. He always feels that the work is too easy and that if he really wanted to do it, he could. Teachers can sometimes be resentful of a student who learns easily.

☐ *CURIOSITY.* Some students drive their teachers crazy with questions. My son nearly did just that to his fourth-grade teacher. Fortunately we were all able to communicate about the issue in a spirit of cooperation, and we solved the problem. But given another type of teacher, he might well have decided that curiosity wasn't welcome in school and turned his energies someplace else.

☐ *HEIGHTENED PERCEPTIONS.* I have found this quality in abundance in underachievers. They can find the inconsistencies in any situation, and if no one ever stops to listen to their ideas or points of view, they will use all of their energies documenting the flaws and weaknesses of the system and using them as an excuse for their lack of effort. I've had hundreds of conferences and developed many work/study contracts with underachieving students. They can always tell me more about the flaws of everyone else than they can about their own.

☐ *DIVERGENT THINKING.* This characteristic goes hand-in-hand with heightened perceptions. Underachievers frequently have little patience with routine. They continually disrupt the classroom with what they are thinking and with what they want to do. When the system can't accommodate them, they can sometimes turn totally off.

Things You Can Do at Home to Help Solve Your Child's Underachievement Problem

Solving an underachievement problem takes a major commitment on your part as a parent. I've worked at solving many underachieving problems in the school setting—reassigning a child to another teacher to give her a fresh start, developing contracts and plans to monitor her work and study habits, providing counseling services so the child can begin to understand what part she can play in the solution. The only real success stories I've had have been those where I've worked hand-in-hand with the parents, and they were willing to change their behaviors as well.

The generic plan and techniques to use are similar at all grade levels. The big difference is that when you're working with older and more mature students, you need to vary your approaches somewhat. Their habits have had much longer to become ingrained; they've been through a variety of different approaches that didn't work and will be very cynical and uncooperative about trying anything new; and they don't have much faith in their parents at this point. I worked with a second grader who I was sure was a misplaced middle-school student. Mike had been wrapping his parents around his little finger since birth and gave every teacher he encountered fits. He was an attention grabber with a booming voice and argumentative style that matched the best Wall Street lawyer. Mike's only problem was that he didn't do anything in school except argue. A variety of school psychologists and behavior management specialists had worked their wonders on Mike, but he always seemed two steps ahead of them. I knew we had a real challenge on our hands when Mike approached me in the hall one day. "Dr. McEwan," he said in his professorial manner, "I'd like to go back on that behavior plan I used in kindergarten. It worked much better than the one we're using now. I got prizes every day. Could you call up that psychologist and get her to come over here?" You can see that a bright child (and underachievers usually have plenty of ability) will soon see through adults who don't follow through or change the rules in the middle of the game.

The first thing you need to realize about solving your child's underachievement problem is that you can't do it on your own. If the problem is a serious one, you've probably done your share to encourage it and you will need backup and support to help you gain the courage and skills to change unhealthy parenting behaviors.

Six steps for solving underachievement problems. The best plan I have seen in writing that approximates what we have been doing in our school for years is Sylvia Rimm's Trifocal Approach. Individuals who attend her clinic in Watertown, Wisconsin, usually enter a structured program that takes about six months. But there are similar clinics and approaches to solving underachievement problems in many cities. Be sure you thoroughly investigate the counselor or program before signing a contract for large sums of money. There are many unscrupulous and incompetent individuals who purport to solve underachievement problems and have no track record.

If you're dedicated and really want to solve your child's underachievement problem, you could consult Rimm's book[17] and work with a team made up of your own family counselor, the school psychologist or behavior management specialist, the school principal, and your child's teacher.

Here are Rimm's six steps for solving underachievement problems. They sound simple (and I have condensed them here), but don't be misled. They will take a serious commitment of time and energy. But I have seen them work.

1. Assessment. You must begin with a complete picture of your child's abilities, achievements, strengths, and weaknesses in order to develop a plan that will work for him or her. Perhaps your child has already been evaluated for placement in some type of alternative or behavior-disorder class if the underachievement problem is severe. If this is the case, then there will have been a great deal of assessment already completed. But this assessment should get at some definitive family information as well. I have found that we do not do a particularly good job of helping families see where their real problems lie. We are often trying to be too polite and thus avoid speaking the truth.

You will definitely need recent IQ and achievement test scores. If your child is older, then collect all of his or her test scores for as long as he has been in school so that a longitudinal picture can be obtained. Rimm has developed a variety of helpful instruments that standardize and organize information gathering. The Achievement Identification Measure is an objective parent report of typical student behaviors based on findings from interviews with parents.[18]

It asks parents to answer yes or no to questions such as "My child is a perfectionist," or "My child forgets to do his homework assignments." This instrument covers many of the issues that were addressed in Greene's parent questionnaire cited earlier but does so in a standardized format that yields a score in each of five dimensions. These dimensions match closely the problems that, according to Rimm, characterize the Underachievement Syndrome. A second test, the Group Achievement Identification Measure, gathers the same types of information from the students themselves. Rimm uses other measures to gather information on creative talents and interests.

2. Communication. At this point all of the parties involved need to sit down and talk with each other. Many of the helpful hints regarding parent-teacher conferences that were shared in Chapter Two should be reviewed at this point. The child should participate in the communication sessions, and regular (weekly or daily) communication should be part of any plan that is developed.

3. Expectation. The third step in Rimm's model is to look at the broad category of expectations. All of the following individuals are involved in changing expectations for achievement, and each plays a critical part: the student, the parent, the sibling, the teacher, and even the peer group in the classroom.

4. Identification. This is a unique aspect to Rimm's model that I have personally used and find extraordinarily important. Underachieving students need someone of achievement with whom to identify. As principal I have frequently served as the mentoring model for underachieving students. But family members, a guidance counselor, and especially another teacher in the school can be excellent role models as well.

5. Correction of deficiencies. This step involves remediating the academic deficiencies that exist because of an underachievement syndrome. If a child hasn't been doing anything in school for one or more years, he or she is now seriously behind in many academic areas. Everyone involved needs to bring the child up to speed academically as quickly as possible.

6. Modifications at home and school. The final step in Rimm's model involves changing conditions at home and school to make sure that the problem is really solved. These corrective measures vary according to which category of underachiever Rimm has assigned them based on the assessment data: dependent conformer, dependent nonconformer, conforming dominant, or nonconforming dominant. The genius of Rimm's model is the suggestions she makes for modifying both the home and school environments based specifically on the type of child involved. But they all involve a restructuring of how you are parenting. So if you're not willing to change, don't expect your child to change. Most other models for helping parents deal with underachievers are much more simplistic and fail to get at some of the subtler aspects of the problem.

Helpful hints for designing your own plan. Rimm's model is an excellent one for helping your underachieving child. I would add the following helpful hints as you begin to design your plan.

- *Make sure that your child has the best teacher and learning environment that you can possibly obtain for her.* This may be a challenging task, but if you approach it in a calm and rational way, I know you can achieve success.

- *Make up your mind that you need to change if you want your child to change.* I have seen many parents who are looking for the "quick fix" for their child from a psychologist, teacher, or administrator. They want to have the problem solved by Monday at the latest. That won't happen if your child is a confirmed underachiever. Remember that at Rimm's clinic the process takes at the very least six months.

- *Read a variety of books from the resource list at the end of this chapter so that you can begin to understand the root of your child's problem.* Many parents discover that problems they are having in their own family go back at least a generation or two in either their or their spouse's family. Developing an insight into the true nature of the problem will enable you to solve it.

- *Develop a network of friends who are going through similar problems or who have achieved success with their underachiever.* You will need support and encouragement as you undertake your plan.

- *Utilize the help of professionals whenever you can.* The objectivity and understanding that can come from involving a professional in helping to solve your problem will be well worth whatever you have to spend.

❖ Resources

If you would like more information on the topics covered in this chapter, the following books and organizations will be helpful to you.

Brooks, Andree Aelion. *Children of Fast-Track Parents.* New York: Viking, 1989.

Cogen, Victor. *Boosting the Underachiever: How Busy Parents Can Unlock Their Child's Potential.* New York: Plenum Press, 1990.

Dr. Sylvia Rimm
Educational Assessment Service, Inc.
W6050 Apple Road
Watertown, WI 53094

Fine, Benjamin. *Underachievers: How They Can Be Helped.* New York: E. P. Dutton & Co., Inc., 1967.

Greene, Lawrence J. *Kids Who Underachieve.* New York: Simon and Schuster, 1986.

Dr. Linnus S. Pecaut
Institute for Motivational Development
200 W. 22nd St., Suite 235
Lombard, IL 60148

Johnson, Eric W. *Raising Children to Achieve: A Guide for Motivating Success in School and in Life.* New York: Walker & Company, 1984.

Pecaut, Linnus S. *The Making of an Underachiever: Growing Up in the Shadow of Success.* Lombard, Ill.: The Institute for Motivational Development, 1986.

Pecaut, Linnus S. *Understanding and Influencing Student Motivation: Assessment and Treatment.* Lombard, Ill.: The Institute for Motivational Development, 1979.

Rimm, Sylvia. *How to Parent So Children Will Learn.* Watertown, Wis.: Apple Publishing Company, 1986.

Vail, Priscilla. *Smart Kids with School Problems: Things to Know and Ways to Help.* New York: New American Library, 1987.

Wlodkowski, Raymond J., and Judith H. Haynes. *Eager to Learn: Helping Children Become Motivated and Love Learning.* San Francisco: Jossey-Bass Publishers, 1990.

6

MAXIMIZING YOUR CHILD'S LEARNING

Learning Styles, Study Skills, and Test-Taking Strategies

In the school district where I served as an elementary principal for eight years, report cards were issued every nine weeks. At some point about halfway through this grading period, "interim reports" began to appear in my mail box. I was required to read and sign each of these reports. They were written by classroom teachers on a multiple copy form, and after I signed them, the original went home to the parents and a copy went into the student's cumulative file. Although the reports were written by a couple of dozen different teachers and dealt with many different students, the substance of each was the same. Sarah or Sam was about to fail one of his or her subjects. The cause was usually poor test grades or failure to complete homework assignments. These reports made for very depressing reading, and I began to wonder what we could do to reduce the number of interim reports and failing grades. I was sure that the parents weren't enjoying the reports any more than I was.

I did two things. First, we instituted a homework assignment book that was mandatory for every student in Grades 3-6 (the highest grade in my school). The junior high (Grades 7 and 8) also began using the same type of book when they saw how well it worked at the elementary level. The second thing I did was to institute lunch study groups in my office. Students could sign up to bring a brown-bag lunch and study for an upcoming test in social studies or science. Teachers let me know when tests were part of the weekly schedule and provided me with a studyguide. We began our sessions about three days before the test and spent about thirty minutes a day. Students who had previously been failing tests would proudly bring in an A or B grade. I'd give them a high five and exclaim, "I knew you could do it." And I did, or I wouldn't have devoted so many lunch hours to reviewing the Civil War or the digestive system of a frog.

You've no doubt turned to Chapter Six because you've been getting a few interim reports from your child's school as well. One thing I've discovered is that most kids don't have the foggiest idea of how to study for a test or how to go about completing a homework assignment they don't understand. The children who get good grades in elementary school do so because learning comes easily for them. Yet there are a few simple strategies that can help any student get better grades. No child is born knowing "how to study." Even the lucky ones, when faced with a large body of new and/or difficult material, can't figure out how to put it all together. Both of my children who are honors college students had to learn how to study in junior high and high school when faced with a subject they didn't understand very well. Learning new information, study skills, classroom test-taking skills, and homework assignments are among the important topics we'll cover in this chapter. We'll also learn how understanding your child's own unique learning style can help you help him or her to be a more successful student.

In addition, we'll talk about another important aspect of school that is often overlooked—standardized testing, both of ability (IQ tests) and achievement (tests like the Iowa Test of Basic Skills, the Metropolitan Achievement Test, or the Stanford Achievement Test). Standardized test scores follow your child throughout his school career and can often open or close academic doors. We'll learn how to interpret and understand these important tests and how to help your child overcome test anxiety.

Standardized Testing Information

What is the difference between an IQ test and an achievement test? An IQ (intelligence) test measures an individual's capacity for learning. It presents students with a set of tasks on which he can demonstrate his skills for learning and then compares the results of his work with a large sample of other people. The comparative aspect of the IQ test is very important to remember. Any score on an IQ test means you've done better or worse than a sample of the population. IQ tests can never really measure innate ability. They represent something that has already been learned. IQ tests can be administered in a group setting or individually. The most popular individual IQ tests for children are the Stanford-Binet Intelligence Scale and the Wechsler Intelligence Scale for Children.

Achievement tests contain items that test students on what they can do with information, skills, and ideas they have already learned in school. The critical difference between the two types of tests is that the IQ test "measures intellectual skills that the individual has acquired over a very long period of time and from many sources, such as home and community, as well as school; the achievement test ordinarily measures knowledge and specialized intellectual skills learned over a shorter period of time—a month, a semester, a year or two—and taught directly in school."[1]

What are the differences between criterion- and norm-referenced achievement tests? Criterion-referenced achievement tests are those that are typically given at the end of a unit in a math or reading book to see how well a student has learned the skills in that unit. The tests are short and don't take more than an hour to administer. The student's scores are not compared to those in a larger population. The teacher only wants to find out how successful her teaching has been and which students need extra help.

In contrast, the norm-referenced achievement test is a battery of tests given over a week-long period. The sections include reading comprehension, vocabulary, spelling, math computation, math problem solving, social studies, and science. The tests are called norm-referenced because your child's scores are compared to a large group of students at the same grade or age level who took the same test. Your child's scores are usually reported in comparison to the national norm (all the kids in the country who took the test) and to a local norm (all the kids at that grade level in the school district who took the test). The most widely used tests are the SRA (Science Research Associates) Achievements, Iowa Tests of Basic Skills, Stanford Achievement Tests, California Achievement Tests, and Metropolitan Achievement Tests.

What other types of standardized tests might be given in school? Beginning in the middle-school years, there are several other types of standardized tests that might be given. These include aptitude, interest, and personality tests. These are especially useful for helping a child look at career and future academic planning. Aptitude tests measure things like clerical speed and accuracy, mechanical reasoning, spatial relations, numerical ability, and verbal reasoning. Interest inventories help students determine what kind of things they like to do. Noting a definite pattern of interests can help a counselor or parent advise a student on a course of study or action. Personality tests would usually only be administered if a child were having a serious emotional or psychological problem.

What do the percentile, stanine, and grade equivalent scores mean on my child's standardized test score report? If your child scored in the 75th percentile, it does not mean that he/she got 75% of the answers correct. It means that he/she scored better on the test than 75% of the students who took it. Twenty-five percent of the students who took it got a better score than your child. Parents often find the following qualitative descriptions of percentile scores more helpful than the actual percentiles. Please remember, however, that these are ranges and very general descriptors.

If your child scored in the 1st to 15th percentile range, he/she has *great difficulty* with the subject matter being tested.

If your child scored in the 15th to 30th percentile range, he/she has *difficulty* with the subject matter being tested.

If your child scored in the 30th to 45th percentile range, he/she has *somewhat below average understanding* of the subject matter being tested.

If your child scored in the 45th to 55th percentile range, he/she has an *average understanding* of the subject matter being tested.

If your child scored in the 55th to 70th percentile range, he/she has a *good understanding* of the subject matter being tested.

If your child scored in the 70th to 90th percentile range, he/she has a *very good understanding* of the subject matter being tested.

If your child scored in the 90th to 99th percentile range, he/she has an *excellent understanding* of the subject matter being tested.

Stanine scores are another way of looking at standardized test scores. There are nine stanines. A score of 5 is average. We label students who score in stanines 1-3 as target students in our school because they need extra help in bringing up their achievement. A score of 4, while below grade level is still considered average by many test experts. A student scoring in stanines 7-9 is considered well above average.

A second grader who gets a 5.6 grade equivalent score isn't necessarily ready for fifth-grade reading. It means he got many more of the items on the test correct than an average second grader did. To judge him ready for fifth-grade reading, he would have to get a 5.6 grade equivalent on the fifth-grade version of the test.

What are the most important questions to ask when looking at my child's standardized test scores?

☐ *WHAT IS MY CHILD'S IQ SCORE?* The first thing most parents want to know is their child's IQ score. While this score only gives you one type of intelligence (most experts recognize there are many different types of intelligence), it does give you an idea of how fast your child will learn traditional school material in comparison to other children of his or her age. Looking at IQ scores from earlier tests can give you an idea if a child's IQ is remaining about the same. A variation of from 5-10 points within several years is not at all unusual and is generally not considered to be a change in IQ score. The average IQ score is 100.

☐ *WHAT IS MY CHILD'S IQ SCORE COMPARED TO THE AVERAGE IQ OF ALL OF THE STUDENTS IN THE SCHOOL? IN THE DISTRICT?* If your child's IQ is 103 and the average of the school or district is 100, then your child should be having no problems whatsoever succeeding in that academic environment. If, however, the average IQ of the school is 120 or 125, then your child is working with a group of students who have more academic ability. The most ideal setting for any child is one in which there is a broad mix of talents and abilities, where teachers recognize the multiple intelligences of children, and where all children are being challenged to the highest level of performance.

☐ *WHAT ARE MY CHILD'S ACHIEVEMENT TEST SCORES? IS MY CHILD ACHIEVING IN A WAY THAT IS COMMENSURATE WITH HER ABILITY?* If your child has an IQ of 120 and isn't getting A's and B's in school, then something is wrong. If your child has an IQ of 100 and is getting A's and B's in school, then she is a motivated, organized, and dedicated student who should be commended for using her talents wisely.

☐ *HOW DOES THE SCHOOL INTERPRET THE TEST RESULTS AND WHAT DO THEY PLAN TO DO ABOUT THEM?* If there are discrepancies between ability and achievement or other problems that become evident upon a closer examination of standardized test scores, the school should be eager to investigate causes and develop a plan of remediation.

How are achievement tests used in school? Achievement tests are used in many ways in the school setting. Of course, the first purpose is to get an accurate picture of how each individual student is learning in school. In my school district we follow students throughout their school career to make sure they are making satisfactory gains from year to year. We expect at least a nine-month increase in grade equivalent scores each year, and from a student who has been targeted for special help, we would like to see at least a two-year gain to make up for lost time.

As students move into middle school or junior high, elementary school achievement tests are frequently used as a criterion for placement in advanced classes.

Schools are being held much more accountable for student learning today than they have been in the past. Achievement tests are one way that administrators and teachers can evaluate whether or not the curriculum and teaching methodologies they are using are effective.

What are the best strategies for helping my child do well on standardized tests? Of course the real preparation for taking standardized tests should be taking place in the classroom day after day and week after week as your child learns the information and skills needed to do well on the test. There are, however, some things that you as a parent should and should not do to help your child.

☐ *TO DO.* Be a good listener and talk with your child about her concerns. Children are sensitive, however, and if you act overanxious and worried about tests, your child may overreact. Make sure that your child has a good night of rest, an adequate breakfast, and a smooth, hassle-free morning on test-taking days. The last thing anyone needs before the big test is an argument.

☐ *NOT TO DO.* You can't study for standardized tests, so please don't start pouring on extra homework in the two weeks prior to the test. On the other hand, don't send the message to your child that the tests are stupid or unimportant. The tests are not games, and your child doesn't have a choice about whether or not he will take them.

Most teachers do some preparation before the test-taking experience regarding what to do when you don't know an answer. Standardized tests are designed to have some questions that almost no one will be able to answer. Be sure your child understands that this test is different from the ones he usually takes in class where everyone is expected to know all of the material because they've been studying it in class.

What is test anxiety and how can I help my child overcome it? Test anxiety is a condition that some people get when faced with any kind of test. They may freeze up, perspire, get headaches, or just plain feel terrible. Where do these fears come from? Perhaps from the strong feelings associated with a past failure. Perhaps from being subjected to some public humiliation associated with a poor test grade. Perhaps from telling oneself over and over that "I can't do it."

If your child suffers from severe test anxiety, you must try to find out why. Are you the guilty culprit? Are you allowing your own text anxiety to creep into the interactions you have with your child? Did something happen to your child that you're unaware of? The best method for overcoming text anxiety that I know about is practice and preparation. Companies have made millions helping adults prepare for real-estate exams, law- and graduate-school entrance tests, and of course the SAT and ACT that every high-school student faces. You can give your child a similar crash course in taking achievement tests by giving her lots of practice in taking short tests and quizzes just for fun. If your child has a truly serious case of test anxiety, you may be able to work with the teacher to figure out alternate forms of assessment. Once your child relaxes and knows that the teacher realizes she isn't "dumb," the problem may resolve itself.

Study Skills and Strategies

What is homework, and why do teachers assign it? Many parents have asked me that question, and most have not been in a particularly good mood during the conversation. Homework assignments are the cause of more confusion and misunderstanding between teachers, parents, and students than just about anything else we do in school. The purpose of homework is to give kids practice and to reinforce what they have learned in school. Good homework assignments should be more than busy work. They should help a child learn. Even if the teacher hasn't assigned any homework, students should be doing independent silent reading every evening.

Ask about your school's homework policy. The policy should delineate the time expectations, what constitutes homework, and what a child should be doing at home if none has been assigned. As a parent you should know what the make-up policy is if your child misses homework assignments and how the teacher will grade and give feedback on the assignment. The best homework assignments should do the following:

1. consider the individual
2. honor developmental levels
3. honor learning styles
4. connect to family and community
5. teach accuracy and precision
6. teach perseverance
7. teach thinking skills
8. show context
9. give feedback other than grades
10. involve all the senses[2]

How long should my child be expected to work on homework? Many school districts have written statements regarding homework. In the absence of that, the following are relatively standard. Kindergarten through second graders should work no longer than fifteen minutes per day.

Third and fourth graders should work about twenty minutes. Fifth and sixth graders can expect to spend about forty-five minutes. And seventh and eighth graders will be working from an hour to an hour and a half.

What about rewards for doing homework? If your child has a long history of refusing to do homework assignments, then most experts recommend some kind of organized plan for changing that history. Some even recommend some type of reward structure. I have found that tokens or rewards are very effective for changing a child's behavior. I worked with a student for three years on a structured homework plan. When we started, his reward was a lunch at McDonald's with me for three days of completed homework. His mother agreed to supply the funds for Donny's lunch. I always bought dessert. This may sound overly generous, but Donny was a hard-core fourth grader who had done no work either in or out of school for two years. His parents and teachers had totally given up on him, but I was willing to try anything. Knowing that Donny was certainly smart enough to do whatever was being asked of him, I wasn't reluctant to put pressure on him. At our first lunch together, Donny was visibly impressed that we'd both actually followed through on a promise. Obviously he wasn't used to promises being kept. We kept this up every three days for about three weeks. He had some ups and downs during that period, a day once in a while that interrupted his unbroken string of successes. But we wiped the slate clean and he tried again. Then I told him that my schedule and budget didn't permit as many lunches. We developed a new schedule that decreased the number of lunches we had together. But by this time, Donny was building new habits and was able to make it on his own. We continued to have lunch together until Donny graduated from my school. We got to be very good friends. Once in a while he still comes back from high school to chat. He's still doing his homework!

You may not be able to afford lunch at McDonald's, but some type of reward system can often make the difference between success and failure in getting your child to complete his homework. Sylvia Rimm suggests a point system for homework completion.[3] It looks like this:

Point System for Typical Homework Schedule
Grades 1-4
15 to 30 minutes of homework time
> 1 point reading story
> 1 point reading workbook page
> 1 point practicing flashcards (ten cards three times)
> 1 point one math or writing page

Set 3-point minimum for daily sticker or baseball card; extra sticker or card for each 3 points; extra points may be added to next day's total.

Point System for Typical Homework Schedule
Grades 5-8
Expected earnings: 20-25 points within one hour
> 1 point for every page read
> 2 points for every page written (e.g. workbooks, social studies or science questions, or copied writing)
> 5 points for every page of math
> 5 points for every page studied (read and outlined)

If your child is motivated to save money to buy something special, Rimm suggests the following monetary reward system based on weekly grade reports you receive from the teacher. A child would receive 50 cents for an A; 30 cents for a B; 10 cents for a C; lose 30 cents for a D; and lose 50 cents for an F. The trick is to make the rewards somewhat immediate. I've rarely seen children respond to a reward system that offers something for grades at the end of a semester or even a grading period.

What are study strategies and why are they important? I well remember the first time my son Patrick was faced with really having to study for a test. Oh, in elementary and middle school he had taken small tests over chapters or units, but this was a semester exam in freshman world history that covered the entire course's content. He sat on the living-room couch, surrounded by books and notes, in the depths of depression. "I don't know where to begin," he moaned. "How do you study for a final?" Although I'd brought some work home from the office, I put it aside and gave him a crash course in "how to study for a final." Fortunately, he had taken good notes, had remembered to bring his textbook home, and his teacher had handed out a studyguide to follow. But there was no way he could possibly remember everything in his notes, his textbook, and the studyguide. The important thing was to narrow down what would probably be on the test, based on all of the clues the teacher had given. These are the key questions I asked him.

- *What kind of a test did the teacher say you were going to have?* The type of test that is being given will dictate how you study and prepare. Each type of test—essay, multiple choice, short answer, true-false—requires a slightly different type of preparation.
- *What does the studyguide indicate will be covered on the test?*

- *Do you have any places in your notes that you high-lighted, underlined, or starred what the teacher said because it was really important?*
- *What chapters of the textbook have been read and discussed in class?*
- *What questions do you think the teacher might ask?*
- *Are there any important names or dates that the teacher said you should know?*
- *What do you already know about the subject?*
- *What are the main ideas you've learned in the class so far?*

The best time to be thinking about these questions is from the very beginning of a unit or course of study. If you know a final exam will be given, encourage your child to pay close attention to those things that the teacher points out as especially important. Your child should be taught all of the reading strategies that were mentioned in Chapter Three. As she completes her reading assignments for the class, she should try to use the appropriate strategy for reading (studying/remembering) what she has read. Studying is simply a method of organizing, making sense of, trying to remember, figuring out what is important about a certain body of subject matter. Study strategies are any tricks you can possibly use that help you do it faster and more efficiently. Individuals who know how to study don't necessarily have better memories than the rest of us, they just know how to figure out what's most important to remember. Their minds aren't all cluttered up with things they don't need to remember.

What are the most important test-taking strategies? Each type of test has its own set of strategies, and it's important for students to understand the differences. As early as second grade, students begin taking standardized tests that are made up completely of multiple-choice items.

☐ *MULTIPLE-CHOICE TESTS.* There are some simple strategies you can share with your child to help improve his scores on multiple-choice tests (including the standardized tests he takes each year). You can also order test-preparation kits from any of the standardized test companies to use with your child.

- *Work quickly.* Standardized tests are timed, and students who move quickly, even if they pick some wrong answers, get better scores than students who know the material better but are slow at taking tests.
- *Read the directions and the questions very carefully.*
- *Guess before you choose.* Figure out the answer to the question on your own before looking at the choices. If your answer is among the choices, you will have saved some time.
- *Choose the closest answer.* Be careful, however, because well constructed multiple-choice tests have several answers that may seem plausible.
- *Eliminate the most ridiculous answer.*
- *Look for clue words or numbers.*
- *If all else fails, guess.*
- *Do change your answers if you have a hunch your first guess was wrong.* But only do it after you've completed the entire test. Then go back and reread the directions. Make sure you've put all your answers in the correct places.

☐ *TRUE-FALSE TESTS.* The true-false test has its own set of pitfalls, especially for students who want to find the hidden meaning in everything they read. Here are some helpful hints on this type of test to share with your child:

- *Read carefully.* Every word in a true-false question is there for a reason.
- *Watch for clue words.* Researchers have found that if the words *all, only, always,* and *because* are in the question, chances are it's false. If the words *none, generally,* or *usually* are found, the question is generally true.
- *Don't try to pick a fight or argue with the question.* Maybe the true statement is only approximately true, but that's good enough for a true answer.
- *Guess.* If you don't know, you have a good chance of guessing right. There are usually more trues than falses on a true-false test because they are easier questions to write.
- *Don't change answers.* In true-false tests, your first guess is usually correct.

☐ *MATCHING TESTS.* Matching tests are favorites of many teachers. They consist of a list of names or dates with corresponding descriptions. Here are some simple strategies to help.

- *Read the directions.* Sometimes you'll need to use an answer more than once. It's important to know this ahead of time.
- *Find out which column has the longest phrases.* Start with that column so you'll be rereading the column with the shortest answers each time.
- *Do the easiest ones first.*
- *Do the toughest ones next.*

☐ *FILL-IN-THE-BLANK AND SHORT-ANSWER TESTS.*
Teachers also love fill-in-the-blank and short-answer tests. Here are some strategies to share with your student to make these tests easier to manage.

- *Look for clues.* Sometimes the very words that are used in the question will help you construct an answer.
- *Don't make things more confusing than they already are.* Don't look for hidden meaning and try to read things into the question that aren't there.
- *Check out the length of the blanks.* If a teacher only gives you enough space for one word, chances are you won't need more than that in the answer.
- *Give the teacher more than is required.* Even if only one answer is required, give two. You might get partial credit.
- *Make educated guesses.* Even if you don't know the exact answer, make up something that sounds logical. You could be right.

☐ *VOCABULARY COMPONENT TESTS.* Most standardized tests (Iowa Test of Basic Skills, Metropolitan Achievement Test, Scholastic Aptitude Test) have a vocabulary component. Here are some useful strategies for helping your student improve her score on these tests.

- *If it seems too easy, watch out.* Test-makers purposefully put in items to trap you into picking the too-obvious answer.
- *If the word seems at all familiar, spend a little time playing around with the word and thinking about it.* You may suddenly recall how and when you heard it and remember the meaning.

- *Make a guess.*
- *Practice.* This is one test that you can continually study for by learning new words and their meanings. My own children benefitted greatly on their SAT's and ACT's by playing vocabulary games on a regular basis.

☐ *NUMBER PROBLEM TESTS.* The trick to doing well on number problems is neatness and carefulness. Researchers have shown that about 20% of the wrong answers on math tests are caused by carelessness and not by ignorance of the problem-solving technique.

- *Work carefully, systematically, and neatly.*
- *Use graphics.* (Remember the problem-solving strategies we introduced in Chapter Four. This is the time to use them. Draw pictures, make charts or lists. Do anything to help you picture what is happening.)
- *Estimate.* Think about what the answer should logically be. Even if you can't compute the exact answer, by estimating you can make an intelligent guess.

☐ *READING COMPREHENSION TESTS.* Success on reading comprehension tests is related to your ability to utilize one or more of the reading strategies mentioned in Chapter Three. Here are some of the most important things you can do to get a good score on this type of test.

- *Instead of reading the passage and then the questions, read the questions first so you'll know what answers you're looking for.* Then you can skim the passage for just the information you need. If you read the passage first, you'll end up reading it twice—once before and once after you read the questions.

- *Use your time wisely.* These tests are nearly always timed.
- *Check your answers by comparing them to actual passages you have read.*

☐ *ESSAY QUESTION TESTS.* The essay question is often the most dreaded. Students have to think, organize, and write from a knowledge base about the subject. If your child has been paying attention, he should have a sample outline well fixed in his mind, as well as a pretty good idea of what essay questions will be included on the test. I always played a game with my teachers (in my head). I would decide what the obvious essay questions would be and then develop an outline before the test. Nine times out of ten I was accurate in my judgment. For younger students, have them practice writing out sample answers to different types of questions.

Learning Styles

How does my child's learning style affect his performance in school? The whole topic of learning styles has only recently been considered an important variable when talking about school problems. In the "olden days," if a student wasn't learning we automatically assumed it was because she was doing something wrong. Now researchers and many educators are beginning to approach learning from the student's viewpoint rather than the teacher's. A student's learning style can be defined as the way in which that student learns most efficiently.

☐ *WAYS TO TAKE IN INFORMATION.* Suppose that someone told you your life depended on mastering seven principles of survival in the wilderness. At the end of the course, you will be sent into the wilderness to survive. The choice of how you want to learn the seven principles is up to you. Would you prefer a lecture on the subject? Then you're probably an auditory learner. Perhaps you'd rather read a textbook. Visual learners need to see what they have to learn in print or in pictures. Or would you choose to have an expert demonstrate each principle and then let you experience them for yourself in a game or simulation? Then you're a kinesthetic learner. You like hands-on experiences and thus learn by doing.

I personally would like to read the material first, then attend the lecture, and finally try out what I've learned in the real world. But there are many who would move to the hands-on experience at the outset and never need to read or hear about what they will be required to do. The efficient learner has a well-developed repertoire of learning styles. But many children, particularly those who have a learning disability and have not received any special training in how to compensate for that disability, can only learn new concepts and skills if they are presented in their primary learning style.

If your child has always loved to sit still and listen to stories, then chances are he's an auditory learner. He can probably understand and remember material better if he hears it. The visual learner, on the other hand, needs to see something written down or illustrated before he can remember it. If your child has to touch everything in sight, take it apart and see how it works, then chances are that the kinesthetic mode is your child's preferred learning style. This particular way of looking at learning styles is the most simplistic. It merely looks at the preferred method of taking information into the brain.

There are many different ways of describing learning styles, almost as many ways as there are theorists who have studied the subject. The theorists apply different labels to the same generic characteristics, and knowing just which labels which theorists use is not particularly important. What is important is having a complete understanding of your child's strengths and weaknesses and how she learns best. Looking at this idea in a variety of ways will help you construct the most complete picture you can of your child.

☐ *THE DIFFERENT SIDES OF THE BRAIN.* Another more complex approach to learning styles originated with the discovery that the brain is divided into two sections or hemispheres. Researchers discovered in working with "split-brain" patients, those who had the corpus callosum (the major connection between the hemispheres) cut due to severe epilepsy, that certain behaviors and ways of thinking seemed to be centered in one hemisphere or the other. Of course, unless our hemispheres have been disconnected, we all use both. But many individuals show a definite preference for either the right or left side; thus the labels "right-brained" and "left-brained."

Distinctly right-brained individuals make better artists and performers. Distinctly left-brained people do better as accountants or chemists. We survived for centuries without knowing about hemisphericity, but an understanding of which thinking or reasoning patterns (learning styles) characterize each hemisphere, along with the related school skills, can be helpful for the parent. This approach to looking at learning styles focuses on what the learner actually does with the information in his brain, once he has successfully learned it either visually, auditorially, or kinesthetically.

Primarily left-brained individuals do their processing (thinking, reasoning) in an *analytical-sequential* fashion. They prefer verbal explanations, use language to remember, produce ideas logically, like structured experiences, and approach problems seriously.[4] The school skills that relate to this type of processing are: symbols, language, reading, phonics, locating details and facts, talking and reciting, following directions, listening, and auditory association.[5]

Individuals who are primarily right-brained do their processing in a *wholistic-simultaneous* way. They prefer visual explanations, use images to remember, produce ideas intuitively, prefer abstract thinking tasks, like open, fluid experiences, and approach problems playfully.[6] The school skills that relate to this type of processing are: spatial relationships, mathematical concepts, color sensitivity, singing and music, art expression, creativity, and visualization.[7] The challenge faced by parents of strongly right-brained children is in finding school settings and teachers that tap into the learning strengths of their children.

Thus far we've looked at learning styles from the standpoint of how information is taken in by the learner (auditory, visual, kinesthetic) and ways in which information is processed by different sides of the brain. A third way of looking at learning styles integrates the child's temperament with his style of learning. This adds another dimension to our understanding.

☐ *TEMPERAMENT CAN AFFECT THE STYLE OF LEARNING.* Dr. Keith Golay has developed this third way of looking at your child's learning patterns and temperaments.[8] He suggests four categories: *actual-spontaneous, actual-routine, conceptual-specific,* and *conceptual-global.*

Children who are described as *actual-spontaneous* are hands-on, active learners. They don't have time to go through the planning and organizing stages of a project. They want to jump right in and do it. They want things to move quickly and be active. Art, music, and physical education are their favorite subjects. They hate homework and can't stand anyone telling them what to do. The actual-spontaneous learner despises the structure of school and can't wait to get out of the classroom. He needs tasks that involve manipulating, constructing, and operating in order to be truly fulfilled.

Actual-routine children are perfect students. Their desks are well organized. They love the systems of school—the rules, the routine, and the memorization and drill. They have to be forced to break out of their molds to try creative writing, drama, or role playing. Just give the actual-routine child a workbook and he or she will be happy all day. The actual-routine child loves helping the teacher and can be found after school emptying wastebaskets or cleaning the blackboard.

The third type of learner is *conceptual-specific.* These children aren't as social as they probably should be. They get impatient when other people don't understand as quickly as they do. They like math, science, engineering, and problem solving. They find group discussions a waste of time and resent the constant repetition of previously mastered material. They have an insatiable desire to learn and pick up information in an effortless way. They are frequently seen by their peers as "different." Unless guided toward appropriate social graces, the conceptual-specific child can become an isolate.

The fourth and final category, *conceptual-global*, contains children who do well in school but thrive on cooperation rather than competition. These children prefer the humanities rather than the sciences and enjoy group discussions, role playing and the good feeling that comes from making a contribution to a group. The conceptual-global child is a "people person" and seems to have an innate sense of how to get along with others. Friends frequently seek her out for assistance and advice.

□ *SCHOOL ACTIVITIES AND TEACHING STYLES*. A fourth way to look at learning styles is to focus on the specific types of school activities and teaching styles that meet the needs of the various learning styles. Bernice McCarthy, author of the 4Mat system (another model for looking at learning styles), warns of the dissonance that can occur when the teacher has a dramatically different learning style from the student. McCarthy has developed four style categories: innovative, analytic, commonsense, and dynamic.[9]

Innovative children learn by listening to others and sharing ideas. They start with what they see and then generalize. They enjoy small-group interaction, role playing, team sports, and simulation, but they don't like timed tests, debates, and computer-assisted instruction. They want to know how things directly affect the lives of those around them.

Analytic learners enjoy listening to the teacher lecture. They are thinkers and watchers with rational and sequential thinking patterns. They enjoy programmed instruction, well-organized lectures or stories, competition, demonstration, and objective tests, but dislike role-play, open discussion, and group projects. They want realistic and practical information and tend to be perfectionistic.

Students with the *commonsense* style enjoy problem solving, debates, logic problems, independent study, and especially experiments that build on what they have learned. They do not value input while they are trying things out. They dislike memorizing, a lot of reading, group work, and writing assignments. They need to be challenged to check the validity of their knowledge. They want to discover how things work and how they can be applied to real life. They may be mislabeled as "hyperactive" but will respond to a teacher who is an intellectual challenger and fellow learner and who is logical and just.

Dynamic children like to see, hear, touch, and feel. They get bored easily unless they can learn by trial and error, taking action, and carrying out plans. They enjoy case studies, guided imagery, drama, creative productions, and assignments that require originality. They dislike assignments without options, standard routines, or activities done in haste. They want a teacher who is a facilitator and stimulator of ideas and who is curious and imaginative, encouraging them to explore the possibilities of what is known.

☐ *ENVIRONMENTAL IMPACTS ON THE LEARNER.*

Still another way to look at learning styles focuses on how various aspects of the environment impact the learner. Kenneth and Rita Dunn have studied how temperature, light, and color can affect the ability of an individual to learn.

Now that I know all this, what difference does it make? Now that you know your child is a right-brained individual who is an auditory learner, or an innovative child who is conceptual-specific, what should you do with this information? There are four reasons for knowing what your child's learning style is: 1) to get the best teacher for your child based on matching her preferred learning style with a compatible teaching style; 2) to help your child with homework and studying at home in her most effective style; 3) to recognize where your child needs to broaden her repertoire of learning styles and encouraging and helping her to grow; and 4) to understand how your learning style differs from that of your child and how that difference can often create problems when you try to help your child.

Things You Can Do at Home to Help Your Child with Homework, Study Skills, and Test-Taking Strategies

Although the subject matter gets more difficult from kindergarten through middle school, the skills to be a successful student never change. If you begin the following routines early in your child's school career, before long he'll be handling most of them on his own. If your child is older and you despair of his ever looking like a student, then begin now to institute these procedures. They include: a monthly calendar; a book bag; a daily assignment notebook; a special place to study and store materials; and a homework (read-aloud) session each evening. As your child gets older, add the following items to the list of must-dos: a schedule of weekly tests that are given (math facts/spelling); and a schedule of unit tests in major subjects.

Post a **monthly calendar** on the refrigerator so that everyone in the family can keep track of what's going on. We started this practice when my daughter began kindergarten, and even though I'm living alone now, the refrigerator calendar is still a part of my life. On this calendar, write school activities (picture day, taffy apple day, band or orchestra lessons, special lunch days). Encourage your child to check this calendar each evening and take the responsibility for getting money, supplies, etc. so that he will be ready for the next day.

Every student needs a **book bag.** This counterpart to the adult briefcase is absolutely essential for your child's success in school. Get in the habit of putting the book bag or backpack in the same place every day. As assignments are completed or items to bring to school are collected, they can be placed in the bag. Part of our yearly getting-ready-to-go-back-to-school routine was purchasing a new book bag because the old one was always worn out. Don't let your child of any age (kindergarten through middle school) leave home without one.

A **daily assignment notebook** is another indispensable item for every student. Perhaps kindergarten and first grade are a bit young, but we start using specially designed assignment notebooks at second grade in my school district. They contain important information about our school and generous spaces in which to write assignments. If your child gets in this habit in her youngest years, much grief will be avoided. If your child needs extra monitoring, have her teacher sign the book each day to show that she completed it correctly. You will then sign it at home to show that you're aware of what she needs to do. This back-and-forth communication system can put even the most disorganized child back on track if she realizes that all of the adults in her life are serious about her completing homework.

Every child needs a **special storage place** for his reference books (dictionary, atlas, encyclopedia, almanac); his school supplies (ruler, pencils, crayons, markers, colored pencils); and his books for recreational reading. In addition, each child needs a **regular place to study.** Although my husband and I purchased very nice student desks for both of our children, our daughter chose to study on her bed and our son sprawled out on the living-room floor in front of the television set. Since they both did very well in their studies, I didn't argue with their choice of location. But if your house is a busy and active place and your child tends to be distracted by what is going on, insist that he choose a quiet spot that doesn't vary from evening to evening in which to do his homework.

A **regular homework session** each evening is important for consistency. If your child doesn't have homework assigned from school, then take advantage of this extra time and do some reading aloud together.

Knowing your child's **weekly schedule of tests** can help you monitor your child's preparation for these important events. In some classrooms, there is a spelling test each Friday. Make sure you as a parent are aware of this and that your child brings home the word list each week. In some math classes there is a quiz every Wednesday. You can find out about these regular tests by attending the open house or curriculum night that is held at your school. If you missed it, call the teacher and ask for a schedule.

In addition to the weekly schedule, be aware of what **units or special projects** your child is working on and when things are due at school. Knowing well in advance can help you plan family activities so that they don't interfere with school.

Your child's desk at school can become a rat's nest of papers and books if he or she has problems with organizational skills. Check in with the teacher on a weekly basis to make sure that homework assignments are being turned in and not getting "lost" in the messy desk.

Helping a child's study skills in kindergarten through second grade.

- *Make sure your child knows and understands the concepts* behind these words: start, stop, every, all, each, missing, matches, now, over, under, before, after, first, last, on, from, to, same, different, beginning, and end. These words are used on a daily basis to give instructions about activities and class assignments. If your child doesn't understand them, she will be confused most of the time.

- *Play games with your child that help him pay attention and concentrate.* Give him plenty of praise for paying attention. The skill of paying attention is critical in school. There are dozens of distractors in the classroom, and children who can't concentrate and focus have a difficult time learning.

- *Encourage an atmosphere of questioning.* Ask your child lots of questions and always encourage her questions about what is going on in her world.

Helping a child's study skills in third through fifth grade. Once your child enters third grade, the skill of studying and taking tests becomes much more important. Begin to work with your child on the study strategies and test-taking skills outlined earlier in the chapter. Talk with your child's teacher to find out how these skills are being incorporated into the curriculum. If they are not included in the school curriculum, then find someone to teach them to your child (or do it yourself).

Helping a child's study skills in sixth through eighth grade. In addition to following all of the good advice from the prior sections, there is one important thing you can do for your middle-school student. Teach her the skill of networking. Teach your child how to tap into the resources of other students in the classroom who may understand the assignment or be studying for the test. Form cooperative study groups and build on the social nature of the middle-school student. If you need to organize and monitor the group, that's all right. But start now to build the skills that your child will need to succeed in high school, college, and life.

❖ Resources

If you would like more information on the topics covered in this chapter, the following books and organizations will be helpful to you.

Bergreen, Gary. *Coping with Study Strategies.* New York: The Rosen Publishing Group, Inc., 1986.

Berry, Marilyn. *Help Is on the Way for: Book Reports.* Chicago: Children's Press, 1984.

Black, Hille. *They Shall Not Pass.* New York: William Morrow and Company, 1963.

Boehm, Ann E., and Mary Alice White. *The Parents' Handbook on School Testing.* New York: Teachers College Press, 1982.

Buzan, Tony. *Use Both Sides of Your Brain.* New York: E. P. Dutton, 1974.

Chauncey, Henry, and John E. Dobbin. *Testing: Its Place in Education Today.* New York: Harper & Row, 1963.

Clark, Faith, and Cecil Clark. *Hassle-Free Homework.* New York: Doubleday, 1989.

Colligan, Louise. *Scholastic's A+ Junior Guide to Book Reports.* New York: Scholastic Inc., 1989.

Divine, James H., and David W. Kylen. *How to Beat Test Anxiety and Score Higher on Your Exams.* Woodbury, N.Y.: Barron's Education Series, Inc., 1979.

Erwin, Bette, and Elza Teresa Dinwiddie. *Tests without Trauma.* New York: Grosset & Dunlap, 1983.

Gall, Meredith D. *Making the Grade.* Rocklin, Calif.: Prima Publishing and Communication, 1988.

James, Elizabeth, and Carol Barkin. *How to Write Your Best Book Report.* New York: Lothrop, Lee & Shepard Books, 1986.

James, Elizabeth, and Carol Barkin. *How to Write a Great School Report.* New York: Lothrop, Lee & Shepard Books, 1983.

Kesselman-Turkel, Judi, and Franklynn Peterson. *Test-Taking Strategies.* Chicago: Contemporary Books, Inc., 1981.

Oppenheim, Joanne. *The Elementary School Handbook: Making the Most of Your Child's Education.* New York: Pantheon Books, 1989.

Rimm, Sylvia. *Underachievement Syndrome: Causes and Cures.* Watertown, Wis.: Apple Publishing Company, 1986.

Vitale, Barbara Meister. *Unicorns Are Real: A Right-Brained Approach to Learning.* Rolling Hills Estates, Calif.: Jalmar Press, 1982.

Warren, Virginia Burgess. *Tested Ways to Help Your Child Learn.* Englewood Cliffs, N.J.: Prentice-Hall, Inc., 1961.

7

NOBODY LIKES ME
Friends and Social Relationships

Ian was a very bright sixth grader. He got straight As, so his parents weren't worried about underachievement or special help for reading problems. But they were in my office several times each month about the social problems he was having. Ian didn't have any friends, and he was miserable. His parents were almost willing to buy him some friends if I could have recommended a store where they could be purchased.

Ian's female counterpart in that same sixth-grade class also had a serious social problem. Her mother waited until 10:00 P.M. one blustery winter night to call me at home. "Are you aware," she challenged me in an imperious tone of voice, "of the problem that exists in the sixth grade?" I imagined sex and drugs, judging from the time of night and her attitude. "There are," she announced, "cliques among the sixth-grade girls." I immediately knew the reason for her call. Her daughter wasn't in the clique and had been crying on her mother's shoulder for the past half hour.

Social Skills

Parents whose children are having problems socially at school often feel powerless to do anything about this problem. Your child comes home from school and complains about getting teased on the bus or not ever getting picked to be on a kickball team until your heart begins to break. You can't hire a tutor to teach your child social skills. Teachers aren't usually that concerned about minor squabbles between elementary-school kids. They address issues as they occur on the playground but often don't see their primary role as one of social arbiter. They see a child who is constantly coming to them with complaints as a whiner or a sissy.

But social skills *can* be taught and nurtured both in the home and in the classroom. You *can* help your child to have more friends, and if you sense that your child may have a problem making friends in kindergarten or first grade, now is the time to begin.

Are there social disabilities similar to learning disabilities? Most definitely! There are many children who need extra help in learning how to act in socially acceptable ways. They seem to walk around with the prickly spines of a porcupine, offending their classmates in a dozen different ways all day long. Not every child who is having friendship problems falls into this category, certainly. But if your child is always complaining about how other children treat him, then chances are he has a mild or even serious social disability. We all know people we try to avoid at the supermarket or the church supper. We don't want to talk with them because they don't seem to have the appropriate social skills. No doubt, they suffered from a social disability when they were young, and no one took the time or effort to help them overcome it.

Are some children predisposed to be friendless? Alexander Thomas and Stella Chess have been studying the temperaments of children since the mid fifties.[1] They identified three categories of temperament in children: easy, difficult, and children who are slow to warm up. Children in the difficult category may be actively disliked by their peers because of disagreeable behavior patterns, while the slow-to-warm-up child may just be shy or lacking in basic social skills. With appropriate guidance, encouragement, and assistance from parents, both kinds of children can learn to make and keep friends.

When do social skills begin to develop? Social skills begin to develop as early as infancy. Burton White, the eminent child-development specialist and researcher, cites several key areas of social development in the very young child that are critical for achieving healthy social relationships when a child reaches school age.[2] They include: knowing how to get and hold the attention of adults in appropriate ways; being able to seek out help from an adult when a task becomes too difficult or frustrating; being able to show both affection and mild annoyance to an adult in an appropriate way; being able both to lead and follow peers; being able to handle some competition; and taking pride in his or her personal accomplishments.

How do friendships change as children get older? Children in kindergarten through second grade develop friendships more on the basis of proximity than on any sense of loyalty or affection. My daughter's best friend in kindergarten lived just down the block, and her mother and I were also best friends. We spent some time together almost every day drinking coffee and sharing a few minutes of conversation. By the time Emily and the neighbor girl had reached middle school, they barely spoke to each other. They had developed into entirely different young people with different interests and values. By middle school, friendships are much more intense and are definitely based on variables such as personality, ability levels, common interests, and shared values.

What are the most serious social problems that educators notice? As an elementary-school principal I faced four types of serious social problems in children: 1) the child who threatens and intimidates other children; 2) the child who acts the part of court jester and is willing to do anything to gain the attention of others; 3) the child who looks for recognition and acceptance from adults because he is unable to relate to his peers; and 4) the child who attempts to buy friendship from both children and adults with gifts and bribes.

Children in the first two categories pose special problems for educators because they are disruptive and sometimes even dangerous. But children who fall into the last two categories are equally as challenging to help. The goal is to help both parents and teachers assist the child in developing a healthy self-image, structuring situations where the child can experience success with his peers, and attempting to eliminate those unpleasant aspects of his behavior.

What kinds of family life produce social problems? For each child I encounter in the school setting who has social problems I can always identify one or more of the following family environments as being present: rejective, hopeless, overprotective, pitying, overly high standards, materialistic, competitive, authoritarian, martyrdom, inconsistent, suppressive, and disparaging.

If you've ever heard yourself making these statements in one form or another, then you're guilty of fostering an unfavorable climate for the development of good social skills.

"You don't belong in this family." (rejective)

"You can't do it." (hopeless)

"You can't make those decisions on your own." (overprotective)

"You poor thing. I feel sorry for you." (pitying)

"You've really let me down." (high standards)

"My possessions are more important to me than you." (materialistic)

"You've got to come in first or I won't love you." (competitive)

"Do it my way." (authoritarian)

"Look what you've done to your mother." (martyrdom)

"Okay, you can do it this time, but never again." (inconsistent)

"Don't say bad things like that." (oppressive)

"You never were very bright." (disparaging)

What other factors besides home environment can affect a child's social development? We have discussed some qualities in the immediate home environment that will help a child to develop socially, but there are some external factors that can impact your child's social development as well.

Your neighborhood and local school are very important factors in continued social development. It is from these environments that children choose their friends. If the majority of children in these environments do not share your work ethic, values, or moral standards, your child will have a difficult time developing positive social relationships.

Your child's appearance will also affect his social development. Although you need not give in to every clothing fad that looms on the horizon, children do like to wear what everyone else is wearing.

Whenever possible, utilize the services of orthodontists, ophthalmologists, orthopedic surgeons, and dermatologists to make sure your children have straight teeth, attractive glasses or contact lenses, straight legs, and clear skin. Problems of this nature can severely frustrate a child's feeling of self-confidence.

As children grow older, the development of competence in a special area may help them gain confidence socially also. Participation in art, music, sports, or drama activities can give any child the feeling that she is special because of her talents.

How can I teach my child to be a good friend? The best way you can teach your child to be a good friend is through modeling what it means to be someone's friend. Schulman and Mekler in their very excellent volume, *Bringing up a Moral Child: A New Approach for Teaching Your Child to Be Kind, Just, and Responsible,* suggest that the following qualities characterize what it means to be someone's friend[3]:

- helping him (your friend) reach his goals (unless you firmly believe he is doing something self-destructive or harmful to others)
- being available when he needs you, even when it's inconvenient

- sharing your possessions with him
- keeping his secrets
- keeping your promises to him
- not allowing jealous feelings to make you possessive. If your friend is really a worthwhile person, other people will like him, too, and he will like them.
- recognizing that there will be times when what he needs from you should take precedence over what you need from him—for example, when he has either serious troubles or great joys that he wants to share
- never making him regret having told you something personal by embarrassing him or using it against him
- not trying to gain his friendship or get him to spend more time with you by making him feel guilty or sorry for you
- enjoying and showing enthusiasm at his successes
- comforting him when he's mad or frightened
- encouraging him when he is discouraged
- respecting his independence as well as your own. If a friend disagrees with you, it should not be taken as a betrayal of the friendship. On the other hand, agreeing with him just to win his friendship is a betrayal of oneself, and in the long run you'll lose the respect of the person you want to have as a friend.

Things You Can Do at Home to Help Your Child Acquire Appropriate Social Skills

You're obviously worried about your child's social development if you've read this far in Chapter Seven already. You've seen some early warning signs of social problems. Your child isn't happy when she comes home from school.

She doesn't get along with other children in the neighborhood when you invite them over to play. Possibly she's moody, bad-tempered, and unpleasant toward her siblings. Maybe she goes right to her room after school and won't talk to anyone.

If you've noticed some of these problems and haven't been contacted by the school, then that is a good sign. The problems have not progressed to a serious state. Call your child's teacher immediately and make an appointment for a conference. Take along the following questions to help you assess the problem:

1. Does my child participate in group activities and class discussions, or is she a loner in the class?
2. Is my child included in play activities at recess or is she turning her classmates off?
3. Does she engage in any specific behaviors that other children find unattractive?
4. Does she work independently, or is she at your desk for help and reassurance too often?
5. Does she have any "friends" at all in the class?
6. What strategies have you as the teacher used to try to help my child?
7. Do you find my child unattractive and put her down in class? (You will have to be subtle in finding out the answer to this question, but it can be done.)

Once you've determined the severity of the problem, you can begin to strategize for what can be done at home, at school, and in the community. Perhaps the problem is only a temporary one. The teacher can help you assess the situation. Together you should develop a plan for what each of you will do to help your child.

Home activities for children in kindergarten through middle school

☐ *ONE-ON-ONE TIME.* You should immediately plan a special time on a regular basis to spend with your child alone. You can do all kinds of things together. One of the things I enjoyed most about being an elementary-school principal was spending time with children who were encountering serious social difficulties and had no one who was willing to spend time with them. They weren't appreciated at home, and their teachers could scarcely get them out of the door fast enough at lunch time. I would often take them to McDonald's for lunch, one of my favorite fast-food places. Here we would practice the fine art of social conversation. Sometimes I had to do some coaching in the area of table manners as well. It was obvious in many cases that this was the first time that anyone had ever taken the time to give this child thirty minutes of uninterrupted attention to listen and talk about anything that was on his mind. All children need this kind of attention from their parents (my children are now in college and still crave it), and it makes a perfect opportunity for modeling the very social skills you so desperately want your child to develop.

The activities you do together should be of the child's own choosing. They could involve playing a video game, making cupcakes, or lying on the bed to talk. Just make sure that nothing interrupts this time together.

☐ *ROLE MODELING.* Give your child a chance to see you in appropriate social interaction. Invite teachers to your home for lunch or dinner. Invite your child to join you if you go places with adult friends. I took my college-aged son to a black-tie dinner recently. It was his first experience in formal dining, and he learned many valuable social lessons from observing me and the adults who attended.

☐ *PRAISE.* Give your child positive feedback whenever you see him do something nice for anyone (family member or friend). I've praised my son on more than one occasion for the wonderful way in which he escorted me to the dinner. He was charming, witty, and a totally captivating companion.

☐ *COOPERATIVE FAMILY ACTIVITIES.* In addition to the one-on-one time that you spend with your child, organize some cooperative family activities that give everyone a chance to practice social skills. Go out for a bite to eat together, play Trivial Pursuit, rake leaves, or go bowling. Every family should have its list of enjoyable things to do together. These family activities will give you a chance to see how well your child is learning some of the lessons you have been teaching.

☐ *LITERATURE.* Use good stories to teach the values of friendship and loyalty. There is much outstanding children's fiction, both Christian and secular, that will give you an opportunity to demonstrate through the printed word what real friendship is all about.[4]

☐ *PLANNING AHEAD / ROLE-PLAYING.* When my children were young, we would often practice how to behave ahead of time if we were going to be heading into a new social situation. I'd play the different parts and demonstrate what my children should say and do to be "socially acceptable." If your child has an explosive temper or tends to say the wrong thing, role-play situations of this type to give him an opportunity to practice appropriate responses.

☐ *TALKING IT THROUGH/DEBRIEFING AND PROCESSING THE DAY.* It's always a good idea to debrief at the end of a school day. This should be done not in the spirit of criticism but in the spirit of "How can I do better tomorrow?" The more you talk about what your child should be doing and let her know that you expect her behavior to change, the greater the chance that a change will actually occur.

☐ *MAKING YOUR HOME A FRIENDLY PLACE.* The Peak Parent Center[5] has published a variety of materials to assist you in the friendship-building process with your child. They have a marvelous bibliography of books to read aloud as well. While their primary focus is on children with disabilities, the strategies and materials they have available will work with all children. They offer the following suggestions for making your home a friendlier place.

- *Create an environment in your home that attracts kids.* Make it a fun place for them to get together. Have snacks available; make children feel welcome to visit or just drop by. Have activities going on that your child and peers enjoy, such as Nintendo, bike-riding, games.

- *Minimize adult presence when children are playing at your house.* Let your child be directly involved with other children without an adult always being right at her side.
- *Invite more than one friend at a time.* To keep things moving, invite two friends at a time over to play with your child. Just be careful that the two you invite aren't best friends who will exclude your child.

School activities for children in kindergarten through middle school. I'm aware that as a parent you have a limited sphere of influence regarding what goes on at school. If you can, however, make the suggestion to your child's teacher that he or she use some cooperative learning activities in the classroom. If you're really resourceful, purchase the books and make a present (or loan) of them to your child's teacher and principal. Perhaps your school already uses some cooperative learning strategies in its classrooms. If so, then you and your child are very fortunate. Cooperative classrooms (rather than competitive ones) foster academic achievement as well as positive social adjustment.

☐ *PEER PAIRING AND BUDDY SYSTEM.* If a teacher expects that students will work together and help each other, there is a greater likelihood that this will happen. If a teacher fosters individualization and doesn't let students interact at all during the school day, children are at a distinct disadvantage for developing their social skills to a higher level.

☐ *DEBRIEFING SESSIONS.* The skilled classroom teacher allows time after a cooperative activity to talk about what happened and why it did or didn't work. Children learn to label their behaviors and praise and reward those students that exhibit positive behaviors.

☐ *SPECIFIC PLANS FOR SPECIAL CASES.* If your child is suffering from a truly severe social problem, then ask for a consultation with the school psychologist and the behavior management specialist. They are skilled in working with classroom teachers and students to enlist help for your child. They often use programs that have been designed to teach social skills. Among the better ones are *Getting Along with Others: Teaching Social Effectiveness to Children,*[6] *The Walker Social Skills Curriculum: The Accepts Program,*[7] *The Walker Social Skills Curriculum: The Access Program: Adolescent Curriculum for Communication and Effective Social Skills.*[8]

Community activities for children in kindergarten through middle school.

☐ *COMMUNITY SERVICE ORGANIZATIONS.* Investigate Scouts, park district programs, YMCA's, or other groups that can provide recreational programs, along with opportunities to meet peers.

☐ *SPECIAL INTERESTS.* Make an effort to figure out what your child's real strengths are. Give him lessons. Karate lessons are often an ego boost for boys who are having social problems. The discipline and mentoring relationships that are found as more proficient students teach the newer ones could be very beneficial to your child. Music, art, and sports can often serve the same purpose.

☐ *ARRANGED FRIENDSHIPS*. Find a way to develop contacts for your child if she is reluctant or unable to do it on her own. Don't force the issue but throw a party, arrange a field trip for a small group, or invite a reluctant playmate for pizza. These arrangements may not always be successful, but keep on trying.

☐ *SOCIAL GAMES AND SKILLS*. Make sure your child knows how to bowl, play volleyball, or roller skate if those activities might facilitate social development. There's nothing worse than being a wallflower at the middle school party because you don't know how to do anything.

☐ *CHURCH GROUPS*. Youth groups at church are the perfect place to use newly developing social skills. Friendship, loyalty, and kindness should flourish in these settings, especially from the adults involved in sponsorship.

❖ Resources

If you would like more information on the topics covered in this chapter, the following books and organizations will be helpful to you.

Gould, Shirley. *The Challenge of Friendship: Helping Your Child Become a Friend.* New York: Hawthorne/Dutton, 1981.

McGinnis, Ellen, and Arnold P. Goldstein. *Skillstreaming the Elementary School Child.* Champaign, Ill.: Research Press Company, 1984.

Oppenheim, Joanne. *Raising a Confident Child: The Bank Street Year-by-Year Guide*. New York: Pantheon Books, 1984.

Osman, Betty B. *No One to Play With: The Social Side of Learning Disabilities*. New York: Random House, 1982.

Peak Parent Center, Inc.
6055 Lehman Drive, Suite 101
Colorado Springs, CO 80918
1-719-531-9400.

Schulman, Michael, and Eva Mekler. *Bringing up a Moral Child*. Reading, Mass.: Addison-Wesley Publishing Company, Inc., 1985.

8

SHE WON'T FOLLOW THE RULES
Behavior Problems at School

In my years as a teacher and elementary-school principal I've seen children do just about everything—from amusing mischief like changing all the teacher name plates to incidents like vandalism or burglary that required police intervention. But in most schools these are rare problems that occur only once in a school year, if at all. The real behavior problems are those that dog us every single day because children can't (or won't) follow the simple school rules that have been established in each classroom. A child's seeming inability or unwillingness to respect her fellow classmates or her teacher, her seeming lack of self-control when it comes to observing the simple amenities of classroom life, or her total disregard for doing anything that interferes with doing it "her way" are all evidences of a school behavior problem. These problems frustrate parents, make teachers think twice about signing their contracts for the next year, and give principals gray hair. What can you as a parent do if your life is plagued by telephone calls and notes from school personnel about your child's behavior problems?

In the sections ahead we'll find answers to these questions about discipline and then look at what you might be doing at each age level if your child won't behave at school.

What Is Discipline?

The word discipline comes from the Latin word *discipulus,* or disciple. Its meaning describes what the relationship between parent and child should be. The parent is the role model and teacher, instilling in his child by example all of the characteristics and values that are worthy in a human being. Unfortunately, the word *discipline* in today's society has come to mean punishment or compliance, both negative connotations. But discipline in the ideal sense is the development of a relationship between parent and child that is built on mutual respect and love. The discipline relationship between parent and child is one that is constantly changing as the child moves from infancy to adulthood. Discipline should take place in the context of empathy, protection, and guidance. Good discipline produces self-confidence, self-control, and self-esteem. Discipline is positive. Discipline is a system, a plan, a belief structure that governs all of your relationships with children. If the plan is working there are few instances when children need consequences. I choose to use the word *consequences* rather than the word *punishment.* Punishment brings with it embarrassment, loss, and even pain (often physical). Punishment is often delivered with anger and harshness. Punishment is usually an act or an episode that is over in a very short time. Punishment usually comes out of the blue and sideswipes a child. Punishment usually makes a child angry and fearful.

I prefer the word *consequences*. Consequences in most cases are quite logical. If you choose to do something, then the choice you make will result in these consequences. Students in my elementary building knew that if they chose to write on the washroom walls, they would have to wash the washroom walls. On more than one occasion, I've taken my chair into the boys' washroom after school to do paperwork while watching an earnest sixth grader scrub the tile walls from top to bottom. Consequences are usually spelled out ahead of time and delivered with calm and even-temperedness, rather than in anger or rage.

Even this early in the chapter, you should already be getting the idea that discipline isn't something you do just once in a while when there's a problem. Discipline is a way of life. Discipline is a plan of action for your family, a set of values and beliefs that govern the way you act toward each other and the world. Discipline is the blueprint for your child's behavior both at home and out in the world.

What Are the Most Common Parental Pitfalls When It Comes to Effective Discipline?

As parents, all of us are susceptible to the following mistakes when it comes to our children and their behavior (particularly their behavior at school): 1) we send mixed messages to our children; 2) our personal goals and values are in conflict with the system (we're still trying to grow up ourselves); or 3) we feel we don't have any control over the situation.

As parents we are often wishy-washy and indecisive about what we want our children to do. We hear about a behavior problem at school and agree that something needs to be done. But we don't follow through on it with any consistency. Perhaps we are in conflict with our spouse about what our family goals should be (e.g. Father is strict and Mother bends the rules behind his back). We can be sure, however, that if we do send mixed messages, our children will receive them loud and clear. When children receive one message from Mom and another from Dad, or one message from the teacher and another from Mom, the problems can become very serious.

A second pitfall I've seen occur with great frequency involves the parents who haven't grown up yet. These individuals set out to redress all of the injustices that were done to them as children by refusing to become the adults in the situation. Their values are in conflict with the system. They give their children permission to act in inappropriate ways and condone unacceptable behavior under the guise of individual rights and expression. The Sloanes* were one such family. Their values were clearly in conflict with those of our school. They believed that if their son Johnny was jostled or bothered on the playground, he had permission to "get physical" with the offender. Johnny had been in my office half a dozen times for fighting, and phone calls to his parents did no good. As the Sloanes sat across from me in my office, I began to understand why Johnny didn't follow our school rules. "Nobody's going to shove my

*Name has been changed.

kid around," announced Mr. Sloan. What he was really saying was, "Nobody's going to shove me around." Before I could deal with Johnny's behavior, I first needed to deal with his father's attitude.

The third major pitfall that parents fall into is the feeling of helplessness. This can be the most debilitating of the pitfalls because it paralyzes parents and renders them impotent to deal with their child's behavior problems at school. They believe that they don't have any control over the situation. They throw up their hands in dismay and say, as so many parents have said in my office, "Do whatever you want to with him. I can't control him at home either." Some parents attribute their child's problems to a learning disability and truly believe that nothing they can do will make a difference. There are other parents who believe that their children are passing through a normal phase or stage in growing up and a little misbehavior is to be expected. They can't understand why we're getting so upset at school about their child's behavior. I call that the "boys will be boys" syndrome. Or, they may feel that their child's behavior problem has been inherited from someone in the family, and they are powerless to change what has been genetically determined.

Children *can* learn to behave and parents *can* take charge of their children and regain control of their family life. It is not always easy, but I've seen it done successfully on countless occasions when everyone has worked together.

Where *Do* School Behavior Problems Come From?

If a child's behavior problems aren't caused by his learning disability, his developmental stage, inherited from Uncle

George, or the result of an emotional trauma in early child-hood, then where *do* they come from? Unfortunately, in most cases they've been learned at home. A child has learned what works for her in her home environment, and when she gets to school, she's only doing what comes naturally. Oh, parents don't set out to teach a child to misbehave in the same way they teach the ABC's, but a child who learns from experience how to control adults at home has a very difficult time unlearning that experience when she gets to school. And the smarter she is, the better she has learned the lesson.

Is It Always My Fault?

I know I've been pretty direct in laying your child's be-havior problems at your doorstep. There are some instan-ces, however, when the school must assume a share of the blame for how your child behaves. If we place your child in a classroom where the teacher is incompetent and lacks basic classroom management skills, even the most obedient of children will forget all about what they've learned at home and follow the crowd. There are other occasions when a child who has never been in trouble before shocks every-one with his behavior. I always encounter at least one or two examples of this phenomenon each school year. These momentary lapses are just that and should be viewed by both the school and parents as a beneficial learning ex-perience in the life of the child. When a pattern of deviant behavior persists over months, then all parties concerned must work on solutions.

What Are the Qualities of a Parent Who Has Good Discipline?

Parents who demonstrate good discipline have some very important qualities in common: 1) they are direct; 2) they are clear; 3) they give reasons honestly and freely; 4) they communicate respect; and 5) they show interest. Examine your own approach to your children to determine if you're missing one or more of these qualities.

Successful parents are **direct.** When they address their children they make statements such as "I want . . . ," "I will not . . . ," "I expect . . . ," or "The rule is . . ." They also let their children know what they as parents need, what they don't like, and how they feel. A successful parent uses the personal pronoun "I" so that children know who is behind the feelings. There is no reticence to let children know exactly what is expected and who is in charge. Successful parents don't equivocate; they are self-confident and certain about what they believe.

Successful parents are also **clear** about what is being said. They communicate their wishes and desires in age-appropriate language that leaves no room for possible misunderstanding.

We must also be ready to **give honest reasons** for any actions we take with our children. "Do it because I said so" is not an acceptable reason. Yes, it may have to do once in a while, but if every action you take as a parent doesn't have some logical and sensible reasons behind it, you need to examine your logic.

Successful parents **communicate respect** to their children. Many parents are direct and clear about what they want their children to do but lose points in the respect department. Their body language, tone of voice, or choice of words are demeaning to the child. If a parent wants respect from the child, he must be willing to give it as well. Successful parents never humiliate or embarrass their children when dealing with behavior problems. They remember how they would like to be corrected by a boss or superior at work.

Finally, successful parents **show interest** in their children. They are eager to talk with their children about what is happening in their lives. They listen with both ears and make sure they have eye contact during conversations. They send a message that is unmistakable—*I love you and I think you're important.*

Which Discipline Method Should I Use?

I'm assuming since you're reading this chapter that your child's behavior is causing a problem at school, and you're looking for a solution to that problem. The discipline plan or method you choose is not nearly as critical as the decision you have made to do something. Recognizing that you alone hold the key to improving your child's behavior both at home and at school is the critical first step. There's no shortage of advice for the parent who's looking for it. Every psychologist in the world has written a book about disciplining children. Some give workshops and sell notebooks and cassettes to help you if their books can't. You can find books on discipline by James Dobson, Lee Canter, and even the gurus of leadership and organizational development Paul Hersey and Kenneth H. Blanchard. There are five basic approaches to discipline that you will read about in the literature: counseling, democratic, behavior modification, logical consequences, and assertive discipline. We'll discuss them in the sections ahead and you'll find many similarities. However, none of them will work without a giant dose of consistency, a generous quantity of love and respect for your child, and a large measure of personal worth and self-esteem for yourself.

In addition, you'll need to believe that all of us (children, parents, and teachers) are capable of change. If you have these key ingredients, then choose a guru or method that makes the most sense to you and stick with it. Perhaps you'll need to attend a class or join a support group. Changing children's behavior is big business these days. But once you've talked, read, and learned, stick to your guns. The worst thing that any parent can do is to keep changing plans, rules, and expectations. Of course, you always have to do some fine-tuning along the way as children become more mature or as family circumstances change, but there should be some bedrock values and rules that never change. If children ever feel that nothing is written in stone and that everything is negotiable, you can kiss good behavior good-bye. If you don't have those key ingredients, or if your child's behavior has gone completely out of your control, then you may need professional help for you or your family. Let's look at each of the popular discipline methods and their pros and cons.

Counseling. The counseling approach to discipline is modeled on the approach a trained counselor would take in working with a patient. Effort is made to explore the reasons behind the misbehavior and to help the child talk about his feelings associated with these reasons. This reasoned and calm approach to solving behavior problems works well with a child like Sam. A fourth grader, he had been a model student for all of his elementary-school career. But when faced with the temptation of a video that he very much wanted and couldn't afford, he stole it from his best friend's desk. Sam knew that what he had done was wrong, suffered great emotional distress after his act, and was relieved to have the whole thing out in the open and receive his consequences. Counseling doesn't work at all, however, with children who have been manipulating adults for years. They will be able to say all of the right things in a counseling session. But minutes after the conversation has ended they'll be right back at it again.

Democratic. This approach to solving behavior problems is particularly attractive to those parents who want to deal with their children as equals. These parents would like to state the problem calmly and then in a spirit of mutual agreement decide with their children how to solve the problem. This approach works beautifully if your children are reasonable and cooperative. You can have a short family meeting or round-table discussion, brainstorm solutions, and implement them immediately. Forget this approach with children who do not possess the maturity and responsibility to follow through on the agreed-upon solution.

Behavior modification. Behavior modification is a methodology that parents can use to increase the rate of a desirable behavior (e.g., getting a student to turn in his homework on a regular basis) or decrease the rate of an unacceptable student behavior (e.g., stop saying inappropriate things to other students in the class). Behaviors are increased or decreased by using positive reinforcement (praise, tokens, rewards) or negative reinforcement (removal of privileges, consequences). Many parents and teachers feel uncomfortable with giving children rewards and praise for doing things that they are supposed to be doing anyway. Indeed, most children perform to a level of expectations with no need for any behavior modification. However, in extreme cases where students have developed long-standing negative behaviors, this process can be very effective. Dr. James Dobson, in his popular book *Dare to Discipline,* devotes an entire chapter to this technique. He calls it a "miracle tool."[1] Behavior modification doesn't always have the expected results, but that's usually the result of procedures that are too complicated, a lack of organization, or the choice of reinforcers that have no meaning for the child. Skilled behavior-management specialists and school psychologists are the best personnel to consult for behavior modification that really works.

What all effective parents know is that they constantly reinforce their children's positive behaviors with smiles, hugs, and words of praise. The children who are usually the most challenging in the behavior department are those who have had very little if any positive reinforcement in their lives. They are looking for any kind of attention, even the negative they receive when they misbehave at home and in school.

Logical consequences. This approach, first described by Rudolph Dreikurs and Loren Grey,[2] advocates letting children suffer the natural consequences that result from misbehavior. The logical consequences of constantly forgetting your lunch money would be to go without lunch. The logical consequence of wasting class time is to add time to the child's school day. This approach can also work well with some children. But there are others who could care less about what the logical consequences are. The child who doesn't turn in his homework and is left to experience the logical consequences will fail the course. This may not be an acceptable alternative to his parents.

Assertive discipline. This popular model for managing a child's behavior was developed by Lee Canter.[3] Canter focuses on the types of responses that parents can make to their children's misbehavior and describes them as either effective (assertive) or ineffective (nonassertive and hostile). An assertive response is a "firm, clear statement—one that you are prepared to back up with actions."[4] A nonassertive response is one that parents are not prepared to back up with action. "When parents respond in a nonassertive manner, they allow their children to take advantage of them because they communicate to the children that they do not mean business and are not prepared to take firm action."[5]

Typical nonassertive statements fall into the following categories: 1) statement of fact: "You're still not doing what I want"; 2) questioning: "Why are you doing that?"; 3) unclear goals: "Try to behave"; 4) demand that children behave but no follow-through: "How many times do I have to tell you?"

The second type of ineffective responses according to Canter is that of hostile responses.[6] Typical hostile responses fall into the following categories: 1) verbal put-downs: "You make me sick"; 2) threats: "You're going to get it"; 3) severe punishment: "You can't leave your room for a week"; 4) physical response: "I'm going to give you what you deserve."

Canter's approach, if followed consistently, can work very effectively. I've seen nonassertive and hostile parents retrain themselves to be positive and assertive in their responses.

What Are the Important Components of a Good Discipline (Good Behavior) Plan?

The best behavior plans are those that have been specially designed for one child. All of the adults that spend time with the child should be a part of the plan's development (day-care providers, grandparents, stepparents, etc.), and they must each agree on the key components: expectations, consequences, and positive reinforcement or rewards.

Expectations. This is the first critical component of the plan. Everyone must agree on what is expected of the child. You may uncover the real root of the problem as you discuss and negotiate a list of behavioral expectations. Keep the first list very simple. It may only have one item (e.g., My child will speak with courtesy to all adults).

Consequences. The second important component is the consequences that will result if the child does not comply with the behavioral expectation. Choosing the appropriate consequence for the age, interests, and maturity level of the child is critical. A consequence for a five-year-old might be a five-minute time-out in his bedroom. A consequence for a fourteen-year-old might mean losing his television privileges for a night. Think about what your child really likes to do and build that into the consequences. If your child likes nothing better than to be alone in his room and listen to music, then sending him to his room is no consequence.

Positive reinforcement/rewards. Don't forget that if you want your plan to succeed you'll have to build in plenty of positive reinforcement. Include a tangible reward as part of the plan. As we discussed earlier, some parents object to providing reinforcers for children doing things they should be doing anyway, but if what you're doing now isn't working, then you don't have the luxury of objecting. You need all the help you can get. Extra privileges like staying up late, a trip to a fast-food restaurant, or watching a TV show are all examples of tangible rewards. Don't forget to include some intangible rewards as well. Your child won't know they're part of the plan, but they will work wonders for his self-esteem. Praise and attention are powerful intangible rewards and you need to use lots of both. If you have a difficult time giving praise, then practice.

Good discipline sounds very easy on paper. It's only when you're confronted with a recalcitrant child that one realizes how difficult it can be. If you don't really believe you can take control of your child, get help for yourself before you begin to work with the child. I've often said in jest that kids are like horses and dogs. Horses and dogs seem to know when we're afraid of them and they take advantage of our fear, becoming aggressive and uncooperative. Children are the same way. They have a sixth sense that tells them when we do or don't mean business. When we don't, they take over. I've seen this phenomenon in dozens of classrooms. Kids know who means business and they fall into line. They'll do the same for parents who mean business. Parents just have to convince themselves they can do it.

What Are the Characteristics of a School with a Good Behavior/Discipline Climate?

You have every right to expect that the climate in your school will support good behavior for all students. This kind of climate will encourage each child to do her best and will offer encouragement and support for those who try. Visit the school and walk through halls. Peek into classrooms. You can tell very quickly if students in the school are well-behaved. Students will be working purposefully in classrooms (not necessarily quietly, but purposefully). Students will be moving quietly through the hallways in an orderly manner. Teachers will be speaking respectfully to all students. Adults will be speaking respectfully to each other. Classrooms will have rules posted where everyone can see them. Teachers will have established consequences and a plan for dealing with students when they break the rules. There is a consistency and cohesion to discipline throughout the school. The rules do not change from classroom to classroom, and all adults in the school take all children as their personal responsibility.

How Can I Work with My Child's School to Develop a Specific Home-School Behavior Plan for My Child?

The following plan is a generic one that is suitable for any grade level. I have used this format with dozens of parents, and when the home and school work closely together, each following through with consistency, school behavior problems can be solved. The key, however, is consistency, and that is a most elusive quality for all of us. Parents are busy. There are many single parents and dual-career parents. Sometimes they forget to sign behavior notices or follow through with positive reinforcement. They lose their tempers and grow impatient with the system.

Teachers are busy, too. They have more than thirty students in a class, and your child isn't the only one with a behavior problem. They get distracted by the academic needs of their students and forget to send home the behavior note or follow through with positive reinforcement. They lose their tempers and grow impatient with the system.

The only individual with consistency, follow-through, and unlimited time and energy is the child. He will consistently exhibit poor behavior if left to his own devices. He will never forget to misbehave. And he loves the present system because he does exactly what he wants to whenever he wants to.

So stop making excuses and get started on a plan to change your child's behavior. The key to improving your child's behavior at school is to let her know that you will under no circumstances tolerate her unacceptable behavior. In my experience, when a parent makes that statement in an unequivocal fashion and follows through at home with consequences when the child misbehaves, school behavior problems gradually fade away. When parents come to a meeting to discuss their child's behavior only to argue, negotiate, make excuses, overprotect, or abdicate, they can only expect their child's problem to escalate into something more serious.

Step One: Gather complete information. Whenever you get a phone call or note from school, respond immediately. If school officials think the problem is serious enough to warrant some form of communication to the parent, it's not going to disappear. Require specifics when school officials talk about your child's behavior. Don't settle for generalities like "Johnny isn't doing well in the behavior department." Exactly what is Johnny doing? How many times has he done it? What interventions have been tried in school? What was Johnny's response? Has the teacher received any help from school support personnel like the school psychologist or behavior-management specialist?

Chances are you will gather this information over the telephone. Once you have all of the facts, ask for a conference to discuss the problem.

Step Two: Meet with school officials to develop a behavior plan. Review the advice about successful parent-teacher conferences in Chapter Two before going to the conference. Ask to have all of the child's teachers present. Sometimes the art or music teacher will have a different perspective relative to your student's behavior. It's important to have the principal present as well. I have found that many heads are better than just a few in the problem-solving process. The plan this team develops should have five parts: 1) the behavior you want your child to exhibit at school; 2) what the teacher and the principal will do when your child does and does not behave; 3) how what happens at school will be communicated to you; 4) what will happen at home when your child does and does not behave at school; and 5) how what you do at home will be communicated to the teacher. All of these parts should be in writing and all of the conference participants should sign the plan.

Step Three: Share the plan with your child. I have found that the plan is best shared with the child in front of the group. One of the conference participants who has especially good rapport and communication skills with the child should share the contents of the plan. That individual should make sure the child can explain and retell the plan and that he or she is absolutely clear on what is expected of him or her. The child should also sign the plan.

Step Four: Follow through on the plan. The best-laid plans of parents and teachers will not work if they do not communicate on a daily basis with one another. Children will do everything in their power to keep this communication from happening. They will tell their parents that the teacher didn't have time to finish the note. They will tell their teacher that Mom lost the note. Children who need this kind of behavior plan are masters at confusing the issue and driving wedges between parents and teachers. Vow that your child will not do this to you and her teacher. If your child is particularly skillful at this, go to school every day and see the teacher face-to-face. I have seen this technique work especially well. The child who sees her mother or father talking with the teacher after school every day will soon decide that her game is over.

Step Five: Monitor, evaluate, and fine-tune the plan. After the first week, have a face-to-face meeting with the teacher to assess how things are going. At this point you may need to change some small details of the plan. But don't give up on the major components, even if they don't seem to be totally successful. The behavior problem has been well-learned, and your child will need a period of time to test both home and school to see if both parties mean business.

If your plan has been successful, you can begin to reduce the heavy-duty monitoring and communicating that has been going on. Show your child that she is beginning to develop self-discipline and can now take responsibility for her own behavior. You will both gain self-esteem through this experience.

❖ Resources

If you would like more information on the topics covered in this chapter, the following books will be helpful to you.

Axelrod, Saul. *Behavior Modification for the Classroom Teacher.* New York: McGraw-Hill Book Co., 1983.

Balter, Lawrence. *Who's in Control? Dr. Balter's Guide to Discipline without Combat.* New York: Poseidon Press, 1988.

Bodenhamer, Gregory. *Back in Control: How to Get Your Children to Behave.* Englewood Cliffs, N.J.: Prentice-Hall Press, 1983.

Canter, Lee. *Lee Canter's Assertive Discipline for Parents.* Santa Monica, Calif.: Canter & Associates, 1982.

Corsini, Raymond J., and Genevieve Painter. *The Practical Parent: ABC's of Child Discipline.* New York: Harper & Row, 1975.

DeRosis, Helen. *Parent Power Child Power: A New Tested Method for Parenting without Guilt.* Indianapolis: The Bobbs-Merrill Company, Inc., 1974.

Dobson, James. *Dare to Discipline.* Wheaton, Ill.: Tyndale House, 1970.

Dodson, Fitzhugh. *How to Discipline with Love: From Crib to College.* New York: New American Library, 1977.

Dreikurs, Rudolf, and Loren Grey. *A New Approach to Discipline: Logical Consequences.* New York: Hawthorn Books, Inc., 1968.

Gibson, Janice T. *Discipline Is Not a Dirty Word: A Positive Learning Approach.* Lexington, Mass.: The Lewis Publishing Company, 1983.

Hersey, Paul, and Kenneth H. Blanchard. *The Family Game: A Situational Approach to Effective Parenting.* Reading, Mass.: Addison-Wesley Publishing Company, 1978.

Kelly, Jeffrey. *Solving Your Child's Behavior Problems: An Everyday Guide for Parents.* Boston: Little, Brown and Company, 1983.

Nelson, Jane, and Lynn Lott. *I'm On Your Side: Resolving Conflict with Your Teenage Son or Daughter.* Rocklin, Calif.: Prima Publishing & Communication, 1990.

Silberman, Melvin L., and Susan A. Wheelan. *How to Discipline without Feeling Guilty: Assertive Relationships with Children.* New York: Hawthorn Books, 1980.

Wood, Paul, and Bernard Schwartz. *How to Get Your Children to Do What You Want Them to Do.* Englewood Cliffs, N.J.: Prentice-Hall, Inc., 1977.

Wyckoff, Jerry L., and Barbara C. Unell. *How to Discipline Your Six to Twelve Year Old.* New York: Doubleday, 1991.

9

LEARNING DISABILITIES AND ATTENTION DEFICIT DISORDER

Are They Real?

Molly didn't do badly in school until she reached fourth grade. She had never been a star student, but she got by, and her teachers usually blamed any problems she had on her lack of concentration and her silliness. She was the "character" in the family, the one who did outrageous things like putting the cornflakes in the refrigerator and the milk in the pantry, like tripping over her own two feet whenever she walked across the room. But when she turned nine, she gradually became angry and depressed. Her parents would learn later that she thought she was crazy and had contemplated suicide. But in the beginning, everyone was confused, most of all Molly. She didn't understand why school kept getting more and more difficult and why the only message she received from her teachers and parents was to try harder. She was already trying as hard as she could, and things just didn't make sense.

Molly's mother thought she might have a learning disability, but the teachers thought she was overreacting. After an extensive workup at a neurological clinic, Molly was diagnosed with Attention Deficit Disorder plus a severe auditory processing learning disability. Suddenly Molly's inability to follow simple directions or even sort her belongings into categories was no longer just lack of trying on her part. There was a reason for her behavior. Now in sixth grade, undergoing counseling to help her overcome some of the negative coping skills she used in the past, Ritalin therapy to help control her ADD, and extensive academic and emotional support from her parents and teachers, she is beginning to deal with her disability as well as utilize the near-genius nonverbal IQ she enjoys. Fortunately for Molly, her high IQ helped her cope with school until the subject matter became too overwhelming and the homework too confusing. Molly is one of the fortunate ones, because her parents have the financial, emotional, and intellectual resources not only to help Molly, but to survive as a couple and family what is a nightmare for most parents, figuring out why their child is having schooling problems and then coping with a diagnosis that for many is devastating.

The topic of learning disabilities is a confusing one for parents. There are a wide variety of professionals who study, diagnose, and treat youngsters with learning disabilities: physicians (pediatricians, neurologists, psychiatrists); psychologists (therapists, counselors); and educators (regular classroom teachers, school psychologists, behavior management specialists, special education teachers, speech and language pathologists, occupational/physical therapists). Depending on where you begin in your search for "truth," you will encounter a variety of terms and diagnoses. In the sections ahead, we will attempt to make sense of the "alphabet soup" that confronts parents and help you determine the best way to get support for your child.

What Is a Learning Disability?

When I began teaching fifth grade in 1963, I had a student in my classroom who couldn't read a word. Ronnie seemed a bright enough boy when we chatted about his family or things that were happening at school. But he couldn't remember from one day to the next the simple sounds I was trying to teach him. I sent him to a special reading teacher, but her efforts failed to break through Ronnie's barrier of misunderstanding and confusion as well. In 1963, the term "learning disability" was rarely if ever heard in education circles. It wasn't until the late 1960s that it was recognized as a field of study. And schools were not required to give special help to students with disabilities until the early 1970s. In 1973, however, Federal Law 94-142 defined learning disabilities and mandated that every school system provide special education appropriate for children with these disabilities. The law defined a learning disability as "one or more significant defects in the essential learning process which may manifest itself in a discrepancy between ability and performance in one or more areas of spoken or written language, the ability to think, read, speak, write, spell, or calculate, including perceptual handicaps, brain injury, dyslexia and aphasia but not learning problems that are the result of visual, auditory or motor handicaps, mental retardation, emotional disturbance, or environmental, cultural or economic handicaps."[1]

In 1981 a new definition was developed by the National Joint Committee for Learning Disabilities, "Learning disabilities is a generic term that refers to a heterogeneous group of disorders manifested by significant difficulties in the acquisition and use of listening, speaking, reading, writing, reasoning, or mathematical abilities. These disorders are intrinsic to the individual and presumed to be due to central nervous system dysfunction. Even though a learning disability may occur concomitantly with other handicapping conditions (e.g., sensory impairment, mental retardation, social and emotional disturbance) or environmental influence (e.g., cultural differences, insufficient/inappropriate instruction, psychogenic factors), it is not the direct result of those conditions or influences."[2] While it is important to be aware of the official definition of learning disabilities because it determines which children are eligible for services under Public Law 94-142, Bloom offers a simpler working definition: "Learning disabled children (and adults) are unable to store, process or produce information in the same way that the rest of us do, although they appear to have no physical, mental, or environmental handicaps to prevent them from doing so."[3]

Learning-disabled children (and adults) do not fail because they lack intelligence. They aren't mentally retarded or mentally ill. They simply have a difficult time learning in the conventional ways in which most schools are structured.

What Are the Symptoms of a Child with a Learning Disability?

A child with a learning disability may exhibit one or more of the following problems on a consistent basis. Although every child exhibits some of the characteristics at some time during his or her development, what distinguishes the child with a learning disability is the number and persistence of the symptoms over an extended period of development.

- Short attention span, easily distracted
- Restless hyperactivity
- Poor letter or word memory
- Poor auditory memory
- Inability to discriminate between letters, numbers, or sounds
- Poor handwriting
- Reads poorly, if at all
- Cannot follow multiple directions
- Erratic performance from day to day
- Impulsive
- Poor coordination
- Late gross or fine-motor development
- Difficulty telling time or distinguishing left from right
- Late speech development, immature speech
- Trouble understanding words or concepts
- Trouble naming familiar people or things
- Says one thing, means another
- Responds inappropriately in many instances
- Adjusts poorly to change[4]

The list above details the symptoms of a child with learning disabilities that may affect his school performance in a negative way. The good news is that learning-disabled children have strengths as well. It is important for you as a parent and for teachers who work with your child to recognize and build on those strengths on a daily basis. Learning-disabled children are often "highly imaginative, creative problem solvers."[5] Learning-disabled children can shine in art or music. They are often very verbal and excel in drama and class discussions.

What Is Dyslexia and How Does It Relate to Learning Disabilities?

Dyslexia is one of the most frequently used terms when discussing learning disabilities. It is, however, only one type of learning disability, the one that affects an individual's ability to learn to read. Dyslexia is often accompanied by other learning disabilities and can frequently run in families. Whether this familial connection is completely biological or has some environmental basis is still a subject for extensive research.

Dyslexia has received a great deal of attention in the popular press, and many famous people of the past have been tentatively identified as dyslexic, offering encouragement to children with learning disabilities. Thomas Edison, Woodrow Wilson, Albert Einstein, and Leonardo da Vinci are all said to have had disabilities. There are many contemporary sports and entertainment stars who also suffer from dyslexia, among them Bruce Jenner, Greg Louganis, Whoopi Goldberg, and Tom Cruise.

How Can I Be Sure That My Child Really Does Have a Learning Disability and It Isn't Something Else That's Causing His Learning Problems?

The answer to this question can usually only be determined with the help of the professionals who work with and test your child. But if your child's learning problem is the result of emotional disturbances, environmental, cultural or economic disadvantages, sensory or motor handicaps, mental retardation, or other factors such as motivational problems (see Chapter Five), a mismatch between previous instruction and curriculum programming (see Chapter Two), then your child should not be diagnosed or labelled as learning-disabled. The fact remains, however, that your child is having problems learning. You will need to be vigorous in pursuit of the reasons, using the problem-solving model suggested in Chapter One. Some questions that are important to answer include:

- Do your child's attendance patterns show that normal achievement gains were not possible because of prolonged illness or frequent moves?
- Have there been any significant traumatic events in your child's life prior to exhibiting the learning problems?
- Has there been extreme disruption or disorganization in your family unit?
- What is the predominant language of your child and has the language difference severely affected your child's academic progress and performance?
- Has your child passed the vision and hearing screening?

- Does your child demonstrate any motor difficulties that affect academic performance?
- Could your child be a slow learner with limited degrees of discrepancy between ability/achievement, cognitive ability/actual achievement?
- Are there motivational problems (insufficient challenge at school, personal problems, inflexible teaching styles)?
- Is there a mismatch between previous instruction and curriculum content and current programming at school?[6]

What Is Attention Deficit Disorder and How Does It Differ from Hyperactivity?

The term Attention Deficit Disorder is a relatively new one but the condition is not. We used to call it *hyperactivity*. However, current research has shown that hyperactivity is only one of a set of symptoms that may or may not be present in a child with ADD. A child can have problems concentrating and paying attention in class without exhibiting any hyperactive symptoms. Professionals have now added a new category called ADHD (Attention Deficit Hyperactive Disorder) to distinguish between children with ADD who have hyperactive symptoms as well. Children with learning disabilities *may* or *may not* have ADD or ADHD. But, nearly without exception, all ADD and ADHD children have some type of learning disability.

The American Psychiatric Associations's Diagnostic and Statistical Manual for Mental Disorder (third edition, revised) gives a list of criteria on which the APA based a diagnosis of ADD with or without hyperactivity. The list stresses the varying degrees of these symptoms and adds that they may be present in other disorders or in the absence of any neurological disorder at all. Children have to give evidence of the symptoms for at least six months, must have at least eight of the symptoms, must have exhibited these symptoms before the age of eight, and must have no other developmental disorder. The manual lists the following symptoms:

- often fidgets with hands or feet or squirms in seat
- has difficulty remaining seated when required to do so
- is easily distracted by extraneous stimuli
- has difficulty awaiting turns in games or group situations
- often blurts out answers to questions before they have been completed
- has difficulty following through on instructions from others (e.g., often fails to finish chores)
- has difficulty sustaining attention in tasks or play activities
- often shifts from one uncompleted activity to another
- has difficulty playing quietly
- often talks excessively
- often interrupts or intrudes on others
- often does not seem to listen to what is being said to him or her
- often loses things necessary for tasks or activities at home or at school
- often engages in physically dangerous activities without considering possible consequences

What Does It All Mean?

Thus far I've tried to keep my explanations simple because too often I've sat in meetings or staffings with parents and watched their eyes glaze over as the professional psychologists and educators read from reports that contained far too many terms that were confusing, if not unintelligible, to the layperson. If, however, you are attempting to understand exactly how your child's learning abilities may be different from those of other children, you will need a more detailed understanding of some basic definitions. For further information, see Appendix H, Learning Disability Definitions.

Larry Silver, in his book, *The Misunderstood Child,*[7] categorizes learning disabilities in four ways: input disabilities, integration disabilities, memory disabilities, and output disabilities.

Input Disabilities exist when the information coming into a child's brain is not perceived correctly in one of three areas: visual, auditory, or tactile. A child may see a different configuration of letters or symbols, hear a different sound, or feel a different shape.

Integration Disabilities are present when the child has a lack of sequencing and abstraction skills. She has a difficult time arranging the symbols as they come into her brain and making any sense of them.

Memory Disabilities exist when a child has a difficult time remembering information or skills. These memory deficits can be observed in several areas: visual short-term (remembering for even a short time the things he sees), auditory short-term (remembering for even a short time the things he hears), visual long-term (remembering for a long period of time the things he sees), and auditory long-term (remembering for a long period of time the things he hears). Memory disabilities can be a great source of frustration to parents and teachers as they grow impatient with a child who seems to understand something one day and has forgotten it the next.

Output Disabilities affect the way information comes out of the brain. This output can occur in the form of spontaneous language (speech we initiate), demand language (speech as a response to others), gross motor skills, and fine motor skills.

How Can I Get an Accurate Diagnosis of *Exactly* What Is Wrong with My Child?

If you suspect your child has a learning disability of any type that is impacting her ability to be successful in school, getting an accurate diagnosis is important. But diagnosing a learning disability is often a complex task involving a number of professionals from a variety of disciplines. And often these professionals don't speak a common language or even have the opportunity to communicate with one another. Medical and psychological experts usually see a child on a one-to-one basis and have a difficult time believing that her problems can be as severe as either her parent and/or teacher believes. Medical personnel aren't always available or eager to discuss a child's problem with school personnel. Finding a clinic setting where medical, educational, and psychological professionals work together as a team will help both you and your child to weather the "storm" of living with a learning disability.

Be wary of a professional who makes any kind of diagnosis without a comprehensive testing program. In order to determine the kind and severity of any learning disability, a variety of tests will be given. The first test that will probably be given is an intelligence test. Truly learning-disabled children have average or above-average levels of intelligence. A test that is being used widely in the testing of elementary school students is the Kaufmann Assessment Battery for Children (KABC). This test gives two scores, one for sequential processing and one for simultaneous processing. Other tests report the IQ in both verbal and nonverbal scores. Many severely learning-disabled children have as much as a thirty-point difference between the intelligence scores on the two sections, with the sequential (verbal) IQ being much lower than the simultaneous (nonverbal) IQ. This test will also give information about any difficulties a child may have with processing (visually or auditorially) and memory. A psychologist will usually administer this test.

A second category of tests revolves around speech and language. These tests measure your child's language abilities in both the receptive (understanding what other people are saying to you) and expressive (being able to talk to others) areas. A speech and language pathologist will administer these tests.

A third category of tests are achievement tests. These tests as described in Chapter Six measure what a child has learned in the academic setting. They will give grade-equivalent scores for each of the subjects like Reading, Mathematics, and Science. If a child has a learning disability but is achieving at grade level (and there are many instances of this happening), you will find it difficult as a parent to get school personnel actively involved in helping your child. They will probably take the position that you are an overanxious parent who is pushing the child too much.

A fourth category of tests that are usually not given in the school setting are tests of emotional development and personality. The presence of a learning disability frequently can have a major impact on a child's emotional development and these tests will help professionals determine if social work and counseling services are needed.

A relatively new area of testing includes a battery of neuropsychological tests that should be given by a qualified neuropsychology evaluator. These tests can often determine the presence of brain dysfunction and various perceptual and cognitive abilities. They are being used increasingly to determine attention and concentration disorders such as those characteristic of ADD and ADHD. Among the tests in this area are the Reitan-Indiana Neuropsychological Test Battery, Vigilance Tests, the Wisconsin Card Sort Test, the Connor Scale of Hyperactivity and Conduct Problems, and the ANSWER System.

Tracking down the existence and possible causes of learning disabilities must also include detailed case histories in prenatal, obstetrical, perinatal, developmental, medical, educational, social, family, behavioral, and nutritional areas. Participating in a workup (done in a doctor's office or clinic) or case study (done in the school setting) to determine the existence of a learning disability if done properly can be an exhausting but very informative exercise needing the complete cooperation of all parties involved, especially the child.

Where Do Learning Disabilities Come From?

It would be nice if we could point to the cause of a learning disability as we do with physical illnesses like strep throat or bronchitis. Then we could prescribe an antibiotic and be assured of a complete cure. But there is no single cause of learning disabilities and that's what makes them so difficult to diagnosis and even more difficult to remediate.

Scientists have discovered much in the past three decades about how the brain operates, and some evidence has been documented showing differences between the brains of learning-disabled individuals, particularly dyslexics, and normal brains. Biology is increasingly being shown to play a role in learning problems. Some learning problems are often found in several generations and many learning-disabled individuals have problems with motor coordination, poor vision, allergies, or stuttering.

But the physical reasons for learning disabilities are seldom clear-cut. The research findings are usually based on the dissection of dead brains of stroke victims, epileptics, or adult dyslexics. How these findings relate to learning problems in children is a subject that may not be completely understood for decades.

In addition to the physical causes of learning disabilities, there are many researchers who believe that emotional and environmental factors play a major role in producing learning-disabled children. They point to the devastating effects that an unfortunate early school experience or an impoverished home environment can produce in the learning capacity of a child.

Gerald Coles is one such individual.[8] He points the finger of blame at parents and educators who have jumped on the "learning disability" bandwagon as a way of absolving themselves from any sense of personal responsibility for an individual child's problems. He posits in his theory of interactivity that only a very few of the diagnosed learning disabled have actual neurological problems. Their problems, he says, are the results of an interaction between the child and his home environment. He lays the blame for many learning problems squarely on the parents and doesn't absolve the schools either. We have misused, he says, the genuinely valid information about the brain that has appeared during the past twenty years to create a scapegoat for our own failures.[9] Coles's theory may make sense unless you've lived or worked with a child who has ADD, ADHD, or a severe learning disability. At that point, no parent or educator needs to be taken on a guilt trip. We need help, support, and encouragement.

Can Learning Disabilities Be Cured?

There are dozens, even hundreds of books that have been written by physicians, psychologists, researchers, educators, and parents promising answers for your learning-disabled child. As an elementary-school principal who has tried to help students with learning disabilities, I can testify that there is no easy answer. But there are answers. These answers only come, however, when all parties, including the child, roll up their sleeves and get to work. Overcoming and compensating for learning disabilities takes a lot of hard work on the part of everyone.

There are three major areas in which all parents and educators must work if the effects of a learning disability are to be minimized or even wiped out: instructional (teaching a student the skills and strategies that will help her to cope with and/or compensate for her learning disability); developmental (bringing a child to the appropriate level so that she can begin to learn the skills and strategies); and biological (administering medication or altering diet or environment to improve a child's behavior and readiness for learning).

What about Drug Therapies or Special Diets for My Learning-Disabled Child?

Some children respond well to the administration of amphetamines that stimulate the nervous system. They are prescribed most frequently to treat ADD and ADHD. Methylphenidate, known commonly by the brand name Ritalin, is used most frequently. Cylert (brand name for pemoline) and Dexdrine (brand name for dextroamphetamine) are prescribed less frequently. While most would agree that Ritalin has a beneficial effect on some learning-disabled children, there is always the danger that doctors and overanxious parents and teachers will rely solely on drug therapy rather than also working to alter instructional and behavioral methodologies for a child. Many parents have also explored allergies or diet as a possible cause of learning disability. While several books have been written and many parents blame sugar and artificial colorings for their child's problems, the scientific community has not found a strong link that is supported by significant research.

How Can I Cope with the Fact that My Child Has a Learning Disability?

Hearing for the first time that your child has a diagnosed learning disability will probably not come as a surprise. You have no doubt been searching for answers about his behavior and learning style for quite some time. But hearing the words said for the first time can still be traumatic. In the words of one mother:

My first response upon learning that my older son had a learning disability was not to tell anyone. It felt like a deep hurt, almost a physical wound that, if touched even slightly would bleed and hurt. While I ached for him, the first hurt was my own. It seemed a condemnation of me, like a secret that somehow had been revealed. All my worst feelings about myself came rushing to the surface.[10]

There are a variety of responses that you as an individual can make to your child's learning disability, and it's important that you make the right one for the good of your child. This is especially true of mothers who have a crucial role as cheerleader and ego-builder for their children. As cited in *Mothers Talk About Learning Disabilities,* Dr. Bob Broad, a senior clinical psychologist at the Communication Disorder Center of Mount Sinai Hospital in New York City, warns against adopting any of the following unproductive attitudes: narcissistic perfectionist, guilt-ridden, defective, denial, overprotective, or excessively concerned.[11] The *narcissistic perfectionist* mother (or father) treats the child's learning disability as a personal injury. The *guilty* parent takes all the blame for what is wrong with his or her child. The *defective* parent feels that the child's disability is proof of his or her own inadequacies and can become depressed as a result of the problem. Another group of parents launches into a full-scale *denial.* The *overprotective* parent is afraid to let the learning-disabled child cope with life and school on his or her own terms and attempts to shelter and keep the child dependent. And there is still another category of parents who sees problems where none exist, causing frustration and consternation for both the child and school personnel.

Coping with a child who has learning disabilities can place an enormous strain on marriage and family life. John Taylor points out a number of destructive marital patterns that result from having a hyperactive child in your family.[12] From my observations, these same patterns can be found in a family coping with any other type of learning disability as well.

Taylor's twelve destructive marital patterns include: *partial denial* (one spouse denies the problem while the other accepts it); *joint denial* (both parents deny the disability); *partial abuse* (one parent abuses the learning-disabled child); *joint abuse* (both parents abuse the child verbally, emotionally, or physically); *partial overinvolvement* (one parent overprotects and overinterferes with the child's life to the point of babying, spoiling, and pitying); *joint overinvolvement* (both parents are overprotective); *partial emotional bankruptcy* (one parent totally abdicates responsibility for dealing with the problem); *joint emotional bankruptcy* (both parents abandon the child psychologically); *partial one-upsmanship* (one parent criticizes the other parent and becomes self-righteous and superior); *mutual one-upsmanship* (both parents engage in this behavior resulting in each criticizing and blaming the other for his or her behavior); *divide and conquer* (the child has come between the two parents and uses deceit to play one parent against the other); and *overcompensation* (one parent responds to a trait in the other parent by going too far in the other direction, e.g., punitive punishment vs. a totally laissez-faire approach).

I have seen nearly all of these patterns at work in families of learning-disabled children and consequently the child's disability is magnified and the possibilities for helping the child are drastically limited. When both parents can get beyond the destructive patterns and adopt the following guidelines that Taylor advises,[13] the learning-disabled child has an excellent chance of compensating for his disability and becoming a successful student.

- **Hunt for the good.** Emphasize the positive aspects of your child and family.
- **Don't expect a perfect solution.** You're not going to find the perfect solution to all of the problems that exist because your child has disabilities. Relax.
- **Seek constant improvement.** Just because you can't find the perfect solution doesn't mean you shouldn't be constantly seeking ways to improve your marriage, family life, and parenting skills. Attend workshops. Read books. Join a support group.
- **Defend against outside criticism.** While we must always remain open to suggestions and helps, keep your mind focused on the positive and don't spend time with people who put you or your child down constantly.
- **Acknowledge your anger.** It's important for everyone to get angry feelings out in a safe environment. Everyone in the family is bound to have some of them. We always do when life doesn't turn out the way we expected it to. But there is great therapeutic value in acknowledging, discussing, and moving on from the anger rather than bottling it up.
- **Recognize your child's manipulations.** Children are masters at manipulating their parents. I'm always amazed at how naive parents are when it come to realizing they've been had. If you don't know whether you're being manipulated, ask your child's teacher and

principal to share their honest observations. You might be surprised at what you hear. Manipulative children are their own worst enemies.

- **Avoid overinvolvement.** Don't protect your child. You and your spouse together should support the child.
- **Accept differences in approach.** Don't fall into the "Who's the better parent?" trap. This will only undermine the united approach that is crucial.
- **Switch parental duties.** The parent who works away from home more should be the primary childcare person every once in while. There's nothing quite so eye-opening as spending a whole day with a child.
- **Be willing to negotiate.** Talk over your problems. Be open to suggestions for improvement relative to your interactions with your child.
- **Use the co-parenting technique.** Always check with your spouse before answering a child's request or making a decision.
- **Arrange for time away.** Make sure you spend time alone together to recharge your batteries and regain your perspective.

What Are the Best Options for Helping My Child at School?

Finding the best learning environment for your learning-disabled child is the most critical thing that you can do. Spending even a month with a poor teacher or in a deprived educational environment can set a learning-disabled child back for years. Susie was an example of just such a deprivation. Although her learning disability was not a severe one, she came to us in third grade unable to read. It wasn't anyone's fault really. But during first grade, the small private school that she had attended hired and fired three different teachers. Susie never learned to read and when she reached second grade she was diagnosed as a slow learner. In second grade she fell victim to the type of teacher that can set any child back: the critic. One study showed that when teachers perceive a child to be "at risk for learning and behavior problems," they are three times as likely to criticize that child in class. Constantly criticized children don't learn as well as those who receive a balance of praise and constructive criticism.[14] When Susie reached our school she was immediately given a crash course in learning to read. She thrived on a diet of praise and encouragement. We told her she wasn't stupid, she just needed some good teaching and hard work. Because everyone involved—Susie, her parents, the teacher, and the reading specialist—worked together, Susie was reading above grade level by sixth grade. Susie's success story certainly illustrates how important finding the right school environment can be for your child.

There are many different responses that your school can make to a problem your child is having with learning, depending upon the severity of the problem, your child's eligibility (based on a case study in which a battery of tests are administered to your child), and the services available. Here's what could possibly happen:

- Nothing is done.
- The classroom teacher does the best she can on her own.
- The classroom teacher does the best she can under the supervision of a specialist.

- The child is removed from the classroom on a regular basis (for varying periods of time, depending on need) to work with a specialist.
- The specialist works separately with the child outside the classroom and helps the classroom teacher in the classroom.
- The child is removed from the classroom (for varying periods of time, depending on need) for LD—learning disabled—tutoring and also for instruction in areas directly affected by his disability (for example, a special math class).
- The child is given all his instruction in a self-contained LD classroom.
- The child goes outside the regular school, either part- or full-time, to a residential, hospital, or at-home program.[15]

In the early 1970s when children with learning disabilities were receiving no special help at all, parents lobbied extensively for special services. They wanted special classes, special teachers, labels and identification to make sure that children with disabilities were given appropriate instruction. Public Law 94-142 brought all of this into existence. What educators and parents failed to recognize at that point was the emotional and psychological fall-out that can often result from separating children from their peers and applying labels to them. Parents and educators found that an entirely different set of problems had been created. A developing trend that holds much promise for not only learning-disabled children but those with other physical and mental disabilities is a program called *inclusion*. In inclusion schools, students with learning disabilities (even the most severe who would previously have been served in a self-contained classroom apart from regular education students), are "included" in the regular classroom. The aides and special teachers who previously worked with students in a classroom set apart from others now work in the regular classroom. The learning-disabled student has the benefit of being with other students socially and developing a healthy self-concept. We have just begun to implement inclusion in the school district where I work, and I am impressed by the benefits that come not only to disabled students, but to all students. We have for too long isolated those students who are "different," creating a most unfortunate elitist academic environment.

Things You Can Do at Home to Help Solve Your Child's Learning Disability or Attention Deficit Disorder (Kindergarten through Middle School)

Engage in creative problem solving. In Molly's situation (see beginning of this chapter), her mother and father engaged in the following process as they tried to find out what exactly was causing the problems in her life. Step One was deciding what it was they wanted to examine about their child. They began with her hearing since it seemed that she was never paying attention or understanding anything they said. Her favorite response was "What?" The audiologist uncovered the incredible difficulties Molly was having in differentiating between some sounds. She described for her parents the "high pitched static" that Molly heard constantly in her ears. These findings led to a complete neurological workup. And that's Step Two. Insure that the proper tests are being done so that the nature of the problem can be determined. This is not always as easy as 1-2-3. Sometimes there will be fits and starts to this part of the process as you attempt to find the right professionals that make sense to you. And that's Step Three. Decide which professionals will do the examining. Step Four involves looking closely at the results of the tests to see if they make sense, and if they don't starting from Step One all over again. The findings of the team that evaluated Molly made perfect sense to her parents. In fact, the findings explained a great deal. Step Five, if you agree with the evaluation, is to decide on a positive achievable goal and a method of remediation. Molly was about to enter middle school when the results of her workup and the recommendations of her evaluation team were completed. Her mom and dad arranged for the psychologists to attend a meeting at school with every one of Molly's teachers. They agreed on what each would do to support Molly in her efforts, the plan was put into writing, and the school counselor agreed to be Molly's advocate or support person at school. And that's Step Six, which is to keep an eye on the remediation process to make sure that the goal is being achieved. Many wonderful plans go down the drain for lack of monitoring and supervision. This process is necessary and works no matter how old your child is—kindergarten through middle school.

Be involved at school. If your child has a learning disability, then you need everyone at school on your side. The best way to keep the school on your side is with positive involvement. The most challenging child to teach will always get the kind of attention he needs if his parents are strong supporters of the school and teachers, and can be counted on to help out when they're needed.

View your child in a positive light. Once you discover your child has a learning disability, it's very easy to look at everything she does in a negative light. You must, however, view her learning behavior as positive. I'm thoroughly delighted by Jill Bloom's way of looking at the learning-disabled child.[16] Rather than learning-disabled, your child is learning different. Rather than labeling your child hyperactive, call her a kinesthetic learner. Instead of calling him dyslexic, stress rather that he is a spatial learner. She isn't aggressive but assertive. Rather than calling your child plodding, change that description to thorough. Your child isn't lazy but relaxed; not immature but late blooming; not phobic but cautious; not scattered but divergent; not a daydreamer but imaginative; not irritable but sensitive; and not perseverative but persistent.

In *Discovering Your Child's Design*, Ralph Mattson and Thom Black hypothesize that each child has a unique design that can be uncovered with some skillful detective work by the parent. They suggest that if we as parents understand our child's design, we can parent at an optimum level. We will be able to "enhance development, affirm uniqueness, appreciate individuality, cultivate appropriate play opportunities, encourage a fitting social style, facilitate formal learning, enhance problem solving, and provide effective career counseling.[17]

Find out what your child's strengths are and highlight these strengths in any way you can. Nathan's parents realize that he has a great deal of trouble dealing with reading and writing in the classroom. But he is a whiz at playing the violin using the Suzuki method. He recently played a solo in the school concert and beamed during the applause.

Have high but realistic expectations for your child. This is a tricky one. You don't want to let your child off the hook, but don't expect your learning-disabled child to excel at the same level or in the same way as her gifted brother or sister.

Be an advocate for your child. You can be an advocate without being overprotective, hostile, and overinvolved. Listen to what your child is saying and support and encourage her in whatever she does.

Involve your child in discussions and plans. You should always invite your child's participation in any meetings or staffings that involve his placement. Talk to him about his feelings and encourage him to share what he is thinking. Many parents and teachers wrongfully assume that children won't have anything to say. More than likely they've never been asked and aren't accustomed to expressing their views. If you want your child to compensate for and overcome his learning disability, you must involve him in whatever you plan from the very beginning. If you share with him what a disability is and what you're going to do together to solve the problem, you will be amazed at the response from your child.

Structure your home environment to maximize your child's efforts. Keep your home environment as organized as possible. In today's busy homes, with two-career families, and activities galore, this will take some doing. But consistency and regularity are a necessity for learning-disabled children. Your child will need a quiet place to work without distractions and fair rules that apply to all family members.

Help your child at home using methodologies from the appropriate chapters in this book. If your child has reading difficulties, then implement the reading strategies at home. If your child is having problems with discipline or friends, then use the ideas from those chapters. Just be aware that your child's problems may be more than you can handle on your own and the problems may interact and connect in ways that are difficult to sort out. Don't frustrate yourself and your child by trying to do everything at once. Select a small goal and work for it before moving to something else.

Keep your cool. It's easy to get angry and impatient with children when we think they have control over what they're doing. Deep down we would like to believe that if our child only tried harder he could control behavior or learn his math facts. But the child's condition is real; he does have some deficits that keep him from doing the very thing you want him to do. He needs your understanding— not your pity, or fear, or anger, or overindulgence—but your understanding and support.

Get professional counseling for your child to help her understand and cope with her learning disability. Learning-disabled children have average to above-average intelligence and know that something is wrong. They just don't have the maturity and experience to know they *do* have the ability and resources to handle it. Counseling can give your child the coping skills she needs to handle life.

Network. Getting to know and talking with other parents is an essential part of helping your learning-disabled child. You will learn about the best professionals to consult, the best schools and teachers for your child, and the best coping strategies for dealing with life. I have included a number of organizations that can help you. Knowing that others have met the challenge and overcome it will give you the faith and energy to go on.

❖ Resources

If you would like more information on the topics covered in this chapter, the following books and organizations will be helpful to you.

Armstrong, Thomas. *In Their Own Way: Discovering and Encouraging Your Child's Personal Learning Style.* New York: St. Martin's Press, 1987.

Association for Children and Adults with Learning Disabilities
4156 Library Road
Pittsburgh, PA 15234
1-412-341-1515

Barkley, Russell A. *Hyperactive Children: A Handbook for Diagnosis and Treatment.* New York: Guilford Press, 1981.

Bloom, Jill. *Help Me to Help My Child: A Sourcebook for Parents of Learning Disabled Children.* Boston: Little, Brown, and Co., 1990.

Brooks, Andree Aelion. *Children of Fast-Track Parents.* New York: Viking, 1989.

Coles, Gerald. *The Learning Mystique: A Critical Look at Learning Disabilities.* New York: Pantheon Books, 1987.

Fisher, Johnanna. *A Parent's Guide to Learning Disabilities.* New York: Charles Scribner's Sons, 1978.

Gardner, Richard A., M.D. *MBD: The Family Book about Minimal Brain Dysfunction.* New York: Jaeson Aronson, Inc., 1973.

Gardner, Richard A., M.D. *The Objective Diagnosis of Minimal Brain Dysfunction.* Cresskill, N.J.: Creative Therapeutics, 1979.

Granger, Lori, and Bill Granger. *The Magic Feather: The Truth about "Special Education."* New York: E.P. Dutton, 1986.

Greene, Lawrence J. *Learning Disabilities and Your Child: A Survival Handbook.* New York: Fawcett Columbine, 1987.

Institute on Community Integration
University of Minnesota
6 Pattee Hall
150 Pillsbury Drive SE
Minneapolis, MN 55455

Knox, Jean McBee. *Learning Disabilities*. New York: Chelsea House Publishers, 1989.

Lamm, Stanley S., and Martin L. Fisch. *Learning Disabilities Explained*. Garden City, N.Y.: Doubleday, 1982.

McGuinness, Diane. *When Children Don't Learn: Understanding the Biology and Psychology of Learning Disabilities*. New York: Basic Books, 1985.

National Center for Learning Disabilities
99 Park Avenue
New York, NY 10016
1-212-687-7211

The Orton Dyslexia Society
724 York Road
Baltimore, MD 21204
1-301-296-0232

Osman, Betty B. *Learning Disabilities: A Family Affair*. New York: Random House, 1979.

Parents for Inclusive Communities (PIC)
39 Regent Drive
Oak Brook, IL 60521

Rosner, Jerome. *Helping Children Overcome Learning Difficulties: Step-by-Step Guide for Parents and Teachers*. New York: Walker, 1979.

Ross, Alan O. *Learning Disability: The Unrealized Potential*. New York: McGraw-Hill Book Company, 1977.

Schools Are for Everyone
1365 Van Antwerp Apartments
Gatehouse
Schenectady, NY 12309

Schrage, Peter, and Diane Divoky. *The Myth of the Hyperactive Child*. New York: Pantheon Books, 1975.

Seligman, Milton. *Strategies for Helping Parents of Exceptional Children*. New York: The Free Press, 1979.

Shapiro, Steven R. *The Learning Connection: The Spiritual Side of Learning Disabilities*. Tulsa, Okla.: Vision Development Center, 1990.

Stevens, Suzanne. *The Learning Disabled Child: Ways That Parents Can Help.* Winston-Salem, N.C.: John F. Blair, Publisher, 1980.

Taylor, Denny. *Learning Denied.* Portsmouth, N.H.: Heinemann, 1991.

Taylor, John. *Helping Your Hyperactive Child.* Rocklin, Calif.: Prima Publishing & Communications, 1990.

Vail, Priscilla. *About Dyslexia: Unravelling the Myth.* Rosemont, N.J.: Modern Learning Press, 1990.

Weiss, Elizabeth. *Mothers Talk about Learning Disabilities.* Englewood Cliffs, N.J.: Prentice-Hall Press, 1989.

Wender, Paul H. *The Hyperactive Child: A Handbook for Parents.* New York: Crown Publishers, 1973.

10

THE TROUBLED STUDENT

Stress and Anxiety

Students troubled with stress, anxiety, and depression are becoming more common in our elementary and middle schools. I was reminded of this in a terrible way last September when I heard of the suicide of a sixth-grade student. I knew this beautiful young girl well. I had watched her grow up as she attended the elementary school where I was principal. I had eaten lunch with her, tried to figure how to get her to do her homework more regularly, and been the recipient of a wonderful farewell poem she had written to me when I left. She was a sensitive and intelligent child. While her friends, parents, and teachers knew she was upset over a recent disciplinary action, there was almost no warning that she was contemplating such an action, let alone that she would follow through on it. In her young life, stress and anxiety had become so unbearable she could no longer face the next day. All who knew her were asking how this could have happened and what they could have done to prevent her tragic death.

In the sections ahead we'll look at common reasons for stress and anxiety in students, warning signs for the presence of problems, and what we can do to help our children be happier and more mentally healthy.

What Is Stress?

Stress is the body's nonspecific response to the demands made on it. Stress is the result of something happening to you. If you are angry, frightened, embarrassed, uncertain, or in pain, you can feel stress. These causes of stress are called *stressors*. Stress can come from both positive and negative situations. Moving to a new home, having a baby, getting married, or inheriting a large sum of money are all positive experiences, but they can cause stress also. People react in different ways to stressors, and even the same people react in different ways to stressors depending on their health, the amount of sleep they have had, their tolerance for ambiguity and change, and what else is happening in their lives.

Adults who are not handling the stress in their lives may exhibit any one of a number of stress-related diseases: ulcers, diarrhea, constipation, cholesterol irregularities; colitis, gastritis, poor appetite, cardiovascular problems, heart attacks, headaches, abnormal blood pressure, asthma, low resistance to disease, skin problems, and sleep problems. Smoking, drinking, and taking drugs can also be stress-related. The stressors in the lives of adults seem obvious enough: worries about money, jobs, marital relationships, and health. In the next section we'll look at what causes stress in children.

What Are the Most Common Causes of Stress in Children and Adolescents?

The Holmes-Rahe Life Stress Inventory is a common scale that is used to measure stress in the lives of adults.[1] Gerald Herzfeld and Robin Powell have adapted the scale for children.[2] They list the following life events from most stressful to least stressful.

1. The death of a parent
2. Parents have divorced
3. Parents have separated
4. Separation from parents (at boarding school or living with another family)
5. Death of a close family member
6. Major personal injury or illness
7. Remarriage of a parent (getting a new parent)
8. A parent was fired from a job or you were expelled from school
9. Parents got back together after separating
10. One parent stops working to stay at home or a parent goes back to work
11. Major change in health or behavior of family member
12. Pregnancy of a family member
13. Problems in school
14. Gaining a new family member (e.g., birth, adoption, grandparent moves in)
15. Major school change (e.g., class or teacher change, failing subjects)

16. Family financial state changes a great deal (much better or worse off)
17. Death or serious illness of a close friend
18. A new activity begins (one that takes up a lot of time and energy, e.g., music lessons, sports team, computer classes after school)
19. Major change in number of arguments with parents or brothers and sisters
20. Feeling threatened (trouble with a bully or a gang)
21. Losing or being robbed of a valuable or important possession
22. Major change in responsibilities at home (e.g., must help with many chores or with raising a younger child)
23. Brother or sister leaves home (e.g. runs away, joins army, goes away to school)
24. Trouble with relatives other than parent or siblings (e.g., grandparents, aunt, uncle)
25. Outstanding personal achievement and recognition
26. Major change in living conditions (e.g., neighborhood gets much improved, fire damages part of home)
27. Personal habits change (e.g., style of dress, manners, people you hang out with)
28. Trouble with a teacher
29. Major change in your school schedule or conditions (e.g., new school schedule, more work demanded, using a temporary building)
30. Change in where you live (even in the same building)
31. Changing to a new school
32. Major change in usual type or amount of recreation (e.g., more or less time to play)

33. Major change in religious activities
34. Major change in school activities (e.g., clubs, movies, visiting friends)
35. Major change in sleep habits
36. Major change in family get-togethers (many more or less)
37. Major change in eating habits
38. Vacation
39. Christmas or birthday
40. Punished for doing wrong

I believe that Herzfeld and Powell have not included several other major stressors in the lives of children. They include abuse from parents, teachers, siblings, or other relatives. This abuse could be physical, psychological, or sexual. This category of stressors, in my opinion, ranks near the top of the list in causing stress for children.

What Are Common Symptoms of Stress?

There are two different ways of coping with stress—"flight" or "fight." In one instance children internalize the stress. They are using the "flight" mechanism of coping with stress.

The following physical symptoms of stress are common in children as well as adults who are internalizing their stress.

- Headaches
- Stomach Problems—diarrhea, constipation, nausea, heartburn

- High blood pressure or heart pounding
- Pain in neck, lower back, shoulders, jaw
- Muscle jerks or tics
- Eating problems—no appetite, constant eating, full feeling without eating
- Sleeping problems—unable to fall asleep, wake up in middle of the night, nightmares
- Fainting
- General feeling of tiredness
- Shortness of breath
- Dry throat or mouth
- Unable to sit still—extra energy
- Teeth grinding
- Stuttering
- Uncontrollable crying or not being able to cry
- Smoking
- Excessive alcohol use
- Drug use
- Increased use of medication—aspirin, tranquilizers, etc.
- General anxiety, nervous feelings, or tenseness
- Dizziness and weakness
- Accident prone[3]

The child or adult who is using the "fight" mechanism to deal with stress generally externalizes it. This child may exhibit symptoms such as frequent crying, nervousness, a short temper, hostility, moodiness, uncooperative behavior, pessimism, uncommunicativeness, whining, complaining, lack of humor, and extreme sensitivity.[4]

What Part Does Substance Abuse Play in Stress and Depression?

Substance abuse can produce stress, anxiety, and depression in young people; on the other hand these factors can be the reason they turn to substance abuse in the first place. Whichever comes first—stress or substance abuse—the combination is a deadly one for your child. The statistics regarding drug and alcohol abuse among young people are horrifying. Christian young people are not immune to the pressures. Three million teenagers between age fourteen and seventeen have a drinking problem. The seeds for that problem were sown in elementary and middle school. Eighty-five percent of children over ten years of age have experimented with drugs. The seeds for that problem were sown in early elementary school also.

There are some important warning signals that your child may be abusing alcohol or drugs.

- Lack of communication: avoiding conversation, memory loss, inability to concentrate or understand, secretive phone calls
- Decrease in family interaction: keeping to one's room, spending longer periods of time with "new" friends who may be older, "cool," sloppy, or secretive
- More criticism of your lifestyle and increased sensitivity to all your demands; disrespectful, abusive language
- Immaturity, apathy, lethargy, lack of motivation

- Physical evidence: drug paraphernalia, extensive use of eyedrops. A child abusing drugs or alcohol may be accident-prone, sensitive to light, frequently sick with respiratory or skin ailments.
- Increased need for money (for drugs) or increased income (from drugs)[5]

What Are the Warning Signals of Suicide?

The following warning signals are based on statistics from the National Center for Health. If your child exhibits any of them, seek professional help immediately. Even if your child makes a statement in anger or passing, take it seriously and do something about it.

- Preoccupation with themes of death or expressing suicidal thoughts
- Giving away prized possessions; making a will or other final arrangements
- Changes in sleeping patterns—too much or too little
- Sudden and extreme changes in eating habits; losing or gaining weight
- Withdrawal from friends and family or other major behavior changes
- Changes in school performance (lowered grades, cutting classes, dropping out of activities)
- Personality changes such as nervousness, outbursts of anger, or apathy about appearance and health
- Use of drugs or alcohol
- Recent suicide of friend or relative
- Previous suicide attempt[6]

What Are the Most Common Stressors in Elementary- and Middle-School Children?

Stress in children can look different at different ages. Dr. Bettie B. Youngs in her excellent book, *Stress in Children: How to Recognize, Avoid and Overcome It,* lists the following sources of stress in children at the different age levels.[7] Knowing the most common fears may help you to uncover the reasons your child is feeling stressed and unhappy.

Kindergarten

☐ *UNCERTAINTY AND FEAR OF ABANDONMENT BY A SIGNIFICANT ADULT.* Symptoms are references to this fear in nap and sleep; daydreaming; crying associated with parental absence; nail-biting.

☐ *FEAR OF WETTING THEMSELVES.* Symptoms include frequent trips to bathrooms; occasional wetting; nail-biting; thumb-sucking; finger twirling in hair.

☐ *FEAR OF PUNISHMENT/REPRIMAND FROM TEACHER.* Symptoms include a strong desire to please the teacher, but a high level of uncertainty about exactly how to do that. There is a constant fear of the teacher's response in expressing disapproval.

First Grade

☐ *FEAR OF RIDING THE BUS.* Symptoms include trying to persuade parents to drive him to school.

☐ *FEAR OF WETTING IN CLASS.* Symptoms include a high level of concern. Much time is devoted to "what if" consequences; daydreaming and occasional wetting in class due to anxiety.

☐ *FEAR OF TEACHER DISAPPROVAL.* Symptoms include continual seeking of teacher approval as opposed to more independent action.

☐ *RIDICULE BY CLASS PEERS AND OLDER STUDENTS IN THE SCHOOL SETTING.* Symptoms include the child becoming inward and expressing a desire to stay home from school.

☐ *RECEIVING FIRST REPORT CARD AND NOT PASSING TO SECOND GRADE.* Symptoms include higher frequency of negative "self-talk" (I can't do it) and low self-esteem.

Second Grade

☐ *FREQUENTLY MISSING A PARTICULAR PARENT.* Symptoms include wanting to go home and be with that parent.

☐ *FEAR OF NOT BEING ABLE TO UNDERSTAND A GIVEN LESSON, OR PASS A TEST.* Symptoms include crying, impatience with self.

☐ *FEAR OF NOT BEING ASKED TO BE A "TEACHER HELPER."* Symptoms include feeling disliked by teacher and consequently seeking any teacher attention, whether positive or negative.

☐ *FEAR OF TEACHER'S DISCIPLINE.* Symptoms include refusing direct eye contact in a teacher-student activity.

☐ *FEAR OF BEING DIFFERENT FROM OTHER CHILDREN IN DRESS AND APPEARANCE.* Symptoms include feeling disliked by other children.

Third Grade

☐ *FEAR OF BEING CHOSEN LAST ON ANY TEAM.* Symptoms include verbal expression of not wanting to play "this stupid game"; being absent ("sick") on a given day.

☐ *FEAR OF PARENT CONFERENCE.* Symptoms include failure to notify parent or take home notices; display of psychosomatic illness on this given day. The opposite extreme is evident in "perfect" behavior on that day.

☐ *FEAR OF PEER DISAPPROVAL AND FEAR OF NOT BEING LIKED BY THE TEACHER.* Symptoms include complaining about being excluded from favorite activities.

☐ *FEAR OF TEST-TAKING AND FEAR OF NOT HAVING ENOUGH TIME TO COMPLETE WORK EXPECTATIONS ON ANY AND ALL TEST ASSIGNMENTS;*

FEAR OF FAILURE TO PERFORM WELL. Symptoms include careless work; absence on a test day; task avoidance.

☐ *FEAR OF STAYING AFTER SCHOOL.* Symptoms include rushing to complete schoolwork; wanting to make sure of getting picked up on certain days.

Fourth Grade

☐ *FEAR OF BEING CHOSEN LAST ON ANY TEAM.* Symptoms include verbal expressions of not want to play "this stupid game" and being absent ("sick") on a given day.

☐ *PEER DISAPPROVAL OF DRESS OR APPEARANCE.* Symptoms include several changes of clothes in the morning before reaching a decision on what they want (and intend) to wear; hostility shown toward adult who selects that day's outfit.

☐ *FEAR THAT A PARTICULAR FRIEND WILL SELECT A DIFFERENT FRIEND OR SHARE "THEIR" SECRETS.* Symptoms include jealously guarding a friendship.

☐ *FEAR OF STUDENT RIDICULE.* Symptoms include name-calling as "fair play."

☐ *FEAR OF NOT BEING PERSONALLY LIKED BY THE TEACHER.* Symptom includes wanting to associate exclusively with the teacher.

Fifth Grade

☐ *FEAR OF BEING CHOSEN LAST ON ANY TEAM.* Symptoms include verbal expression of not wanting to play "this stupid game" and being absent ("sick") on a given day.

☐ *FEAR OF LOSING "BEST FRIEND" OR THAT FRIEND WILL SHARE "SECRETS."* Symptoms include a jealous guarding of that best friend.

☐ *FEAR OF BEING UNABLE TO COMPLETE SCHOOL-WORK.* Procrastinates on tasks and assignments; completes work carelessly.

☐ *FEAR OF PEER DISAPPROVAL.* Symptoms include expecting to select own clothing, own activities, and own friends.

☐ *FEAR OF NOT BEING A "BIG SIXTH GRADER" NEXT YEAR.* Symptoms include the continual generation of information/concerns on grades or "passing."

Sixth Grade

☐ *FEAR OF BEING CHOSEN LAST ON ANY TEAM.* Symptoms include verbal expression of not wanting to play "this stupid game" and being absent ("sick") on a given day.

☐ *FEAR OF THE UNKNOWN CONCERNING OWN SEX-UALITY.* Share gossip, myths, rumors, jokes concerning sexuality in all species.

☐ *FEAR OF NOT PASSING INTO MIDDLE SCHOOL/ JUNIOR-HIGH SCHOOL.* Symptoms include renewed concentration on homework, or pronounced procrastination.

☐ *FEAR OF PEER DISAPPROVAL OF APPEARANCE.* Symptoms include renewed emphasis on appearance; experimentation with appearance (hair, clothes, etc.).

☐ *FEAR OF BEING UNPOPULAR.* Symptoms include the selection of numerous friends but the jealous guarding of one selected friend of the same sex.

Seventh Grade

☐ *FEAR OF BEING SELECTED FIRST (AND HAVING TO LEAD) AND FEAR OF BEING PICKED LAST (INTERPRETED AS BEING DISLIKED OR UNPOPULAR).* Symptoms include the exhibition of extreme shyness or boldness; introvert or extrovert behavior becomes evident.

☐ *FEAR OF THE UNKNOWN CONCERNING OWN SEXUALITY.* Shares gossip, rumors, myths concerning human sexuality; personal exploration and quest of facts concerning sexuality; careful observation of peers.

☐ *EXTREME CONCERN AND WORRY ABOUT EMOTIONAL HAPPINESS AND UNHAPPINESS (EMOTIONAL FITNESS).* Symptoms include exhibiting little consistency in behavior; being withdrawn and a crowd-pleaser; being a loner or an extrovert, long periods of depression.

☐ *FEAR OF NOT BEING ABLE TO COMPLETE HOME-WORK/SCHOOLWORK/TASK ASSIGNMENT.* Symptoms include either perfectionism or procrastination.

☐ *FEAR OF SCHOOL CALLING HOME.* Symptoms include worrying, being overly concerned, and being defensive.

Eighth Grade

☐ *FEAR OF BEING SELECTED FIRST (AND HAVING TO LEAD) AND FEAR OF BEING PICKED LAST (INTERPRETED AS BEING DISLIKED OR UNPOPULAR).* Symptoms include exhibition of extreme shyness or boldness, introverted or extroverted behavior becomes evident.

☐ *FEAR OF COMING TO TERMS WITH OWN SEXUALITY (BASED ON BITS AND PIECES AND LACK OF INFORMATION CONCERNING SEX).* Symptoms include serious exploration of facts and information concerning human sexuality, as well as examination of self as sexual being.

☐ *EXTREME CONCERN AND WORRY ABOUT EMOTIONAL HAPPINESS AND UNHAPPINESS (EMOTIONAL FITNESS).* Symptoms include beginning to reject feelings associated with being unhappy; avoiding dealing with specific issues.

☐ *FEAR OF ACTIVITIES THAT REQUIRE EXPOSURE OF THE BODY, SUCH AS PHYSICAL EDUCATION.* Symptoms include occasionally being absent from specific activities; feigning illness as avoidance; showing extreme shyness or crudeness regarding human sexuality.

☐ *FEAR OF BEING "THE BIG NINTH GRADER" BUT ALSO OF NOT PASSING INTO THE NINTH GRADE.* Symptoms include being tough, withdrawn, wanting to know grades but doing little with information.

How Can I Help My Child Cope with Stress?

Given the enormous possibilities for stress in the lives of our children, how can we help them at the various developmental stages to cope with stress in productive and growth-evoking ways? We can't do everything for them. We can't save them from the ups and downs of life. But we can run interference for them and teach them some strategies that we have found helpful for dealing with stress in our own lives. Here are some that I have found helpful with my own children as well as others from a variety of sources. Build them into your lives on a daily basis.

Listening. Being a good listener is one of the most important things you can do for your stressed child. This is a difficult role to play. We want to give advice and direction. We want to solve the problem. But sometimes, kids just need a listening ear.

Conversation/Advice/Role Modeling. At times you will sense a need for some good old-fashioned advice—perhaps a similar situation occurred when you were a child. Perhaps you're encountering a stressful situation at work and can empathize. Be sensitive to your child's need for a listening ear, but be ready to give advice if it's warranted. Showing a child by example how you cope with stress in your own life is most effective. If you are not dealing well with the stressors in your life, then your child will probably be following your example.

Prayer. Prayer and meditation are absolutely essential for dealing with stress. Pray with your child, asking God to help you both deal with whatever is making your child fearful, anxious, or depressed.

Physical Relaxation Techniques (Imagery, Deep Breathing). My technique for stress relief is a weekly massage. During a ten-minute soak in the hot tub where I clear my mind of the worries and concerns of the week, I often pray or meditate, breathing deeply and letting the hot water wash away my cares. On the massage table I continue to breathe deeply and listen to the soft music that is a backdrop for the ministering hands of the masseuse. If you can teach your child a deep-breathing technique to use whenever he is feeling stressed, he will have a tool to use for the rest of his life. Breathing should be deep, from the belly, the way babies and animals breathe, not the shallow type of breathing that most of us use frequently, especially when we are stressed.

Environment. Encourage your child to create an environment that she likes in her bedroom. Choose colors, pictures, and music that make her feel good.

Hobbies/Exercise/Extracurricular Activities. We all need outside interests apart from school and work to refresh our minds and bodies. Caring for a pet, working on a stamp collection, or singing or dancing can reduce stress.

Physical Activities/Exercise. Middle school is a particularly stressful time for most young people. My son was no exception. Many classes, many teachers, lockers, and kids who were bigger and more assertive than he was were all stressors. Karate classes not only gave my son a marvelous physical outlet, but strengthened his body, helped him get an A in physical education, and gave him self-confidence. Any type of sports or physical fitness activity that you can do with your child on a regular basis is a perfect way to control stress. One of the ways in which I have coped with the first year of being a widow is a daily workout at the health club. Some of the benefits of exercise include:

- enhancement of ability to handle daily stressful encounters
- increase in circulation
- assistance to heart
- additional oxygen to the body
- benefits from the body's endorphins
- aid to digestion
- relaxation of nerves, balanced emotions
- increased resistance to disease
- reduced fatigue
- strengthened muscles, bones, and ligaments
- improved complexion and skin tone
- sharpened mental powers
- increased self-confidence

Shared Activities. Spending time with your child can be a wonderful stress reducer for both of you. Watching television, going shopping, reading aloud, going to the movies, or playing games are all wonderful ways to focus on the fun of being a family.

Anticipation/Awareness. An important part of dealing with stress is anticipating what will cause a stress or anxiety problem and developing a repertoire of positive behaviors to deal with it.

Diet. Children who are under stress exhibit many of the following symptoms: anxiety, blurred vision, craving for sweets, dizziness, feelings of doom, headaches, insomnia, irritability, nervousness, temporary muscle aches, tiredness, weakness, and weight problems. Researchers have found that children under stress typically eat no breakfast or a breakfast high in sugar. They either skip meals or eat lightly during the day and heavily at night. They typically eat refined carbohydrates for snacks. The recommended diet for children who experience high levels of stress includes:

- three evenly spaced, well-balanced meals each day
- adequate protein daily, whether animal or vegetable
- fresh fruits and vegetables daily
- whole grains only
- legumes and nuts
- snacks allowed if a fruit, vegetable, or protein

Role Playing. An important activity for parent and child in dealing with stress is role playing. If your child is anxious because of a possible stressor, acting out what might be said or done in such a situation can help a child know how to deal with a problem. Rehearsing ahead of time what you'll say or do when confronted with a stressor is also a helpful technique for adults.

Time Management. A major source of stress in older children is time pressure. Parents eager to expose their children to a wide range of opportunities and activities do not stop to think that an overloaded schedule can be a major source of stress for children just as it is for adults. If your child appears stressed, examine the schedule and reduce the number of outside activities.

Love and Affection. A sign I saw recently prescribed a certain number of hugs each day as essential for good health. Your child needs plenty of verbal and physical affection to cope with stress. That well-worn bumper sticker "Have you hugged your kid today?" is especially important to your child who is stressed.

Professional Help. Don't be afraid to seek professional help for your troubled child. Very often we are too close to the problem to be either objective or helpful and we need to seek outside resources.

❖ Resources

If you would like more information on the topics covered in this chapter the following books will be helpful to you.

Elkind, David. *The Hurried Child: Growing Up Too Fast Too Soon.* Reading, Mass.: Addison-Wesley, 1984.

Elkind, David. *All Grown Up and No Place to Go: Teenagers in Crisis.* Reading, Mass.: Addison-Wesley, 1984.

Ferguson, Sherry, and Lawrence E. Mazin. *Parent Power: A Program to Help Your Child Succeed in School.* New York: Clarkson N. Potter, Inc./Publishers, 1989.

Herzfeld, Gerald, and Robin Powell. *Coping for Kids: A Complete Stress-Control Program for Students 8-18.* West Nyack, N.Y.: The Center for Applied Research in Education, Inc., 1986.

Phillips, Beeman. *School Stress and Anxiety.* New York: Human Sciences Press, 1978.

Youngs, Bettie B. *Stress in Children: How to Recognize, Avoid, and Overcome It.* New York: Arbor House, 1985.

CONCLUSION
The Spiritual Side of
Solving School Problems

If you've been reading this book carefully, you've no doubt noticed that the "spiritual" aspects of solving school problems have been conspicuously absent. Perhaps you've wondered why I haven't quoted any Bible verses or sermonized along the way. As the author I made a conscious decision to take that approach from the very beginning. There is always the danger of trivializing the part that our Christian faith can play in helping us to parent effectively. Prayer can't take the place of having the appropriate skills and knowledge to help your children be the best they can. We've all known godly people who seemed to do everything wrong in the child-rearing department. But trying to be the "super parent" without relying on God's guidance and direction can also have disastrous results. What kind of perspective does God expect us to take as we attempt to solve school problems? What kind of model does he wish us to follow as we teach and correct our children?

God's Perspective for Parents

You don't have to solve it alone. Whatever the problem, help is on the way. God expects, even commands us, to bring our problems, large and small, to him for help. "Let him have all your worries and cares, for he is always thinking about you and watching everything that concerns you" (1 Peter 5:7). "Commit everything you do to the Lord. Trust him to help you do it and he will" (Psalm 37:5).

Don't be angry and don't worry. Sometimes our first tendency when faced with a school problem is to get angry. We either get angry at ourselves, at our child, or at school personnel. Then we begin to worry and fret over the problem. Both approaches are counterproductive. "Stop your anger! Turn off your wrath. Don't fret and worry—it only leads to harm" (Psalm 37:8). Turn your energies to productive solutions.

Forget the past. Another trap we fall into when faced with a school problem is to focus on past mistakes and failures—ours, our children's, and the school's. "I don't mean to say I am perfect. I haven't learned all I should even yet, but I keep working toward that day when I will finally be all that Christ saved me for and wants me to be. No, dear brothers, I am still not all I should be but I am bringing all my energies to bear on this one thing: Forgetting the past and looking forward to what lies ahead, I strain to reach the end of the race and receive the prize for which God is calling us up to heaven because of what Christ Jesus did for us" (Philippians 3:12-14).

Rearrange your priorities. Solving your child's school problems should be a high priority in your life. It's more important than job or career, personal hobbies or interests, or even church. Our children are one of our most precious resources. "Children are a gift from God; they are his reward. Children born to a young man are like sharp arrows to defend him. Happy is the man who has his quiver full of them" (Psalm 127:3-5). How we shape and mold their young lives will impact the future for good or evil. "Teach a child to choose the right path, and when he is older he will remain upon it" (Proverbs 22:6). "I will bring the curse of a father's sins upon even the third and fourth generation of the children of those who hate me; but I will show kindness to a thousand generations of those who love me and keep my commandments" (Deuteronomy 5:9-10).

Don't be a wimp. Don't be afraid to provide structure and leadership in solving school problems at your house. Your child is powerless to solve his problems without your help. "Don't fail to correct your children; discipline won't hurt them" (Proverbs 23:13). Have confidence in your role as a parent. Invoke the biblical advice from Proverbs often and loudly in your children's presence: "Young man, obey your father and your mother. . . . Take to heart all of their advice. Every day and all night long their counsel will lead you and save you from harm; when you wake up in the morning, let their instructions guide you into the new day" (Proverbs 6:20-22).

Use resources that are available to you. God knows and understands our weaknesses and he can help us. This help will come in the form of friends, relatives, professionals, and reading material. God doesn't answer prayer only in miraculous ways. He does it in ordinary, everyday ways through the people he sends into our lives. "For the eyes of the Lord search back and forth across the whole earth, looking for people whose hearts are perfect toward him, so that he can show his great power in helping them" (2 Chronicles 16:9).

Know the real source of confidence. Our true source of confidence is not in experts who have written books, but the Lord himself. "But when I am afraid, I will put my confidence in you. Yes, I will trust the promises of God" (Psalm 56:3).

Pray. Pray both with and for your child. If your child is uncomfortable praying with you about solutions to his school problem, then do it on your own—and tell him you are praying for him. "The earnest prayer of a righteous man has great power and wonderful results" (James 5:16). God "delights in the prayers of his people" (Proverbs 15:8). And "he hears the prayers of the righteous" (Proverbs 15:29).

Celebrate uniqueness. We are fearfully and wonderfully made. Your child has unique gifts and strengths. Discover them and celebrate them often. Continually build up your child. Help her to understand that she is God's special creation and that God will help her become the best she can. "So God made man like his Maker. Like God did God make man, man and maid did he make them" (Genesis 1:27).

Approach solving the problem with your Christian witness in mind. We want what is best for our children in the context of our values and beliefs. We also want our faith to shine through our relationships and interactions with school personnel.

Recognize your own personal limitations. Without help and guidance from the Lord, you can read all of the parenting books that have been published and still fall flat.

Our true strength is in the Lord. "Oh, praise the Lord, for he has listened to my pleadings! He is my strength, my shield from every danger. I trusted him, and he helped me" (Psalm 28:6-7).

Be willing to grow and change. Model that openness for your children. Confess mistakes to your spouse, your child, and his or her teacher. "A man who refuses to admit his mistakes can never be successful. But if he confesses and forsakes them, he gets another chance" (Proverbs 28:13).

Honor and respect your child. Whenever we approach our children to offer them our help (with homework, tutoring, advice about friends) or to give them directives about their behavior, we must take care that it is done in the spirit of respect and honor for each child as God's unique creation. "And now a word to you parents. Don't keep on scolding and nagging your children, making them angry and resentful. Rather bring them up with the loving discipline the Lord himself approves, with suggestions and godly advice" (Ephesians 6:4). "Fathers [and mothers] don't scold your children so much that they become discouraged and quit trying" (Colossians 3:21).

God's Perspective for Children

In addition to providing advice for parents as they seek to help their children solve school problems, God's Word also provides an excellent process for training and teaching our children in any of the areas mentioned in Chapters Two through Ten. The four steps to this model are: 1) teaching, 2) internalizing, 3) correcting, and 4) training. They come from 2 Timothy 3:16. "The whole Bible was given to us by inspiration from God and is useful to teach us what is true (teaching) and to make us realize what is wrong in our lives (rebuking); it straightens us out (correcting) and helps us do what is right (training)." These four steps need always to be present as we teach and train our children. The learner (the child) receives the information from the teaching process; he realizes that his prior lack of information and understanding was creating a school problem for him (behavior, lack of academic skills, not using his talents wisely); he begins to work on correcting the problem (he begins to correct his deficiencies); and finally through practice and repetition (training) the skills, knowledge, and behavior become permanent.

The process is progressive; it has a beginning and an end. We can chart our accomplishments. But it is also cyclical. Once we have reached the end, there is always a new beginning—a new skill to be learned, more knowledge to acquire, and behaviors that exemplify the best in your child. That is the joy of parenting. That is the joy of helping our children solve their school problems. This is the joy of raising children who can truly be God's best.

APPENDIX A

Resources for Kindergarten through Second Grade

Parent Read-Aloud Resources

The following books contain hundreds of suggestions for books to read aloud to your child. The most important thing you can do today is to buy one from a bookstore or borrow one from a library and begin reading. Every day that passes when you are not reading aloud is valuable time lost that could be helping your child.

American Library Association. *Let's Read Together: Books for Family Enjoyment.* Chicago: American Library Association, 1981.

Boegehold, Betty D. *Getting Ready to Read.* New York: Ballantine Books, 1984.

Copperman, Paul. *Taking Books to Heart: How to Develop a Love of Reading in Your Child.* Reading, Mass.: Addison-Wesley, 1986.

Graves, Ruth. ed. *The RIF Guide to Encouraging Young Readers.* Garden City, N.Y.: Doubleday & Company, Inc., 1987.

Gross, Jacquelyn. *Make your Child a Lifelong Reader.* New York: St. Martin's Press, 1986.

Kimmel, Margaret Mary and Elizabeth Segel. *For Reading Out Loud! A Guide to Sharing Books with Children.* New York: Delacorte Press, 1988.

Kobrin, B. *Eyeopeners! How to Choose and Use Children's Books about Real People, Places, and Things.* New York: Viking/Penguin Inc., 1988.

Laughlin, Midred Knight and Claudia Lisman Swisher. *Literature-Based Reading: Children's Books and Activities to Enrich the K-5 Curriculum.* Phoenix, Ariz.: Orynx Press, 1990.

McEwan, Elaine K. *How to Raise a Reader.* Elgin, Ill.: David C. Cook, 1987.

Nehmer, Nancy L. A. *A Parent's Guide to Christian Books for Children*. Wheaton, Ill.: Tyndale House Publishers, 1984.

Smith, Charles A. *From Wonder to Wisdom: Using Stories to Help Children Grow*. New York: New American Library, 1989.

Trelease, Jim. *The New Read Aloud Handbook*. New York: Penguin, 1989.

The following organizations provide reading lists and/or resource materials for parents:

International Reading Association
P.O. Box 8139
Newark, NJ 19714-8139

NAESP Educational Products
1615 Duke Street
Alexandria, VA 22314
Order a kit that encourages reading at home using the newspaper. There is a kit for both elementary and middle-school students:

Reading Is Fundamental, Inc.
600 Maryland Ave., SW, Suite 500
Washington, DC 20024-2520

Parent-Child Read Together Resources

The following companies publish read-together materials that can help you read with your kindergarten through second-grade child. The key difference between read-aloud and read-together books is the level of difficulty and predictability of language.

Modern Curriculum Press
13900 Prospect Rd.
Cleveland, OH 44136

> Any of the following kits/units from this company would be an excellent investment for your home library. Star Series; Begin to Read; Language Works; Exploring This World; Reading Friends; Integrated Language Arts; and Concept Science.

Children's Press
P.O. Box 71049
Chicago, IL 60694

Steck-Vaughn
P.O. Box 26015
Austin, TX 78755

McDougal & Littell Co.
P.O. Box 1667
Evanston, IL 60204

Rigby Education
P.O. Box 797
Crystal Lake, IL 60014

If you cannot purchase materials for reading together, you can find what you're looking for at the public library, if you look carefully. Choosing read-together books is time-consuming, but I have included one or two examples from the very beginning level (Level One) through Level Twenty (the level numbers are arbitrary and given to indicate a progression of difficulty).

Level 1   Arugo, Jose. *Look What I Can Do.* Scribner, 1971.
           Carle, Eric. *Do You Want to Be My Friend?* Crowell, 1971.

Level 2   Pienkowski, Jan. *Colors.* Simon & Schuster, 1989.
           Ziefert, Harriet. *Where Is My Dinner?* and *Where Is My Friend?* Putnam, 1985.

Level 3   Hutchins, Pat. *1 Hunter.* Greenwillow Books, 1982.
           Wildsmith, Brian. *All Fall Down.* Oxford University Press, 1987.

Level 4   Martin, Bill. *Brown Bear, Brown Bear, What Do You See?* Holt, Rinehart &
           Winston, 1983.

Level 5   Berenstain, Stan and Jan. *Bears in the Night.* Random House, 1971.

Level 6   Burningham, John. *The School.* Crowell, 1975.
           Ginsburg, Mirra. *The Chick and the Duckling.* Macmillan, 1972.

Level 7   Kraus, Robert. *Herman the Helper.* Simon & Schuster, 1987.
           Shaw, Charles G. *It Looked Like Spilt Milk.* Harper & Row, 1947.

Level 8   Burningham, John. *The Blanket.* Crowell, 1976.
           Seuss, Dr. *The Foot Book.* Random House, 1968.

Level 9   Asch, Frank. *Just Like Daddy.* Prentice-Hall, 1981.
           Hutchins, Pat. *Rosie's Walk.* Scholastic, Inc., 1971.

Level 10   De Regniers, Beatrice. *Going for a Walk.* Harper & Row, 1982.
Hurd, Edith. *Johnny Lion's Rubber Boots.* Harper & Row, 1972.

Level 11   Hutchins, Pat. *Titch.* Macmillan, 1971.
Kraus, Robert. *Whose Mouse Are You?* Macmillan, 1969.

Level 12   Carle, Eric. *The Very Busy Spider.* Philomel, 1984.

Level 13   Alexander, Martha G. *The Blackboard Bear.* Dial, 1969.

Level 14   Adams, Pam. *There Was an Old Lady Who Swallowed a Fly.* Child's Play, 1973.
Brown, Margaret. *Good Night Moon.* Harper & Row, 1947.

Level 15   Seuss, Dr. *Green Eggs and Ham.* Random House, 1960.
Galdone, Paul. *Henny Penny.* Seabury Press, 1968.

Level 16   Bonsall, Crosby. *And I Mean It Stanley.* Harper & Row, 1974.
Hutchins, Pat. *Good Night Owl.* Macmillan, 1972.

Level 17   Johnson, Crockett, *Harold and the Purple Crayon.* Harper & Row, 1955.
Lobel, Arnold. *Mouse Soup.* Harper & Row, 1977.

Level 18   Bridwell, Norman. *Clifford the Big Red Dog.* Scholastic, 1975.
Minarik, Else. *Little Bear.* Harper & Row, 1957.

Level 19   Hutchins, Pat. *The Surprise Party.* Macmillan, 1969.
Lobel, Arnold. *Frog and Toad Are Friends.* Harper & Row, 1970.

Level 20   Allen, Pamela, *Who Sank the Boat?* Coward, 1985.
Sendak, Maurice. *Chicken Soup with Rice.* Harper & Row, 1962.

Writing Resources

The following books will give you more ideas on how to help your child with writing.

Lamme, Linda Leonard. *Growing Up Writing.* Washington, D.C.: Acropolis Books Ltd., 1984.

Lee, Barbara, and Masha Kabakow Rudman. *Mind over Media: New Ways to Improve Your Child's Reading and Writing Skills.* New York: Seaview Books, 1982.

Vail, Priscilla L. *Clear and Lively Writing: Language Games and Acitivities for Everyone*. New York: Walker and Company, 1981.

Wiener, Harvey S. *Any Child Can Write: How to Improve Your Child's Writing Skills from Preschool through High School*. New York: Bantam Books, 1990.

APPENDIX B

Resources for Third through Fifth Grade

Independent Reading Resources

Here are some series books that are fairly easy to read, have a predictable plot, and have characters to whom children can relate. Ask your public or school librarian for more ideas. Christian series are indicated with an asterisk.

*Ashley, Meg
BOARDING HOUSE ADVENTURE SERIES
Regal Books

*Bly, Stephen and Janet
CRYSTAL BLAKE BOOKS
David C. Cook

Cleary, Beverly
HENRY BOOKS
William Morrow
RAMONA BOOKS
William Morrow

CHOOSE YOUR OWN ADVENTURE SERIES

*Clifford, Laurie B.
PEPPERMINT GANG SERIES
Tyndale House

*Courtney, Dayle
THORNE TWINS ADVENTURE BOOKS
Standard

Hicks, Clifford B.
ALVIN FERNALD SERIES
Holt, Rinehart, & Winston

*Hutchens, Paul
SUGAR CREEK GANG SERIES
Moody Press

*Jenkins, Jerry B.
THE BRADFORD FAMILY ADVENTURES
Standard
DALLAS O'NEIL AND THE BAKER STREET SPORTS CLUB
Moody Press

*Johnson, Ruth I.
JOY SPARTON SERIES
Moody Press

*Leppard, Lois Gladys
MANDIE BOOKS
Bethany House Publishers

*Lutz, Norma Jean
MARCIA STALLINGS SERIES
David C. Cook

*McEwan, Elaine K.
JOSHUA MCINTIRE SERIES
David C. Cook

MacGregor, Ellen and Dora Pantell
MISS PICKERELL SERIES
McGraw Hill

*Nielsen, Shelly
VICTORIA MAHONEY SERIES
David C. Cook

Robertson, Keith
HENRY REED SERIES
Viking

*Smith, Bonnie Sours
DORRIE BOOKS
David C. Cook

Sobol, Donald J.
ENCYCLOPEDIA BROWN SERIES
E.P. Dutton (hardcover) Bantam (paperback)

Williams, Jay, and Raymond Abrashkin
DANNY DUNN SERIES
McGraw-Hill

Graphic Representations*

Following is a sample procedure students can follow when webbing and an actual web that was constructed by a student.

Procedure

1. Tell the student he/she is going to use a new type of review procedure called *webbing* to assist him as he studies for his unit test on teeth. (See sample web on following page.)

2. Tell the student to write the word "teeth" in the center of his own paper and draw lines and circles radiating out from the center.

3. Direct the student to skim the section on teeth in his textbook and identify the secondary category headings. (Depending on the student's ability level, you may have to help him identify what the secondary headings are during the first use of webbing).

4. Have the student write in the parts of his web the secondary category headings from the chapter.

*Material taken from Beau Fly Jones, Jean Pierce, and Barbara Hunter, "Teaching Students to Construct Graphic Representations," in Educational Leadership, December 1988/January 1989, pp. 20-25. Used by permission.

5. Tell the student to close his book. Then ask him to recall all of the details or facts from the book about each of the categories and add it to his own web.

6. If this technique is used in a group setting, students will then contribute their findings and the instructor will write them on the large chart. If a tutor is working individually with a child, he/she may wish to contribute some ideas of his/her own.

7. The web can then be used to study for the test.

Web

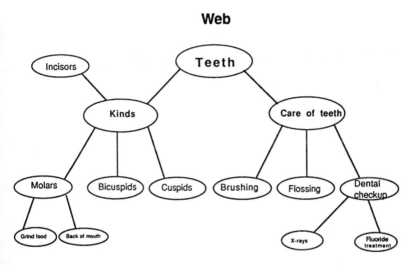

Sample web using subject of teeth

In addition to using webs as a study skill for test preparation, visual organizers (graphic representations) can be constructed before, during, or after reading as a way of remembering the information. As students (particularly those in fourth through eighth grade) read different types of textbooks and assignments, they will need to be able to decide just what type of graphic representation will be most helpful to organize the material. They can benefit from an introduction to a variety of different graphic forms (spider map, continuum scale, compare/contrast matrix; series of events chain; problem/solution outline; network tree; human interaction outline; and cycle. The following illustrations will help you understand what graphic organizers are and how they work for different types of reading and writing.

Spider Map

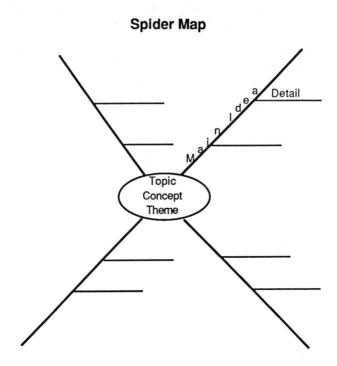

The **spider map** is used to describe a central idea such as a geographic region (the Northeastern states); a concept (patriotism); a process (photosynthesis); or a proposition with support (abortion should be outlawed in the United States). The key questions to ask are: What is the central (main) idea? What are its attributes? What are its functions?

Continuum/Scale

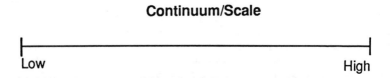

The **continuum scale** is used for time lines showing historical events or ages (grade levels in school); degrees of something (weight); shades of meaning (Likert scales) or rating scales (achievement in school). The key questions to ask are: What is being scaled? What are the end points?

Compare/Contrast Matrix

	Name 1	Name 2
Attribute 1		
Attribute 2		
Attribute 3		

The **compare/contrast matrix** is used to show similarities and differences between two things (people, places, events, ideas, etc.) The key questions to ask are: What things are being compared? How are they similar? How are they different?

Series of Events Chain

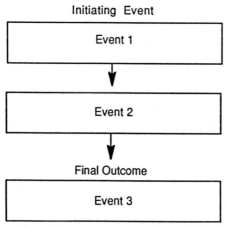

Initiating Event

Event 1

Event 2

Final Outcome

Event 3

The **series of events chain** is used to describe the stages of something (the life cycle of a primate); the steps in a linear procedure (how to neutralize an acid); a sequence of events (how feudalism led to the formation of nation states); or the goals, actions, and outcomes of a historical figure or character in a novel (the rise and fall of Napoleon). The key questions to ask are: What is the object, procedure, or initiating event? What are the stages or steps? How do they lead to one another? What is the final outcome?

Problem/Solution Outline

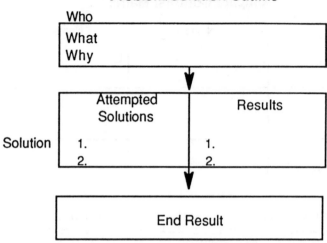

The **problem/solution outline** is used to represent a problem, attempted solutions, and results (the national debt). The key questions to ask are: What was the problem? Who had the problem? Why was it a problem? What attempts were made to solve the problem? Did those attempts succeed?

Network Tree

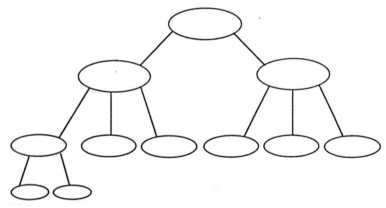

The **network tree** is used to show causal information (causes of poverty), a hierarchy (types of insects), or branching procedures (the circulatory system). The key questions to ask are: What is the superordinate category? What are the subordinate categories? How are they related? How many levels are there?

Fishbone Map

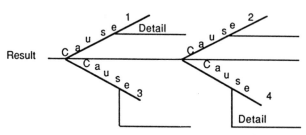

The **fishbone map** is used to show the causal interaction of a complete event (an election, a nuclear explosion) or complex phenomenon (juvenile delinquency, learning disabilities). The key questions to ask are: What are the factors that cause X? How do they interrelate? Are the factors that cause X the same as those that cause X to persist?

Human Interaction Outline

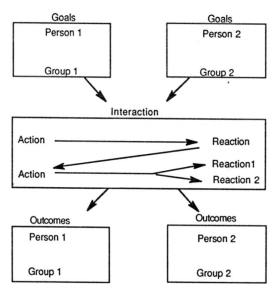

The **human interaction outline** is used to show the nature of an interaction between persons or groups (European settlers and American Indians). The key questions to ask are: Who are the persons or groups? What were their goals? Did they conflict or cooperate? What was the outcome for each person or group?

Cycle

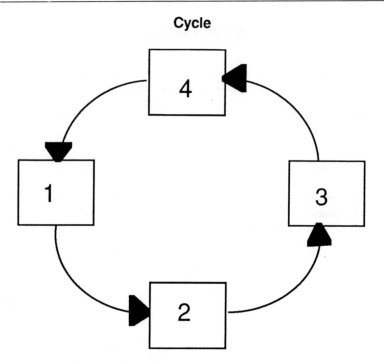

The **cycle** is used to show how a series of events interact to produce a set of results again and again (weather phenomena, cycles of achievement and failure, the life cycle). The key questions to ask are: What are the critical events in the cycle? How are they related? In what ways are they self-reinforcing?

APPENDIX C

Resources for Sixth through Eighth Grade

Independent Reading Resources**

The following companies publish series of books for less able readers. The books are written around a specific theme of high interest to adolescents but have an easier, somewhat controlled reading level. Before you purchase any of these, consult with a reading specialist in your school district to see if they can be borrowed or ask for a review copy of one of the books in the series.

Addison-Wesley Publishing Co.
2725 Sand Hill Road
Menlo Park, CA 94025
Series titles are Checkered Flag, Deep Sea Adventure, Happenings, Morgan Bay Mysteries, and Top Flight Readers.

Allyn and Bacon, Inc.
470 Atlantic Avenue
Boston, MA 02210
Series is titled Breakthrough.

Benefic Press
10300 West Roosevelt Rd.
Westchester, IL 60153
Series titles are Horses and Heroines, Mystery Adventure, Space Science Fiction, and Sports Mystery.

Bowmar Publishing Company
4563 Colorado Boulevard
Los Angeles, CA 90039
Series titles are Play the Game, Reading Incentive, Search, and Young Adventurers.

**This list was taken from Michael F. Graves, Judith A. Boettcher, and Randall A. Ryder, Easy Reading (Newark, Del.: International Reading Association, 1979).

Crestwood House
515 N. Front St.
P.O. Box 3427
Mankato, MN 56001
Series is titled Monster Series.

Dexter and Westbrook, Ltd.
958 Church St.
Baldwin, NY 11510
Series is titled Incredible Series.

Economy Company
1901 N. Walnut
Oklahoma City, OK 73125
Series is titled Guidebook to Better Reading.

Educational Activities, Inc.
P.O. Box 392
Freeport, NY 11520
Series is titled Hawk Books.

Fearon-Pitman Publishers, Inc.
6 Davis Drive
Belmont, CA 94002
Series titles are Adventures in Urban Reading, American West, Fearon Racing, Pacemaker
Bestsellers, Pacemaker Classics, Pacemaker Storybooks, and Pacemaker True Adventures.

Follett Publishing Company
1010 W. Washington Blvd.
Chicago, IL 60607
Series is titled Venture.

Globe Book Company, Inc.
50 W. 23rd St.
New York, NY 10010
Series is titled Adapted Classics.

D.C. Heath and Company
125 Spring St.
Lexington, MA 02173
Series is titled Teenage Tales.

Jamestown Publishers
P.O. Box 6743
Providence, RI 02940
Series titles are Attention Span Series and Jamestown Classics.

McCormick-Mathers Publishing Co.
7625 Empire Drive
Florence, KY 41042
Series is titled Turning Point.

McDougal, Littell & Company
Box 1667
Evanston, IL 60204
Series is titled Adapted American Classics.

New Reader Press
Division of Laubach Literacy International
Box 131
Syracuse, NY 13210
Series is titled News for You.

Pendulum Press, Inc.
Saw Mill Rd.
West Haven, CT 06516
Series is titled Now, Age Illustrated.

Reader's Digest Services, Inc.
Educational Division
Pleasantville, NY 10570
Series is titled Reader's Digest Adult Readers.

Scholastic Book Services
904 Sylvan Avenue
Englewood Cliffs, NY 07632
Series are titled Action Libraries, Contact, Double Action Libraries, Firebird Books, Scholastic Action, Scholastic Scope, Scholastic Sprint, and Spring Libraries.

Webster/McGraw-Hill Book Company
1221 Avenue of the Americas
New York, NY 10020
Series is titled City Limits.

Xerox Education Publications
1250 Fairwood Avenue
Columbus, OH 43216
Series titles are Know Your World, Pal Paperbacks, Scrambler Reading, and You and Your World.

Young Readers Press
A Simon Schuster Company
One West 39th St.
New York, NY 10018
Series is titled Raceway Paperbacks.

APPENDIX D

Math Learning Outcomes for Each Grade Level

Kindergarten

Applications

Talking about mathematics used in our daily lives.

Numbers/Numeration

Learning to estimate how many.

Counting objects, up to about 15 or 20.

Putting out objects to match a number.

Comparing two sets of objects.

Recognizing numerals up to 20.

Writing numerals, 0 through 9.

Learning about ordinal numbers, such as first, second, third.

Measurement

Estimating and comparing: taller or shorter; longer or shorter; largest or smallest; heavier or lighter.

Geometry

Recognizing and classifying colors and simple shapes.

Patterns

Recognizing simple patterns, continuing them, and making up new patterns.

Probability and statistics

Making and talking about simple graphs of everyday things, such as birthdays, pets, food, and so on.

First Grade

Applications

Talking about mathematics used in daily living.

Learning strategies such as using manipulatives or drawing diagrams to solve problems. **See section on problem-solving strategies in Chapter Four.**

Arithmetic and numbers

Practicing estimation skills.

Counting through about 100.

Recognizing, writing, and being able to order numbers through about 100.

Counting by twos, fives, and tens.

Using ordinal numbers, such as first, second, tenth, and so on.

Learning basic addition and subtraction facts up to $9 + 9 = 18$ and $18 - 9 = 9$.

Developing understanding of place value using tens and ones with manipulatives, including base ten blocks, Cuisenaire rods, abaci, play money, and so on.

Developing the concept of fractional values such as halves, thirds, and fourths.

Measurement

Telling time to the hour or half-hour (but don't press if not mastered).

Recognizing and using calendars, days of the week, months.

Estimating lengths and measuring things with non-standard units, such as how many hand-prints across the table.

Understanding uses and relative values of pennies, nickels, dimes.

Geometry and patterns

Working with shapes, such as triangles, circles, squares, rectangles.

Recognizing, repeating, and making up geometric and numeric patterns.

Probability and statistics

Making and interpreting simple graphs, using blocks or people, of everyday things such as color preferences, number of brothers and sisters, and so on.

Second Grade

Applications

Talking about mathematics used in daily life.

Creating and solving word problems in measurement, geometry, probability, and statistics, **as well as arithmetic.** I have emphasized the phrase about arithmetic, because in many classrooms that is the only emphasis. Make sure your child has experiences doing problem solving using all areas of mathematics, not just computation.

Practicing strategies for solving problems, such as drawing diagrams, organized guessing, putting problems into own words, and so on. **See section on problem-solving strategies in Chapter Four.**

Numbers

Practicing estimation skills.

Reading and writing numbers through about 1,000, playing around with numbers up to 10,000.

Counting by twos, fives, and tens, and maybe some other numbers for fun.

Learning about odd and even numbers.

Using ordinal numbers such as first, second, and tenth.

Identifying fractions such as halves, thirds, quarters.

Understanding and using the signs for greater than (>) and less than (<).

Arithmetic

Knowing addition and subtraction facts through $9 + 9 = 18$ and $18 - 9 = 9$. **Notice that in first grade these facts are learned, but in second they are mastered.**

Estimating answers to other addition and subtraction problems.

Practicing addition and subtraction with and without regrouping (carrying), such as:

```
 27    27    27    27
 +2    +8    -2    -8
 29    35    25    19
```

Adding columns of numbers such as

```
  2
  8
  9
+ 7
 26
```

Exploring uses of a calculator.

Being introduced to multiplication and division.

Geometry

Finding congruent shapes (same size and shape).

Recognizing and naming squares, rectangles, circles, and maybe some polygons.

Informally recognizing lines of symmetry.

Reading and drawing very simple maps.

Measurement

Practicing estimation of measurements—how many toothpicks long is the table?

Comparing lengths, areas, weights.

Measuring with non-standard units (**a non-standard unit is anything you choose— toothpick, hand, pencil**) beginning to use some standard units such as inches or centimeters.

Telling time to the nearest quarter-hour, maybe to the minute.

Making change with coins and bills, doing money problems with manipulatives. **See the section on manipulatives in Chapter Four.**

Knowing days of the week and months, and using the calendar to find dates.

Probability and statistics

Making and interpreting simple graphs, using physical objects or manipulatives.

Doing simple probability activities

Patterns

Working with patterns of numbers, shapes, colors, sounds, and so on, including adding to existing patterns, completing missing sections, making up new patterns.

Third Grade

Applications

Talking about mathematics seen in students' lives.

Creating, analyzing, and solving word problems in all of the concept areas.

Practicing a variety of problem-solving strategies with problems of more than one step. **See section on problem-solving strategies in Chapter Four.**

Numbers

Practicing estimation skills with all problems.

Reading and writing numbers through about 10,000, exploring those beyond 10,000.

Counting by twos, threes, fours, fives, tens, and other numbers.

Naming and comparing fractions such as $\frac{1}{2}$ is greater than $\frac{1}{4}$.

Identifying fractions of a whole number such as $\frac{1}{2}$ of 12 is 6.

Exploring concepts of decimal numbers such as tenths and hundredths, using money to represent values.

Using the signs for greater than (>) and less than (<).

Arithmetic

Learning how to use calculators effectively.

Using calculators to solve problems.

Continuing to practice basic addition and subtraction facts and simple addition and subtraction problems.

Doing larger and more complicated addition and subtraction problems.

```
  3897   8342
+ 8342  -3897
```

Beginning to learn multiplication and division facts through 9 x 9 = 81 and 81 ÷ 9 = 9.

Beginning to learn multiplication and division of two- and three-digit numbers by a single-digit number.

```
 27   124        4
x 3   x 8     6 ) 24
```

Learning about remainders.

```
       4    R1
  7 ) 29
     28
      1
```

Geometry

Recognizing and naming shapes such as squares, rectangles, trapezoids, triangles, circles, and three-dimensional objects such as cubes, cylinders, and the like.

Identifying congruent shapes (same size and shape).

Recognizing lines of symmetry, and reflections (mirror images) and translations (movements to a different position) of figures.

Reading and drawing simple maps, using coordinates.

Learning about parallel and perpendicular lines.

Measurement

Estimating before doing measurements.

Using non-standard and some standard units to measure:

- Length (toothpicks, straws, paper strips, string lengths/non-standard units; centimeters, decimeters, meters, inches, feet, yards/standard units)
- Perimeters (same as length)
- Area (paper squares, tiles, and so on/non-standard units; square centimeters, meters, inches, feet, yards/standard units)
- Weight (paper clips, rocks, blocks, beans, and so on/non-standard units; grams, kilograms, ounces, pounds/standard units)
- Volume and capacity (blocks, rice, beans, water; in cans, gallons, pints, quarters/standard units)
- Temperature (Celsius, Fahrenheit)

Telling time, probably to the nearest minute.

Continuing to use money to develop understanding of decimals.

Using calendars.

Probability and statistics

Being introduced to probability concepts, such as the chance of something happening.

Using tally marks, collecting and organizing informal data.

Making, reading, and interpreting simple graphs.

Patterns

Continuing to work with patterns, including those found on addition and multiplication charts.

Fourth Grade

Applications

Talking about uses of mathematics in students' lives and in their futures.

Creating, analyzing, and solving word problems in all of the concept areas.

Using a variety of problem-solving strategies to solve problems with multiple steps.

Working in groups to solve complex problems.

Using calculators for problem solving.

Developing formal and informal mathematical vocabulary.

Numbers and operations

Practicing rounding and estimation skills with all problems.

Using calculators with some proficiency for all operations.

Reading and writing numbers to 10,000 and beyond.

Learning about special numbers, such as primes, factors, multiples, square numbers.

Recognizing equivalent fractions, such as $\frac{1}{2} = \frac{2}{4}$.

Finding fractions of whole number such as $\frac{1}{8}$ of 72 = 9.

Maintaining and extending work with operations of addition, subtraction, multiplication, and division of whole numbers.

Adding and subtracting simple decimal numbers.

Learning about simple percents such as 10%, 50%, and 100%.

Geometry

Using geometric shapes to find patterns of corners, diagonals, edges, and so on.

Recognizing right angles, exploring terminology of other angles.

Continuing to explore ideas connected with symmetry.

Reading and drawing simple maps, using coordinates.

Exploring terminology and uses of coordinate grid.

Identifying parallel and perpendicular lines.

Exploring how differing shapes fill a flat surface (tiling).

Measurement

Estimating before measuring.

Using non-standard and standard units to measure length, area, volume, weight, temperature.

Telling time for a purpose.

Making simple scale drawings.

Exploring terminology and uses of geometric grind.

Probability and Statistics

Using sampling techniques to collect information or conduct a survey.

Discussing uses and meanings of statistics, such as how to make a survey fair, how to show the most important information, how to find averages.

Making, reading, and interpreting graphs.

Performing simple probability experiments, discussing results.

Fifth and Sixth Grade

Applications

Talking about mathematics used in present and future lives.

Creating, analyzing, and solving word problems in all of the concept areas.

Using a variety of problem-solving strategies to solve problems with multiple steps. **See section on problem-solving strategies in Chapter Four.**

Working in groups to solve complex problems. (Mathematics in the real world often involves working with a team of people. Children should have opportunities on a weekly basis to solve problems in cooperative groups.)

Using calculators for problem solving.

Developing mathematical vocabulary.

Numbers and arithmetic

Practicing rounding and estimation skills with all problems.

Using calculators effectively for appropriate problems.

Expanding understanding and use of special numbers such as primes, composite numbers, square and cubic numbers, common divisors, common multiples.

Increasing and understanding of fraction relationships:

Comparisons, such as $\frac{2}{3} > \frac{1}{2}$
Equivalence, such as $\frac{2}{3} = \frac{4}{6}$
Reducing, such as $\frac{10}{20} = \frac{1}{2}$
Relating mixed numbers and improper fractions, such as $2\frac{1}{3} = \frac{7}{3}$.

Developing skills in adding, subtracting, multiplying, dividing fractions (mastery not expected).

Maintaining skills in basic addition, subtraction, multiplication, and division of whole numbers.

Adding, subtracting, multiplying, and dividing decimal numbers.

Computing percents, and relating percents to fractions and decimals.

Developing some understanding of ratio and proportion.

Exploring scientific notation, such as $3 \times 10^8 = 300,000,000$.

Geometry

Using the concept of parallel and perpendicular lines.

Measuring and drawing angles of various kinds.

Understanding circle relationships, including diameter, circumference, radius.

Recognizing shapes that are congruent, or the same size and shape.

Recognizing shapes that are similar, or the same shape but a different size.

Developing understanding of symmetry, reflections, and translations of figures.

Drawing constructions such as equal line segments or perpendicular bisectors.

Understanding coordinate graphing.

Drawing and reading maps.

Doing perspective drawing.

Measurement

Continuing to use hands-on experience with the tools of measurement, estimating first in all cases, for length, area, volume and capacity, mass or weight, temperature (Celsius and Fahrenheit), and telling time accurately.

Probability and statistics

Performing and reporting on a variety of probability experiments.

Collecting and organizing data.

Displaying data in graphic form, such as bar, picture, circle, line, and other graphs.

Beginning to develop understanding of statistical ideas such as mean, median, and mode.

Seventh and Eighth Grades

Applications

Talking about uses of mathematics and its importance to students' present and future lives.

Creating, analyzing, and solving word problems in all of the concept areas.

Using a variety of problem-solving strategies to solve problems with multiple steps.

Working in groups to solve complex problems.

Using calculators for problem solving.

Numbers and arithmetic

Practicing rounding and estimation skills with all problems.

Using calculators with proficiency for appropriate problems.

Expanding understanding and use of special numbers such as primes, composite numbers, square and cubic numbers, common divisors, common multiples.

Increasing understanding of fraction relationships: comparisons such as $2/3 > 1/2$; equivalence, such as $2/3 = 4/6$; reducing, such as $10/20 = 1/2$; relating mixed numbers and improper fractions, such as $2\frac{1}{3} = 7/3$.

Adding, subtracting, multiplying, and dividing fractions.

Adding, subtracting, multiplying, and dividing decimal numbers.

Maintaining skills in basic addition, subtraction, multiplication, division of whole numbers.

Computing percents, and relating percents to fractions and decimals.

Understanding of ratio and proportion.

Using scientific notation such as $3 \times 10^8 = 300,000,000$.

Learning about positive and negative numbers.

Finding greatest common factors (GCF) and least common multiples (LCM).

Finding square roots.

Learning about special number relationships such as ⅖ is a reciprocal of 5½.

Geometry

Using the concept of parallel and perpendicular lines.

Measuring and drawing angles of various kinds.

Understanding circle relationships, including diameter, circumference, radius.

Using correct formulas to calculate areas of rectangles, triangles, circles, and so on.

Recognizing shapes that are congruent, or the same size and shape.

Developing understanding of symmetry, reflections, and translations of figures.

Making constructions such as equal line segments or perpendicular bisectors.

Understanding coordinate graphing.

Drawing and reading maps.

Doing scale and perspective drawings.

Measurement

Continuing to have hands-on experience with the tools of measurement, estimating first in all cases, for length, area, volume and capacity, mass or weight, temperature (Celsius and Fahrenheit), telling time correctly.

Probability and statistics

Performing and reporting on a variety of probability experiments.

Collecting and organizing data.

Displaying data in graphic form, such as bar, picture, circle, line, and other graphs.

Developing understanding of statistical ideas such as mean, median, and mode.

APPENDIX E
Math Resources

Read-Aloud Math Books for Kindergarten through Second Grade

Anno, Mitsumasa. *Anno's Counting Book.* New York: Thomas Crowell, Publishers, 1986.

Anno, Mitsumasa. *Anno's Hat Tricks.* New York: Philomel Publishers, 1985.

Aylsworth, Jim. *One Crow: A Counting Book.* New York: Harper & Row, 1988.

Bang, Molly. *10, 9, 8.* New York: Scholastic, 1988.

Birch, David. *The King's Chessboard.* New York: Dial, 1988.

Brown, Richard. *100 Words About My House.* New York: Harcourt Brace Jovanovich, Publishers, 1988.

Carle, Eric. *The Grouchy Ladybug.* New York: Harper & Row, 1977.

Crews, Donald. *Ten Black Dots.* New York: Greenwillow, 1986.

Hutchins, Pat. *Changes, Changes.* New York: Macmillan, 1986.

Hutchins, Pat. *The Doorbell Rang.* New York: Greenwillow, 1986.

Hutchins, Pat. *Rosie's Walk.* New York: Scholastic Inc., 1971.

McMillan, Bruce. *Counting Wildflowers.* New York: Lothrop, 1986.

Read-Aloud Math Books for Third through Fifth Grades

Adler, David A. *Roman Numerals.* New York: Harper/Crowell, 1977.

Anno, Mitsumasa, and Masaichiro Manno. *Anno's Mysterious Multiplying Jar.* New York: Putnam/Philomel, 1983.

Burns, Marilyn. *The I Hate Mathematics! Book*. Boston: Little, Brown and Company, 1975.

Burns, Marilyn. *Math for Smarty Pants*. Boston: Little, Brown, & Company, 1982.

Dennis, J. Richard. *Fractions Are Parts of Things*. New York: Harper/Crowell, 1971.

Froman, Robert. *Angles Are Easy as Pie*. New York: Harper/Crowell, 1976.

Froman, Robert. *The Greatest Guessing Game*. New York: Harper/Crowell, 1978.

Mori, Tsuyoshi. *Socrates and the Three Little Pigs*. New York: Putnam/Philomel, 1986.

Phillips, Louis. *263 Brain Busters: Just How Smart Are You Anyway?* New York: Viking, 1985.

Sachar, Louis. *Sideways Arithmetic from Wayside School*. New York: Scholastic, 1989.

Sitomer, Mindel, and Harry Sitomer. *How Did Numbers Begin?* New York: Harper/Crowell, 1976.

Srivastava, Jane Jonas. *Number Families*. New York: Harper/Crowell, 1979.

Watson, Clyde. *Binary Numbers*. New York: Harper/Crowell, 1977.

White, Laurence B., and Ray Brocket. *Math-a-Magic*. New York: Albert Whitman, 1990.

Zalavsky, Claudia. *Count on Your Fingers African Style*. New York: Harper/Crowell, 1980.

Math Manipulatives

The following publishers and suppliers can provide books and information about the use of manipulatives with your child.

Activity Resources Co., Inc.
P.O. Box 4875
Hayward, CA 94540

Addison-Wesley Publishing Co.
2725 Sand Hill Rd.
Menlo Park, CA 94025

Creative Publications
P.O. Box 10328
Palo Alto, CA 94303

Cuisenaire Company of America
12 Church St., Box D
New Rochelle, NY 10805

Lawrence Hall of Science
University of California Berkeley
Berkeley, CA 94720

Dymax
Box 310
Menlo Park, CA 94025

Math/Science Resource Center
Mills College
Oakland, CA 94613

Midwest Publications
P.O. Box 448
Pacific Grove, CA 93950

National Council of Teachers of Mathematics
1906 Association Drive
Reston, VA 22091

Sybex Inc.
2344 Sixth St.
Berkeley, CA 94710

APPENDIX F

Impact of Family Behavior on Child's Success in School

The following research was gathered by the National Association of Elementary School Principals in 1991. Principals indicated the importance of each of the behaviors in providing a nurturing home learning environment and ensuring success in school. The percentage figure indicates the percentage of principals who thought that the behavior was essential or highly desirable. The single number in parentheses indicates the ranking of this item as it relates to all twenty-two items (1 is highest ranking; 22 is lowest ranking).

Family Work Habits

How important is it for parents to emphasize regular, planned used of time in the home for studying, playing, and eating meals? 94.5% (7)

How important do you consider structure, routine, and punctuality for activities at home? 86.8% (14)

How important is it to give priority to schoolwork, reading, and other academic activities over non-academic endeavors like television, music, videos, recreation? 94.5% (6)

How important is it for parents to instill a strong work ethic in a child? 96.3% (4)

Family Support for Academics

How important is it for a child to have a quiet place to study, with appropriate reference materials available for use? 85.9% (6)

How important is it to have parents regularly encourage children with their school work? 97.3% (3)

How important is it to have parents give support to a child and help with homework when it is needed? 91.6% (11)

How important is it for parents to know a child's academic strengths and weaknesses? 87.2% (13)

Family Participation in Stimulating Activities

How important is it for a family to be active in hobbies, games, and activities that have educational value? 72.1% (17)

How important is it for the family to make frequent use of libraries, museums, and cultural activities? 68.9% (18)

How important is it to have the family make frequent use of books, newspapers, and periodicals? 86.5% (15)

Family Emphasis on Language Development

How important is it for the parent and child to read aloud to each other? 92.8% (8)

How important is it for the parent and child to have regular discussions and opportunities to enlarge vocabulary and sentence patterns? 90.5% (12)

How important is it to have parents correct a child's use of language at very early stages of his/her development? 61.4% (21)

How important is it to have parents continue to correct and develop a child's language (and grammar) throughout his/her development? 62.5% (20)

Family Academic Expectations

How important is it to have parents set standards and expectations for a child? 92.4% (9)

How important is it for parents to know their child's current schoolwork and school activities? 91.7% (10)

How important is it for parents to expect a child to go on to higher education (college)? 46.7% (22)

How important is it for parents to introduce the idea of educational and career aspirations to a child as early as elementary school? 66.4% (19)

Family Reinforcement of Child's Self-Esteem

How important is it for parents to help a child perceive himself or herself as a capable problem-solver? 96.2% (5)

How important is it for parents to show pride in their child's academic growth and accomplishments? 97.8% (2)

How important is it for parents to listen to and to talk with a child, paying consistent attention to the child's questions and feelings? 98.2% (1)

APPENDIX G

School Success Questionnaire

The following questionnaire appeared in the December, 1986 issue of the *Reader's Digest*. I've added the editorial comments.

Reader's Digest Questionnaire

Score two points for each statement that is "almost always true" of your home; score one point if it's "sometimes true"; score zero if it's "rarely or never true."

1. Everyone in my family has a household responsibility, at least one chore that must be done on time.

It's never too late to begin giving your child some responsibility around the house, if you haven't up to this point. If your child has not been made accountable for the little things at home, he will have a difficult time assuming responsibility for work at school.

2. We have regular times for members of the family to eat, sleep, play, work, and study.

If your household is characterized by a total lack of organization and structure, then your child will have a difficult time adapting to the expectations of most school environments. See what you can do to get your own life organized and you will find that the benefits spill over to your children.

3. Schoolwork and reading come before play, TV, or even other work.

Make sure you build in a regular read-aloud time every evening for your kindergarten child. Try not to let anything interfere with this time together. Your child will soon get the message that reading and school responsibilities are important!

4. I praise my child for good schoolwork, sometimes in front of other people.

Don't overdo the praise of your child in front of other people, especially when they have children of the same age. Praising to grandma and grandpa is always acceptable! Display schoolwork on a cork bulletin board or on the refrigerator. Your child will be eager to share her work with you.

5. My child has a quiet place to study, a desk or table at which to work, and books, including a dictionary or other reference material.

Even if you don't have the space or resources for a desk for your child, make sure he has a space where he can save his school papers (cardboard files are wonderful for this), a spot to show off his best work (affix to the refrigerator with magnets), a shelf to hold his own books (boards and bricks make good bookshelves), and a table where he can work on projects of his own.

6. Members of my family talk about hobbies, games, news, the books we're reading, and movies and TV programs we've seen.

Set aside time at the dinner table each evening to share conversation about the above topics. Don't worry if what you're talking about sometimes seems to go over your child's head. You'll be surprised at how much he's absorbing.

7. The family visits museums, libraries, zoos, historical sites, and other places of interest.

8. I encourage good speech habits, helping my child to use the correct words and phrases and to learn new ones.

If your grammar isn't the best or if you have sloppy speech patterns, it's never too late to remediate your own speech. It will certainly benefit your child. Encourage him to help you.

9. At dinner, or some other daily occasion, our family talks about the day's events, with a chance for everyone to speak and be listened to.

The old addage "A child should be seen and not heard" is definitely not recommended for those parents who want lively, intelligent, inquisitive, and interesting children. Of course, all children need to develop a sense about when it's appropriate to talk or not. Good manners never go out of style. But make sure that you talk about what happened in school every day. In the beginning, you may have to ask many leading questions, but never permit your child to answer the question: "What happened in school today?" with a "Nothing."

10. I know my child's current teacher, what my child is doing in school, and which learning materials are being used.

Always learn as much as you can about your child's teacher and the curriculum. This information will help you understand what goes on each day at school. You can then encourage and reinforce.

11. I expect quality work and good grades. I know my child's strengths and weaknesses and give encouragement and special help when they're needed.

Never downgrade or make fun of anything your child does in school, no matter how simple or uninspired. Children are most sensitive, and a thoughtless comment can damage a tender ego. Listen to what your child's teacher asks of you and cooperate to the fullest.

12. I talk to my child about the future, about planning for high school and college, and about aiming for a high level of education and vocation.

It's a little early for applying to Harvard, but you can talk about saving money for college and even open a savings account.

If you scored ten or more, your home ranks in the top one-fourth in terms of the support and encouragement you give your child for school learning. If you scored six or lower, your home is in the bottom one-fourth. If you scored somewhere in-between, you're average in the support you give your child for school learning. Work as a family to bring your score up to ten or more!

Parent Questionnaire

In addition to the preceding questionnaire from the *Reader's Digest*, I'd like to add my own set of questions. These have been developed from my years as an elementary-school principal working with parents. I find that the families who can answer "yes" to most of them have children who are successful in school.

1. I'm not afraid to say "no" to my child. I believe that parental discipline is an important prerequisite to self-discipline.

Children who have never heard the word "no" or learned the difficult lesson of letting someone else have the spotlight have a very difficult time in school. They are so worried about getting their share of the attention, they have little time left for learning.

2. I find out what is happening at school by asking good questions and then carefully listening to what my child is saying about his "school life."

Not every child is willing to share every detail of what happens in school. Many children will respond to parental questions with little if any information. But don't give up. Keep asking and then be prepared to listen!

3. I attend all of the conferences, open houses, musical programs, and special events I possibly can.

Being on the scene at school is a perfect way to meet other parents, get to know teachers on a more personal basis, and get a sense of what your child's school is really all about. Even if school wasn't your favorite place to be as a child or young person, put aside your own hesitant feelings and get involved!

4. I model goal-setting and task completion so that my child can see good work habits. I understand that what I do is far more important than anything I say.

You cannot expect your child to finish assignments or start homework without nagging if you keep putting off required tasks or never complete the needlework or remodeling project you started last year. Children need to see that adults overcome procrastination and fear of failure before they themselves are able to do it.

5. I am always willing to learn something new and model being a learner in front of my child.

Get excited about learning a new skill. Sign up for a class at church or community college. Read a book. Talk about a new idea. Demonstrate that learning is a lifelong activity and is NOT limited to school and classrooms.

6. I am willing to admit that I am wrong or have made a mistake and am ready to apologize, even to my own child for my wrongdoing.

We all admit that we're not perfect (to ourselves and a few close friends). We also need to be ready to admit it to our children. They will be able to pick themselves up after failure and defeat when they see that their parents do the same.

7. I encourage my child to talk about her friends and plan activities and outings that give her an opportunity to make friends and play with them. I make an effort to talk with her about friendships and model the act of making and keeping friends.

The best way to keep track of what's going on in your child's life is to know who her friends are. This process doesn't begin in high school; it begins in nursery school. Invite friends in to play. Meet and talk with other parents. Keep your child involved in an active social life that you can guide and monitor.

8. I support and encourage my child's interests and am willing to let him learn something new or try an unusual hobby or activity from time to time.

There will be times when you don't have the financial resources to sign your child up for another round of music lessons, but give him the benefit of the doubt once in awhile. Children need to experiment with a variety of interests before they find out where their talents and interests lie.

9. I respect my child as an individual and am a good listener when she has problems at school.

You don't need to solve all of the social, emotional, and academic problems that your child may encounter, but you do need to provide a listening ear and a sympathetic attitude when she feels like talking.

10. I respect my child's principal and teachers and let my child know that he should do the same.

Even if you violently disagree with a stand or action taken by a member of the school staff, try not to let those feelings undermine your child's feelings of respect and cooperation for these important adults. School personnel can make mistakes, but you should never give your child an excuse for unacceptable behavior by permitting him to think he doesn't have to follow the rules and meet the standards.

If you scored 8 or more, you rank in the top one-fourth of families in the kind of environment you are creating that will enhance your child's chances of school success. If you scored 5 or lower, your home is in the bottom one-fourth. If you scored somewhere in-between, you're average in structuring the type of home environment that will help your child be a successful student. Work as a family to bring your score up to eight or more.

APPENDIX H

Definitions of Learning Disabilities

These definitions are taken from Jill Bloom's very excellent book, *Help Me to Help My Child: A Sourcebook for Parents of Learning Disabled Children.** I have added several of my own that I have found particularly helpful in working with parents. I have also added some "plain language" definitions in italics.

Attention Deficit Disorder (ADD)—the chronic inability to focus on pertinent stimuli for an enduring period of time. *(Your child has a hard time concentrating on what's going on in school.)*

Attention Deficit Hyperactive Disorder (ADHD)—the chronic inability to focus on pertinent stimuli for an enduring period of time, combined with unusual energy, restlessness, and frequent aggressive and impulsive behavior. *(Your child has a hard time concentrating, can't sit still, and bothers his classmates.)*

Agnosia—the loss or impairment of ability to recognize the form and nature of objects. *(Your child may have difficulty recognizing and differentiating objects held in his hand when his eyes are closed. He may be colorblind or unable to discriminate between various sounds or letters.)*

Alexia—the loss or impairment of the ability to read. *(This is even more severe than dyslexia. In either case your child will have a difficult time linking the spoken word with symbol.)*

Anomia, Aphasia, and Apraxia—these three A's are typically seen in their most severe forms in adult stroke patients. Anomia is the loss or impairment of the ability to remember words or names. Aphasia is the inability to evoke spoken or written language. Apraxia is the inability to reproduce written or spoken language. *(In children with learning disabilities these problems are usually mild and often mixed in with a variety of symptoms. They rarely appear in a pure form.)*

Auditory Perceptual Disorder—the inability to identify, organize, and interpret what is perceived by the ear. *(The child with this disorder has a terrible time learning phonics*

*Boston: Little, Brown and Company, 1990, pp. 23-24.

because what you think he should be hearing and what he is actually perceiving are two different things.)

Cognitive Disabilities—disturbances in perception, conception, reasoning, and judging—the skills by which knowledge is acquired. *(Cognitive refers to the thinking process. Cognitive impairment means your child will have a problem thinking and reasoning. Learning new things will be difficult for your child.)*

Dyscalculia—disturbances in quantitative reasoning due to neurological disorders. *(Your child will have a hard time learning math.)*

Dysgraphia—a neurological disorder leading to the inability to transfer visual patterns to motor patterns in writing. *(Your child will have a difficult time with handwriting.)*

Dyslexia—an impairment of the ability to read due to neurological dysfunction. One of a variety of learning disabilities. *(Your child will have a hard time learning to read because he will often see letters and numerals as reversed or inverted.)*

Fine-Motor Problems—a disorder in the use of hands necessary to perform precision tasks such as writing or object manipulation. *(Your child will have a hard time holding a pencil and learning to write.)*

Gross-Motor Problems—a disorder in the use of large muscle groups used in running, jumping, hopping. *(Your child will look clumsy and won't do well in physical education or outdoor play.)*

Hyperactivity—increased or excessive muscular activity as a result of neurological disorder. *(Your child won't sit still for more than a few minutes at a time.)*

Hyperkinesis—a restless behavior syndrome, usually connected to learning problems. *(This term is often used interchangeably with hyperactivity and Attention Deficit Disorder. Some practitioners view hyperactivity as a label for the increased activity while hyperkinesis and ADD describe syndromes that involve a cluster of symptoms.)*

Hypoactivity—reduced muscular activity as a result of neurological disorder. *(Your child will exhibit a low activity level.)*

Information Processing Disorder—an inability to organize, interpret, and store information after it has been received via the senses. *(This is the same general category as Cognitive Disabilities. Your child will have difficulty dealing with new information he has learned.)*

Language Disability—the impairment of the learning systems involving the use of symbols to communicate. *(Your child will have a difficult time understanding language or communicating through the spoken word.)*

Maturational Lag—a delay in the process of becoming fully developed in character and mental capacity. *(Your child will learn to do something later than most children his or her age, but will eventually reach the desired level of performance.)*

Minimal Brain Dysfunction—This term was formerly applied to a wide variety of learning disabilities, including deficits in language, memory, attention, and motor control, thought to be the result of impairment in various areas of the brain. This term is not as widely used by professionals today.

Perceptually Handicapped—a disorder in the way one receives, comprehends, and organizes impressions via the senses. *(Your child won't take in information through his or her senses in quite the same way as others.)*

Specific Learning Disability—a learning problem involving a particular sensory disorder or a combination of disorders that affect the ability to absorb and organize information. *(Your child will have a difficult time learning in the same way that most others do.)*

Visual Perceptual Disorder—the inability to identify, organize, and interpret what is perceived by the eye. *(Your child will not see things in quite the same way as others.)*

NOTES

Chapter One/What's the Problem?

1. Cliff Schimmels, *How to Help Your Child Thrive and Survive in the Public Schools* (Old Tappan, N.J.: Fleming H. Revell Co., 1982). Terry Frith, *Secrets Parents Should Know about Public Schools* (New York: Simon & Schuster, 1986). Marty Nemko, *How to Get a Private School Education in a Public School* (New York: Acropolis Books, 1986).

2. Elaine K. McEwan, *Schooling Options: Choosing the Best for You and Your Child* (Wheaton, Ill.: Harold Shaw Publishers, 1991).

3. Linwood Laughy, *The Interactive Parent: How to Help Your Child Survive and Succeed in the Public Schools* (Kooskia, Idaho: Mountain Meadow Press, 1988), pp. 113-122.

4. Terry Frith, *Secrets Parents Should Know about Public Schools* (New York: Simon and Schuster, 1986), p. 53.

5. Jeannie Oakes and Martin Lipton, *Making the Best of Schools* (New Haven, Conn.: Yale University Press, 1990), p. 269.

Chapter Two/It's All Their Fault

1. Terry Frith, *Secrets Parents Should Know about Public Schools,* p. 117.

2. Ibid., p. 116.

3. Jeannie Oakes and Martin Lipton, *Making the Best of Schools,* p. 159.

4. Jeannie Oakes, *Keeping Track: How Schools Structure Inequality* (New Haven, Conn.: Yale University Press, 1985). Robert E. Slavin, *Ability Grouping and Student Achievement in Elementary Schools: A Best Evidence Synthesis.* Report of the National Center for Effective Elementary Schools (Baltimore: Johns Hopkins University, 1986).

5. Elaine K. McEwan, *Schooling Options.*

6. The Council for Basic Education, 725 Fifteenth Street, NW, Washington, D.C. 20005

Chapter Three/Reading and Writing

1. Albert J. Harris and Edward R. Sipay, *Effective Teaching of Reading* (New York: McKay, 1971), p. 13.

2. Tony Buzan, *Use Both Sides of Your Brain* (New York: E.P. Dutton, 1983), pp. 27-28.

3. Burton J. White, *The First Three Years of Life* (Englewood Cliffs, N.J.: Prentice-Hall, 1975), p. 111.

4. Priscilla Vail, *Common Ground: Whole Language and Phonics Working Together* (Rosemont, N.J.: Modern Learning Press, 1991), p. 4.

5. Marilyn Adams, *Beginning to Read: Thinking and Learning about Print* (Cambridge, Mass.: The MIT Press, 1990), p. 13.

6. Ibid., p. 416.

7. Vail, op. cit., p. 4.

8. Ibid., p. 7.

9. Marie Clay, *The Early Detection of Reading Difficulties* (Portsmouth, N.H.: Heinemann, 1979).

10. J.S. Chall and B. Jacobs, "Writing and Reading in Elementary Grades: Developmental Trends Among Low SES Children" in *Language Arts*, 60, pp. 617-626.

11. Marie Clay, *Reading: The Patterning of Complex Behaviour* (Auckland, New Zealand: Heinemann, 1972). John Downing, *Reading and Reasoning* (New York: Springer-Verlag, 1979).

12. Marie Clay, *Stones—The Concepts about Print Test* (Exeter, N.H.: Heinemann, 1979).

13. Marie Clay, *The Early Detection of Reading Difficulties.*

14. Adams, op. cit., pp. 334-335.

15. J. Collins, "Discourse Style, Classroom Interaction and Differential Treatment" in *Journal of Reading Behavior*, 14, pp. 429-37.

16. Barbara J. Fox, *RX for Reading: How the Schools Teach Your Child to Read and How You Can Help* (New York: Penguin Books, 1989).

17. Ibid.

18. Elaine K. McEwan, *Project Cockroach* and *The Best Defense* (Elgin, Ill.: David C. Cook, 1991).

19. Arthea J.S. Reed, *Comics to Classics: A Parent's Guide to Books for Teens and Preteens* (Newark, Del.: International Reading Association, 1988).

Chapter Four/Two Plus Two Equals Five

1. Marilyn Burns, *The I Hate Mathematics! Book* (Boston: Little, Brown and Company, 1975), p. 7.

2. Robert T. Green and Veronica J. Laxon, *Entering the World of Number* (London: Thames and Hudson, 1978), p. 15.

3. Ibid., p. 16.

4. M. Behr, S. Erlwanger, and E. Nichols, "How Children View the Equals Sign," in *Mathematics Teaching*, 92, pp. 13-15.

5. Jean Kerr Stenmark, Virginia Thompson, and Ruth Cossey, *Family Math* (Berkeley, Calif.: University of California, 1986), p. 19.

6. Martin Hughes, *Children and Numbers: Difficulties in Learning Mathematics* (London: Basil Blackwell, 1986), p. 8.

7. Stenmark, Thompson, and Cossey, op. cit., pp. 299-310.

8. Iris M. Carl, "Better Mathematics for K-8," in *Streamlined Seminar* (Alexandria, Va.: National Association of Elementary School Principals, 1991).

9. National Council of Teachers of Mathematics, *Professional Standards for Teaching Mathematics* (Reston, Va.: National Council of Teachers of Mathematics, 1991), pp. 3-4.

10. *The Problem Solver: Activities for Learning Problem Solving Strategies* (Palo Alto, Calif.: Creative Publications).

11. Stenmark, Thompson, and Cossey, op. cit., pp. 18-20.

Chapter Five/He Won't Do It

1. Benjamin Fine, *Underachievers: How They Can Be Helped* (New York: E.P. Dutton & Co., Inc., 1967), p. 10.

2. Lawrence Greene, *Kids Who Underachieve* (New York: Simon and Schuster, 1986), pp. 40-42.

3. R.W. White, "Motivation Reconsidered: The Concept of Competence," in *Psychological Review*, 66 (1959), pp. 297-333.

4. Raymond J. Wlodkowski and Judith H. Jaynes, *Eager to Learn: Helping Children Become Motivated and Love Learning* (San Francisco: Jossey-Bass Publishers, 1990), pp. 7-11.

5. Ibid., p. 8.

6. Ibid., pp. 13-22 and Greene, op. cit., p. 46.

7. J.K. Morishima, "Academic Characteristics of Asian/Pacific Americans," in *Cultural and Ethnic Factors in Learning and Motivation: Implications for Education*, W.J. Lonner and V.O. Tyles, Jr. (eds.). From the 12th Western Symposium on Learning, Western Washington University, Bellingham, 1988. S.D. Holloway, "Concepts of Ability and Effort in Japan and the United States," in *Review of Educational Research*, 58 (1988), pp. 327-345.

8. Elaine K. McEwan, *Raising Balanced Children in an Unbalanced World* (Elgin, Ill.: David C. Cook Publishing Co., 1988).

9. Linnus S. Pecaut, *The Making of an Underachiever: Growing Up in the Shadow of Success* (Lombard, Ill.: The Institute for Motivational Development, Inc., 1986).

10. Sylvia B. Rimm, *How to Parent So Children Will Learn* (Watertown, Wis.: Apple Publishing Company, 1990) and *Underachievement Syndrome: Causes and Cures* (Watertown, Wisc.: Apple Publishing Company, 1986).

11. Rimm, *Underachievement Syndrome.*

12. Elaine K. McEwan, *Raising Balanced Children* and *Will My Child Be Ready for School?* (Elgin, Ill.: David C. Cook Publishing, 1990).

13. Paul Meier, *Christian Child-Rearing and Personality Development* (Grand Rapids, Mich.: Baker Book House, 1977).

14. Rimm, *Underachievement Syndrome*, pp. 35-62.

15. Greene, op. cit., pp. 267-270.

16. Priscilla Vail, *Smart Kids with School Problems* (New York: New American Library, 1987).

17. Rimm, *Underachievement Syndrome*.

18. Ibid., p. 134.

Chapter Six/Maximizing Your Child's Learning

1. Henry Chauncey and John E. Dobbin, *Testing: Its Place in Education Today* (New York: Harper & Row, Publishers, 1963), p. 37.

2. Faith Clark and Cecil Clark, *Hassle-Free Homework* (New York: Doubleday, 1989), p. 165.

3. Sylvia Rimm, *Underachievement Syndrome: Causes and Cures* (Watertown, Wis.: Apple Publishing Company, 1986), pp. 208-209.

4. James T. Webb, Elizabeth A. Meckstroth, and Stephanie Tolan, *Guiding the Gifted Child* (Columbus, Ohio: Psychology Publishing Company, 1982), p. 52.

5. Barbara Meister Vitale, *Unicorns are Real: A Right-Brained Approach to Learning* (Rolling Hills Estate, Calif.: Jalmar Press, 1982), p. 9.

6. Webb, Meckstroth, and Tolan, op. cit.

7. Vitale, op. cit.

8. Keith Golay, *Learning Patterns and Temperament Styles* (Fullerton, Calif.: Manas-Systems, 1982), pp. 27-44.

9. Bernice McCarthy and Susan Leflar, eds. *4Mat in Action: Creative Lesson Plans for Teaching to Learning Styles with Right/Left Mode Techniques* (Barrington, Ill.: Excel, 1983).

Chapter Seven/Nobody Likes Me

1. Alexander Thomas, Stella Chess, and Herbert G. Birch, *Temperament and Behavior Disorders in Children* (New York: New York University Press, 1968).

2. Burton J. White, *The First Three Years of Life* (Englewood Cliffs, N.J.: Prentice-Hall, 1975), pp. 180-182.

3. Michael Schulman and Eva Mekler, *Bringing Up a Moral Child: A New Approach for Teaching Your Child to Be Kind, Just, and Responsible* (Reading, Mass.: Wesley Publishing Company, Inc., 1985), p. 245.

4. I have written two books in a series for junior boys that focus on the issue of friendship and how to choose good friends, *Project Cockroach* and *The Best Defense* (David C. Cook Publishing, 1991).

5. Peak Parent Center, Inc. 6055 Lehman Drive, Suite 101, Colorado Springs, CO 80918 1-719-531-9400.

6. Nancy F. Jackson, Donald A. Jackson, and Cathy Monroe, *Getting Along with Others: Teaching Social Effectiveness to Children* (Champaign, Ill.: Research Press, 1983).

7. Hill M. Walker et. al., *The Walker Social Skills Curriculum: The Accepts Program* (Austin, Tex.: Pro-Ed, 1988).

8. Hill M. Walker et. al., *The Walker Social Skills Curriculum: The Access Program: Adolescent Curriculum for Communication and Effective Social Skills* (Austin, Tex.: Pro-Ed, 1988).

Chapter Eight/She Won't Follow the Rules

1. James Dobson, *Dare to Discipline* (Wheaton, Ill.: Tyndale House, 1981).

2. Rudoph Dreikurs and Loren Grey, *A New Approach to Discipline: Logical Consequences* (New York: Hawthorn Books, Inc., 1968).

3. Lee Canter with Marlene Canter, *Lee Canter's Assertive Discipline for Parents* (Santa Monica, Calif.: Canter & Associates, 1982).

4. Ibid., p. 40.

5. Ibid., p. 41.

6. Ibid., p. 45.

Chapter Nine/Learning Disabilities and Attention Deficit Disorder

1. Jill Bloom, *Help Me to Help My Child: A Sourcebook for Parents of Learning Disabled Children* (Boston: Little, Brown and Company, 1990), p. 18.

2. D.D. Leigh, G. McNitt, and S.C. Larsen, "A New Definition of Learning Disabilities," in *Learning Disabilities Quarterly*, 4 (1981), p. 336.

3. Bloom, op. cit., p. 19.

4. Jean McBee Knox, *Learning Disabilities* (New York: Chelsea House Publishers, 1989), p. 25.

5. Priscilla Vail, *About Dyslexia: Unravelling the Myth* (Rosemont, N.J.: Modern Learning Press, 1990), p. 2.

6. Illinois State Board of Education, "Criteria for Determining the Existence of a Learning Disability" (Executive Summary, Springfield, Ill., 1990).

7. Larry Silver, *The Misunderstood Child* (New York: McGraw-Hill, 1987).

8. Gerald Coles, *The Learning Mystique: A Critical Look at Learning Disabilities* (New York: Pantheon Books, 1987).

9. Ibid., pp. 196-197.

10. Elizabeth Weiss, *Mothers Talk about Learning Disabilities: Person Feelings, Practical Advice* (Englewood Cliffs, N.J.: Prentice-Hall Press, 1989), p. 1.

11. Ibid., pp. 17-18.

12. John F. Taylor, *Helping Your Hyperactive Child* (Rocklin, Calif.: Prima Publishing & Communication, 1990), pp. 220-227.

13. Ibid., pp. 228-234.

14. Thomas Armstrong, *In Their Own Way: Discovering and Encouraging Your Child's Personal Learning Style* (New York: St. Martin's Press, 1987), pp. 125-126.

15. Bloom, op. cit., p. 122.

16. Bloom, op., cit. p. 128.

17. Ralph Mattson, and Thom Black, *Discovering Your Child's Design* (Elgin, Ill.: David C. Cook Publishing, 1989), pp. 62-65.

Chapter Ten/The Troubled Student

1. Thomas Holmes and Richard Rahe, "Holmes-Rahe Social Readjustment Rating Scale," in *Journal of Psychosomatic Research*, Vol. II, (New York: Pergamon Press, Ltd., 1967).

2. Gerald Herzfeld and Robin Powell, *Coping for Kids: A Complete Stress-Control Program for Students 8-18* (West Nyack, N.Y.: The Center for Applied Research in Education, Inc., 1987).

3. Ibid.

4. Sherry Ferguson and Lawrence E. Mazin. *Parent Power: A Program to Help Your Child Succeed in School* (New York: Clarkson N. Potter, Inc., Publishers, 1989), p. 131.

5. Ibid., p. 129.

6. Pamela Cantor, "These Teenagers Feel They Have No Options," in *People Magazine*, February 18, 1985, p. 87.

7. Bettie B. Youngs, *Stress in Children: How to Recognize, Avoid and Overcome It* (New York: Arbor House, 1985), pp. 55-60.

BIBLIOGRAPHY

Adams, Marilyn Jager. *Beginning to Read: Thinking and Learning about Print.* Cambridge, Mass.: The MIT Press, 1990.

Amabile, Teresa. *Growing Up Creative: Nurturing a Lifetime of Creativity.* New York: Crown Publishers, Inc., 1989.

Armstrong, Thomas. *In Their Own Way: Discovering and Encouraging Your Child's Personal Learning Style.* New York: St. Martin's Press, 1987.

Axelrod, Saul. *Behavior Modification for the Classroom Teacher.* New York: McGraw-Hill Book Co., 1983.

Balter, Lawrence. *Who's in Control? Dr. Balter's Guide to Discipline without Combat.* New York: Poseidon Press, 1988.

Barkley, Russell A. *Hyperactive Children: A Handbook for Diagnosis and Treatment.* New York: Guilford Press, 1981.

Barth, Roland. *Improving Schools From Within.* San Francisco: Jossey-Bass Inc., Publishers, 1990.

Bergreen, Gary. *Coping with Study Strategies.* New York: The Rosen Publishing Group, Inc., 1986.

Berry, Marilyn. *Help Is on the Way for: Book Reports.* Chicago: Children's Press, 1984.

Black, Hille. *They Shall Not Pass.* New York: William Morrow and Company, 1963.

Bloom, Jill. *Help Me to Help My Child: A Sourcebook for Parents of Learning Disabled Children.* Boston: Little, Brown & Company, 1990.

Blumenfield, Samuel L. *How to Tutor.* New Rochelle, N.Y.: Arlington House, 1973.

Bodenhammer, Gregory. *Back in Control: How to Get Your Children to Behave.* Englewood Cliffs, N.J.: Prentice-Hall Press, 1983.

Boegehold, Betty D. *Getting Ready to Read.* New York: Ballantine Books, 1984.

Boehm, Ann E., and Mary Alice White. *The Parents' Handbook on School Testing.* New York: Teachers College Press, 1982.

Brooks, Andree Aelion. *Children of Fast-Track Parents.* New York: Viking, 1989.

Burns, Marilyn. *The I Hate Mathematics! Book.* Boston: Little, Brown & Company, 1975.

Buxton, Laurie. *Do You Panic About Math? Coping With Math Anxiety.* London: Heinemann Educational Books, 1981.

Buzan, Tony. *Use Both Sides of Your Brain.* New York: E.P. Dutton, 1983.

Canter, Lee, with Marlene Canter. *Lee Canter's Assertive Discipline for Parents.* Santa Monica, Calif.: Canter & Associates, 1982.

Chauncey, Henry, and John E. Dobbin. *Testing: Its Place in Education Today.* New York: Harper & Row, 1963.

Chess, Stella. *How to Help Your Child Get The Most Out of School.* Garden City, N.Y.: Doubleday, 1974.

Clabby, John F., and Maurice J. Elias. *Teach Your Child Decision Making.* Garden City, N.Y.: Doubleday, 1986.

Clark, Faith, and Cecil Clark. *Hassle-Free Homework.* New York: Doubleday, 1989.

Clay, Marie. *The Early Detection of Reading Difficulties.* Portsmouth, N.H.: Heinemann, 1979.

———. *Reading: The Patterning of Complex Behaviour.* Auckland, New Zealand: Heinemann, 1972.

———. *Stones—The Concept about Print Test.* Exeter, N.H.: Heinemann, 1979.

Cogen, Victor. *Boosting the Underachiever: How Busy Parents Can Unlock Their Child's Potential.* New York: Plenum Press, 1990.

Coles, Gerald. *The Learning Mystique: A Critical Look at Learning Disabilities.* New York: Pantheon Books, 1987.

Colligan, Louise. *Scholastic's A+ Junior Guide to Book Reports.* New York: Scholastic Inc., 1989.

Copeland, Richard W. *How Children Learn Mathematics: Teaching Implications of Piaget's Research.* London: Collier-Macmillan Limited, 1970.

Corsini, Raymond J., and Genevieve Painter. *The Practical Parent: ABC's of Child Discipline.* New York: Harper & Row, 1975.

Cutright, Melitta. *The National PTA Talks to Parents: How to Get the Best Education for Your Child.* New York: Doubleday, 1989.

Deppe, Philip R. and Judith L. Sherman. *The High Risk Child: A Guide for Concerned Parents.* New York: Macmillan Publishing Co., Inc., 1981.

DeRosis, Helen. *Parent Power Child Power: A New Tested Method for Parenting without Guilt.* Indianapolis: The Bobbs-Merril Company, Inc., 1974.

Dickman, Irving, with Dr. Sol Gordon. *One Miracle at a Time.* New York: Simon and Schuster, 1985.

Divine, James H., and David W. Kylen. *How to Beat Test Anxiety and Score Higher on Your Exams.* Woodbury, N.Y.: Barron's Education Series, Inc., 1979.

Dobson, James. *Dare to Discipline.* Wheaton, Ill.: Tyndale House, 1970.

Dodson, Fitzhugh. *How to Discipline with Love: From Crib to College.* New York: New American Library, 1977.

Downing, John. *Reading and Reasoning.* New York: Springer-Verlag, 1979.

Dreikurs, Rudolf, and Loren Grey. *A New Approach to Discipline: Logical Consequences.* New York: Hawthorn Books, Inc., 1968.

Dyer, Wayne. *What Do You Really Want for Your Children?* New York: William Morrow and Company, Inc., 1985.

Eby, Judy W., and Joan F. Smutny. *A Thoughtful Overview of Gifted Education.* New York: Longman, 1990.

Elkind, David. *The Hurried Child: Growing Up Too Fast Too Soon.* Reading, Mass.: Addison-Wesley, 1984.

———. *All Grown Up and No Place to Go: Teenagers in Crisis.* Reading, Mass.: Addison-Wesley, 1984.

Erwin, Bette, and Elza Teresa Dinwiddie. *Test without Trauma.* New York: Grosset & Dunlap, 1983.

Ferguson, Sherry, and Lawrence E. Mazin. *Parent Power: A Program to Help Your Child Succeed in School.* New York: Clarkson N. Potter, Inc. Publishers, 1989.

Fine, Benjamin. *Underachievers: How They Can Be Helped.* New York: E.P. Dutton & Co., Inc., 1967.

Fisher, Johnanna. *A Parent's Guide to Learning Disabilities.* New York: Charles Scribner's Sons, 1978.

Flesch, Rudolph. *Why Johnny Still Can't Read: A New Look at the Scandal of Our Schools.* New York: Harper & Brothers, 1981.

Fox, Barbara J. *Rx for Reading: How the Schools Teach Your Child to Read and How You Can Help.* New York: Penguin Books, 1989.

Frith, Terry. *Secrets Parents Should Know About the Public Schools.* New York: Simon & Schuster, 1986.

Gall, Meredith D. *Making the Grade.* Rocklin, Calif.: Prima Publishing and Communication, 1988.

Gardner, Richard A. M.D. *MBD: The Family Book About Minimal Brain Dysfunction.* New York: Jaeson Aronson, Inc., 1973.

———. *The Objective Diagnosis of Minimal Brain Dysfunction.* Cresskill, N.J.: Creative Therapeutics, 1979.

Gibson, Janice T. *Discipline Is Not a Dirty Word: A Positive Learning Approach.* Lexington, Mass.: The Lewis Publishing Company, 1983.

Golay, Keith. *Learning Patterns and Temperament Styles.* Fullerton, Calif.: Manas-Systems, 1982.

Gould, Shirley. *The Challenge of Friendship: Helping Your Child Become a Friend.* New York: Hawthorne/Dutton, 1981.

Granger, Lori, and Bill Granger. *The Magic Feather: The Truth About "Special Education."* New York: E.P. Dutton, 1986.

Green, Robert T., and Veronica J. Laxon. *Entering the World of Number.* London: Thames and Hudson, 1978.

Greene, Lawrence J. *Kids Who Underachieve.* New York: Simon and Schuster, 1986.

———. *Learning Disabilities and Your Child: A Survival Handbook.* New York: Fawcett Columbine, 1987.

Harris, Albert J., and Edward R. Sipay. *Effective Teaching of Reading.* New York: McKay, 1971.

Hersey, Paul, and Kenneth H. Blanchard. *The Family Game: A Situational Approach to Effective Parenting.* Reading, Mass.: Addison-Wesley Publishing Company, 1978.

Herzfield, Gerald, and Robin Powell. *Coping for Kids: A Complete Stress-Control Program for Students 8-18.* West Nyack, N.Y.: The Center for Applied Research in Education, Inc., 1986.

Holt, John. *How Children Fail.* New York: Delacorte Press, 1964.

———. *How Children Learn.* New York: Delacorte Press, 1967.

———. *Instead of Education.* New York: E.P. Dutton, 1976.

———. *Learning All the Time.* Reading, Mass.: Addison-Wesley Publishing Company, Inc., 1989.

———. *Teach Your Own.* New York: Delacorte Press, 1981.

Holt, Michael, and Zoltan Dienes. *Let's Play Math.* New York: Walker & Company, 1973.

Hughes, Martin. *Children and Numbers: Difficulties in Learning Mathematics.* New York: Basil Blackwell, 1986.

Hulme, Charles. *Reading Retardation and Multi-Sensory Teaching.* London: Routledge & Kegan Paul, 1981.

Jackson, Nancy S., Donald A. Jackson, and Kathy Monroe. *Getting Along with Others: Teaching Social Effectiveness to Children.* Champaign, Ill.: Research Press, 1983.

James, Elizabeth, and Carol Barkin. *How to Write Your Best Book Report.* New York: Grosset & Dunlap, 1983.

———. *How to Write a Great School Report.* New York: Lothrop, Lee, & Shepard Books, 1983.

Jansky, Jeannette, and Katrina deHirsch. *Preventing Reading Failure.* New York: Harper & Row, 1972.

Johnson, Eric W. *Raising Children to Achieve: A Guide for Motivating Success in School and in Life.* New York: Walker & Company, 1984.

Jones, Claudia. *More Parents Are Teachers, Too.* Charlotte, Vt.: Williamson Publishing Co., 1990.

Kalina, Sigmund. *How to Sharpen Your Study Skills.* New York: Lothrop, Lee, and Shepard Company, 1975.

Kaye, Peggy. *Games for Math: Playful Ways to Help Your Child Learn Math from Kindergarten to Third Grade.* New York: Pantheon Books, 1987.

———. *Games for Reading: Playful Ways to Help Your Child Read.* New York: Pantheon Books, 1984.

Kelly, Jeffrey. *Solving Your Child's Behavior Problems: An Everyday Guide for Parents.* Boston: Little, Brown & Company, 1983.

Kesselman-Turkel, Judi, and Franklynn Peterson. *Study Smarts: How to Learn More in Less Time.* Chicago: Contemporary Books Inc., 1981.

———. *Test Taking Strategies.* Chicago: Contemporary Books, Inc., 1981.

Knox, Jean McBee. *Learning Disabilities.* New York: Chelsea, House Publishers, 1989.

Lamm, Stanley S., and Martin L. Fisch. *Learning Disabilities Explained.* Garden City, N. Y.: Doubleday, 1982.

Lamme, Linda Leonard. *Growing Up Writing.* Washington, D.C.: Acropolis Books Ltd., 1984.

Laughy, Linwood. *The Interactive Parent: How to Help Your Child Survive and Succeed in the Public Schools.* Kooska, Idaho: Mountain Meadow Press, 1988.

Lee, Barbara, and Masha Kabakow Rudman. *Mind Over Media: New Ways to Improve Your Child's Reading and Writing Skills.* New York: Seaview Books, 1982.

Lewontin, R.C., Steven Rose, and Leon J. Kamin. *Not in Our Genes: Biology, Ideology, and Human Nature.* New York: Pantheon Books, 1984.

Mattson, Ralph, and Thom Black. *Discovering Your Child's Design.* Elgin, Ill.: David C. Cook, 1989

McEwan, Elaine K. *How to Raise a Reader.* Elgin, Ill.: David C. Cook, 1987.

———. *Raising Balanced Children in an Unbalanced World.* Elgin, Ill.: David C. Cook, 1990.

———. *Schooling Options: Choosing the Best for You & Your Child.* Wheaton, Ill.: Harold Shaw Publishers, 1991.

———. *Will My Child Be Ready for School?* Elgin, Ill.: David C. Cook, 1990.

McGinnis, Ellen, and Arnold P. Goldstein. *Skillstreaming the Elementary School Child.* Champaign, Ill.: Research Press, 1984.

McGuinness, Diane. *When Children Don't Learn: Understanding the Biology and Psychology of Learning Disabilities.* New York: Basic Books, 1985.

Meier, Paul. *Christian Child-Rearing and Personality Development.* Grand Rapids, Mich.: Baker Book House, 1977.

Melton, David. *Promises to Keep: A Handbook for Parents of Learning Disabled, Brain-Injured, and Other Exceptional Children.* New York: Franklin Watts, 1984.

Nelsen, Jane, and Lynn Lott. *I'm On Your Side: Resolving Conflict with Your Teenage Son or Daughter.* Rocklin, Calif.: Prima Publishing & Communications, 1990.

Nemko, Marty. *How to Get a Private School Education in a Public School.* New York: Acropolis Books, Ltd., 1986.

Oakes, Jeannie. *Keeping Track: How Schools Structure Inequality.* New Haven, Conn.: Yale University Press, 1985.

Oakes, Jeannie, and Martin Lipton. *Making the Best of Schools:* New Haven, Conn.: Yale University Press, 1990.

Oppenheim, Joanne. *The Elementary School Handbook: Making the Most of Your Child's Education.* New York: Pantheon Books, 1989.

———. *Raising a Confident Child: The Bank Street Year-By-Year Guide.* New York: Pantheon Books, 1984.

Osman, Betty B. *Learning Disabilities: A Family Affair.* New York: Random House, 1979.

———. *No One to Play With: The Social Side of Learning Disabilities.* New York: Random House, 1982.

Parsons, Cynthia. *Seeds: Some Good Ways to Improve Our Schools.* Santa Barbara, Calif.: Woodbridge Press, 1985.

Pecaut, Linnus S. *The Making of an Underachiever: Growing Up in the Shadow of Success.* Lombard, Ill.: The Institute for Motivational Development, 1986.

———. *Understanding and Influencing Student Motivation: Assessment and Treatment.* Lombard, Ill.: The Institute for Motiviational Development, 1979.

Phillips, Beeman. *School Stress and Anxiety.* New York: Human Sciences Press, 1978.

Popkin, Michael. *Active Parenting: Teaching Cooperation, Courage, and Responsibility.* San Francisco: Harper & Row, 1987.

Reed, Arthea J. S. *Comics to Classics: A Parent's Guide to Books for Teens and Preteens.* Newark, Del.: International Reading Association, 1988.

Rich, Dorothy. *Megaskills.* Boston: Houghton Mifflin Company, 1988.

Rimm, Sylvia. *How to Parent So Children Will Learn.* Watertown, Wis.: Apple Publishing Company, 1986.

———. *Underachievement Syndrome: Causes and Curses*. Watertown, Wisc.: Apple Publishing Company, 1986.

Rioux, William. *You Can Improve Your Child's School: Practical Answers to Questions Parents Ask Most about Their Public Schools*. New York: Simon & Schuster, 1980.

Rosenberg, Nancy. *How to Enjoy Mathematics with Your Child*. New York: Stein and Day, 1970.

Rosner, Jerome. *Helping Children Overcome Learning Difficulties: Step-By-Step Guide for Parents and Teachers*. New York: Walker, 1979.

Ross, Alan O. *Learning Disability: The Unrealized Potential*. New York: McGraw-Hill Book Company, 1977.

Schimmels, Cliff. *How to Help Your Child Thrive and Survive in the Public Schools*. Old Tappan, N.J.: Fleming H. Revell, 1982.

Schrage, Peter, and Diane Divoky. *The Myth of the Hyperactive Child*. New York: Pantheon Books, 1975.

Schulman, Michael, and Eva Mekler. *Bringing Up a Moral Child*. Reading, Mass.: Addison-Wesley Publishing Company, Inc., 1985.

Seligman, Milton. *Strategies for Helping Parents of Exceptional Children*. New York: The Free Press, 1979.

Shapiro, Steven R. *The Learning Connection: The Spiritual Side of Learning Disabilities*. Tulsa, Okla.: Vision Development Center, 1990.

Silberman, Melvin L., and Susan A. Wheelan. *How to Discipline without Feeling Guilty: Assertive Relationships with Children*. New York: Hawthorn Books, 1980.

Silver, Larry. *The Misunderstood Child*. New York: McGraw-Hill, 1987.

Slavin, Robert E. *Ability Grouping and Student Achievement in Elementary Schools: A Best Evidence Synthesis*. Baltimore, Md.: Johns Hopkins University, 1986.

Smith, Charles A. *From Wonder to Wisdom: Using Stories to Help Children Grow*. New York: New American Library, 1989.

Sobol, Tom. *Your Child in School: Kindergarten Through Second Grade*. New York: Arbor House, 1987.

Stenmark, Jean Kerr, Virginia Thompson, and Ruth Cossey. *Family Math*. Berkeley, Calif.: University of California, 1986.

Stevens, Suzanne. *The Learning Disabled Child: Ways That Parents Can Help*. Winston-Salem, N.C.: John F. Blair, Publisher, 1980.

Taylor, Denny. *Learning Denied*. Portsmouth, N.H.: Heinemann, 1991.

Taylor, John F. *Helping Your Hyperactive Child*. Rocklin, Calif.: Prima Publishing & Communication, 1990.

Thomas, Alexander, Stella Chase, and Herbert G. Birch. *Temperament and Behavior Disorders in Children*. New York: New York University Press, 1968.

Tobias, Sheila. *Overcoming Math Anxiety*. New York: W.W. Norton & Company, Inc., 1978.

———. *Succeed with Math: Every Student's Guide to Conquering Math Anxiety*. New York: College Entrance Examination Board, 1987.

Toole, Amy L., and Ellen Boehm. *Off to a Good Start: 464 Readiness Activities for Reading, Math, Social Studies, and Science*. New York: Walker & Company, 1983.

Unger, Harlow G. *What Did You Learn in School Today? A New Parent's Guide for Evaluating Your Child's School*. New York: Warner Books, 1975.

Vail, Priscilla. *About Dyslexia: Unravelling the Myth*. Rosemont, N.J.: Modern Learning Press, 1990.

———. *Clear and Lively Writing: Language Games and Activities for Everyone*. New York: Walker & Company, 1981.

———. *Common Ground: Whole Language and Phonics Working Together*. Rosemont, N.J.: Modern Learning Press, 1991.

———. *Gifted, Precocious, or Just Plain Smart*. Rosemont, N.J.: Programs For Education, 1987.

———. *Smart Kids with School Problems: Things to Know and Ways to Help*. New York: New American Library, 1987.

Vitale, Barbara Meister. *Unicorns are Real: A Right-Brained Approach to Learning.* Rolling Hills Estates, Calif.: Jalmar Press, 1982.

Warren, Virginia Burgess. *Tested Ways to Help Your Child Learn.* Englewood Cliffs, N.J.: Prentice-Hall, Inc., 1961.

Webb, James T., Elizabeth A. Meckstroth, and Stephanie Tolan. *Guiding the Gifted Child.* Columbus, Ohio: Psychology Publishing Company, 1982.

Wender, Paul H. *The Hyperactive Child: A Handbook for Parents.* New York: Crown Publishers, 1973.

Weiss, Elizabeth. *Mothers Talk about Learning Disabilities.* Englewood Cliffs, N.J.: Prentice-Hall Press, 1989.

White, Burton J. *The First Three Years of Life.* Englewood Cliffs, N.J.: Prentice-Hall, 1975.

Wiener, Harvey S. *Any Child Can Write: How to Improve Your Child's Writing Skills from Preschool through High School.* New York: Bantam Books, 1990.

Wlodowski, Raymond J., and Judith H. Haynes. *Eager to Learn: Helping Children Become Motivated and Love Learning.* San Francisco: Jossey-Bass Publishers, 1990.

Wood, Paul, and Bernard Schwartz. *How to Get Your Children to Do What You Want Them to Do.* Englewood Cliffs, N.J.: Prentice-Hall, Inc., 1977.

Wyckoff, Jerry L., and Barbara C. Unell. *How to Discipline Your Six to Twelve Year Old.* New York: Doubleday, 1991.

Youngs, Betty B. *Stress in Children: How to Recognize, Avoid, and Overcome It.* New York: Arbor House, 1985.

Zaslavsky, Claudia. *Preparing Young Children for Math: A Book of Games.* New York: Shocken Books, 1979.

INDEX